IMAGES
of America

BUFFALO'S EAST SIDE INDUSTRY

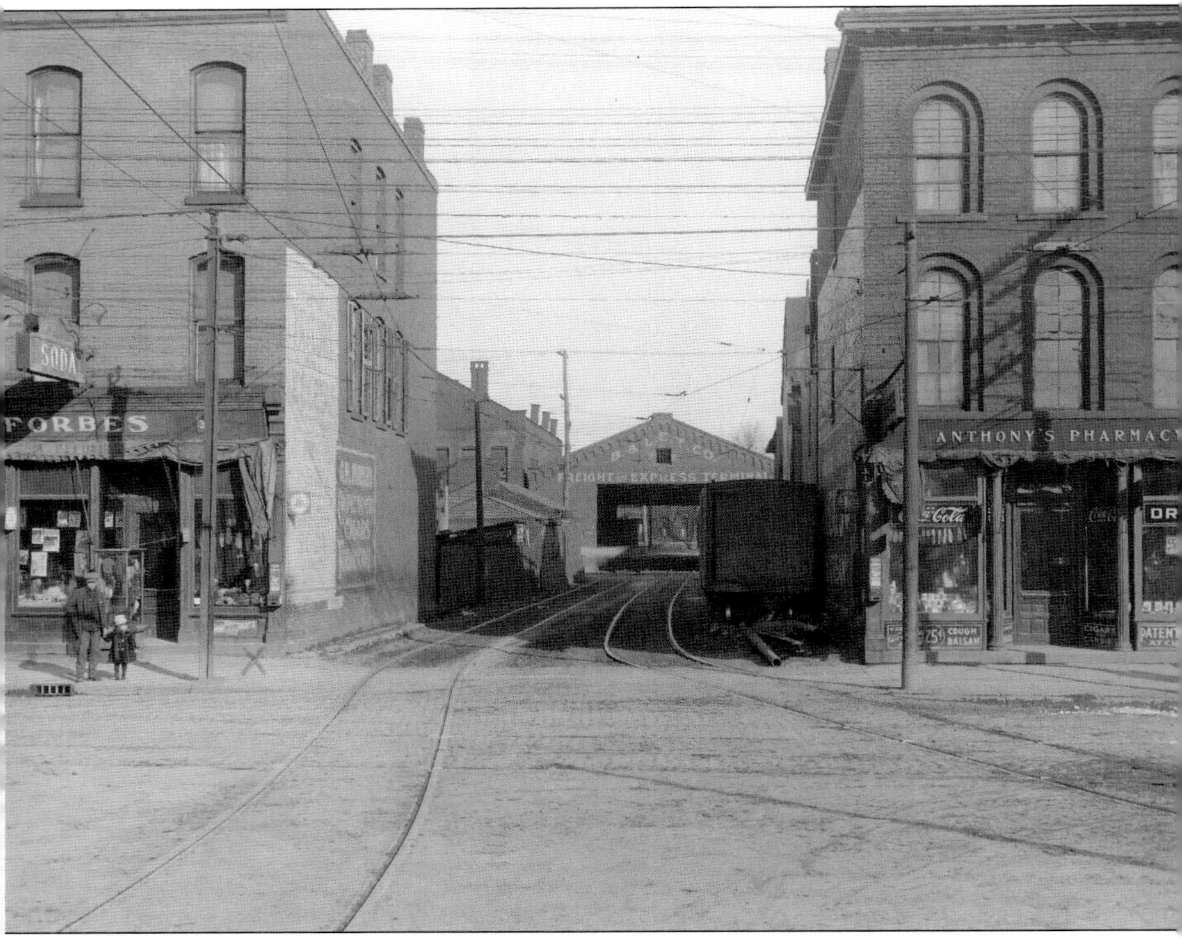

The Buffalo and Lake Erie Traction Company, as shown from 382 Seneca Street, operated the "Grape Line" of railroads and trolleys that ran along the Lake Erie shoreline toward Erie, Pennsylvania, from 1906 to 1934. In this undated photograph, the freight and terminal house is shown between Anthony's Pharmacy and A.P. Forbes General Store. Currently, the terminal sits a few doors east and one block north of DiTondo's Restaurant, where the terminal house can be seen from the restaurant's gravel parking lot. (Courtesy of the Buffalo History Museum.)

On the Cover: Jacob Koebel, at far left (with the moustache), started the pictured blacksmithing business at 258 Broadway between Pine and Ash Streets. He entered into business with Frank and George Eberl when he married into the Eberl family. In 1923, Koebel and the Eberls opened Eberl Iron Works at Michigan Avenue and Sycamore Street, where it still is in operation today. Eberl Iron Works currently has five divisions and is a worldwide distributor for Unistrut products. (Courtesy of the Eberl family.)

IMAGES
of America

BUFFALO'S EAST SIDE INDUSTRY

Shane E. Stephenson

ARCADIA
PUBLISHING

ISBN 978-1-4671-3489-7

Published by Arcadia Publishing
Charleston, South Carolina

Printed in the United States of America

Library of Congress Control Number: 2015943628

For all general information, please contact Arcadia Publishing:
Telephone 843-853-2070
Fax 843-853-0044
E-mail sales@arcadiapublishing.com
For customer service and orders:
Toll-Free 1-888-313-2665

Visit us on the Internet at www.arcadiapublishing.com

This book is dedicated to the thousands of men and women who worked in the industries and companies listed within. I hope this is a worthy remembrance.

Contents

ACKNOWLEDGMENTS

This research and book project would not have been possible without the generosity, understanding, and guidance of the Buffalo History Museum, a place I am honored to be a part of. The executive director, Melissa Brown, and the director of library and archives, Cynthia Van Ness, worked with me in all facets and were infinitely flexible regarding the needs of this project. An appreciation goes to Trish Kibler, who enthusiastically helped turn this idea of an East Side industry book into reality. A "thank you" also goes out to Amy Miller, librarian assistant and archivist at the museum. Her research assistance and attention to detail when I felt stuck is so very appreciated. For their guidance and patience, I would like to thank Sara Miller, Henry Clougherty, and Sharon McAllister at Arcadia Publishing for being there for me. Many thanks to Dan DiLandro, archivist and special collections librarian at SUNY Buffalo State. Familial acknowledgement is instinctively due; from them, I learned that setting and reaching a goal can only come from focus and a willingness to embrace hard work. Appreciative feelings also go out to everyone who came into contact with this work and shared my enthusiasm for it.

Unless otherwise noted, all images are courtesy of the Buffalo History Museum.

INTRODUCTION

To understand the East Side of today requires comprehending the East Side of yesterday. The history of its various neighborhoods cannot be understood by viewing the area with modern eyes. Diversity, growth, power, and collapse have shifted slowly and steadily over the course of 190 years, and through all this, the city of Buffalo has remained a thoroughly spontaneous uprising based around industry.

The area's growth first took place on the waterfront and in the Hydraulics neighborhood. As the city continued expanding, the natural tendency was to move east and north, where farmland, forests, and creeks could be manipulated to establish bigger and more complex industries. People from diverse backgrounds joined in this manipulation of natural resources. Following a radial street pattern established by Joseph Ellicott, the major east-west thoroughfares of the East Side began to take shape between 1826 and 1831.

The southernmost streets of South Park Avenue, Perry Street, Scott Street, Exchange Street, Seneca Street, Myrtle Avenue, Swan Street, North and South Division Streets, and Eagle Street run in a gentle southeast—but seemingly straight—pattern perpendicular to lower downtown. At Clinton Street, they shift to a more angled northeast pattern. It is on these northeast streets that many East Side industries took hold. Major arterials Clinton Street, William Street, Batavia (Broadway), Sycamore Street, and Genesee Street—along with minor arterials Howard Street, Peckham Street, Lovejoy Avenue (Paderewski Drive), and Stanislaus Street—formed the heart of the inner East Side located west of the Buffalo Belt Line. East of the belt line, streets such as Walden and Doat continue the pattern. In 1832, the newly incorporated city of Buffalo encompassed four and a half square miles, with Jefferson Avenue as the easternmost street. The city limits still in place today were established by 1854, setting the square mileage at 42 miles.

For these first 22 years, between 1832 and 1854, the East Side was surveyed and its streets laid out four to six rods wide to Jefferson Avenue. Much of this area is vernacularly known as the Fruit Belt, though "Fruit and Timber Belt" may be a clearer designation. Pine, Ash, Hickory, Cedar, Walnut, Spruce, and Maple Streets were named to complement the northerly Lemon, Grape, Peach, Cherry, and Orange Streets, giving a simple yet satisfying description of the land from which they were carved. All of the streets mentioned above are listed in the 1840 city directory for Buffalo, along with 193 other roadways throughout the city.

Settlements began to appear east and north of the lower downtown area as early as 1826, when certain streets were surveyed. Immigrants were drawn to the area by cheap housing and workable land. German and Jewish immigrants began settling around Michigan Avenue, one of the first major north-south streets that might be deemed a part of the East Side. The migration continued north to the Fruit Belt. Within a decade or two, African Americans started establishing neighborhoods around Michigan Avenue, and in 1837, some of these settlers founded a congregation that would fill the Michigan Avenue Baptist Church once it was built in 1845. This church became an intellectual center for the abolitionist movement; both W.E.B. Du Bois and Booker T. Washington attended meetings there. Farther east, Polish immigrants began to lay down roots after the original St. Stanislaus Bishop and Martyr Church was constructed in 1874.

Many of the companies listed in this book started out near the water or in the core of downtown. When they were ready to expand, they looked east to the open, affordable land there. Once newer and larger business operations were established, the nearly empty streets began filling with houses and people. With the new people came stores that catered to the necessities of daily living. In 1890, Buffalo had 76 dry good stores, and of those, 51 were clustered around the major arterials on the East Side, showing its development into a major population center. This eastward expansion was also made possible with the 1842 arrival of the Buffalo & Albany Railroad, which connected the western part of the state with the expanding cities on the eastern seaboard for the first time via rail. This was the first of many railroads—an industry that experienced additional expansion after the Civil War, including the opening of the all-important Buffalo Belt Line in 1883. By 1907, there were 16 distinct railroad lines entering the city. The Buffalo Belt Line, which proved instrumental to the growth of the East Side, was originally intended to serve passengers, but industries realized the potential for cheap transport to other rail lines and began building factories and plants in a cluster around the line. Companies such as Niagara Machine & Tool Works, Curtiss-Wright Corporation, Otis Elevator, Houde Engineering, and Buffalo Foundry & Machine Company gathered around the Northland-Grider section of the belt line. In the southern part of the belt line, the Lisk-Savoy Corporation, Wiesner-Rapp Corporation, American Car & Foundry, and George Laub & Sons Tannery took advantage of their proximity to it through short connecting rails.

After 100 years as a seat of industrial power, the East Side was left battered and bruised by suburbanization, racial tensions, and deindustrialization. The immigrants who settled in a myriad of neighborhoods watched their children follow jobs to other parts of Buffalo, Western New York, or the rest of the country. This, predictably, created an urban vacuum similar to those happening in other northeastern industrial cities.

One solution may be to create an environment friendly to business with the goal of bringing industry back into East Side neighborhoods. There has been progress with the creation of the Northland Corridor Light Industrial Hub, and there are companies in the area that still remain strong. The businesses in this book—and the hundreds not represented—reflect a different time in the country's growth. They also represent an immensely diverse collection of industries and offer a testament to the human spirit, innovation, opportunity, and a desire to help make our neighbors' lives better.

One

Streetscapes
The Way It Was

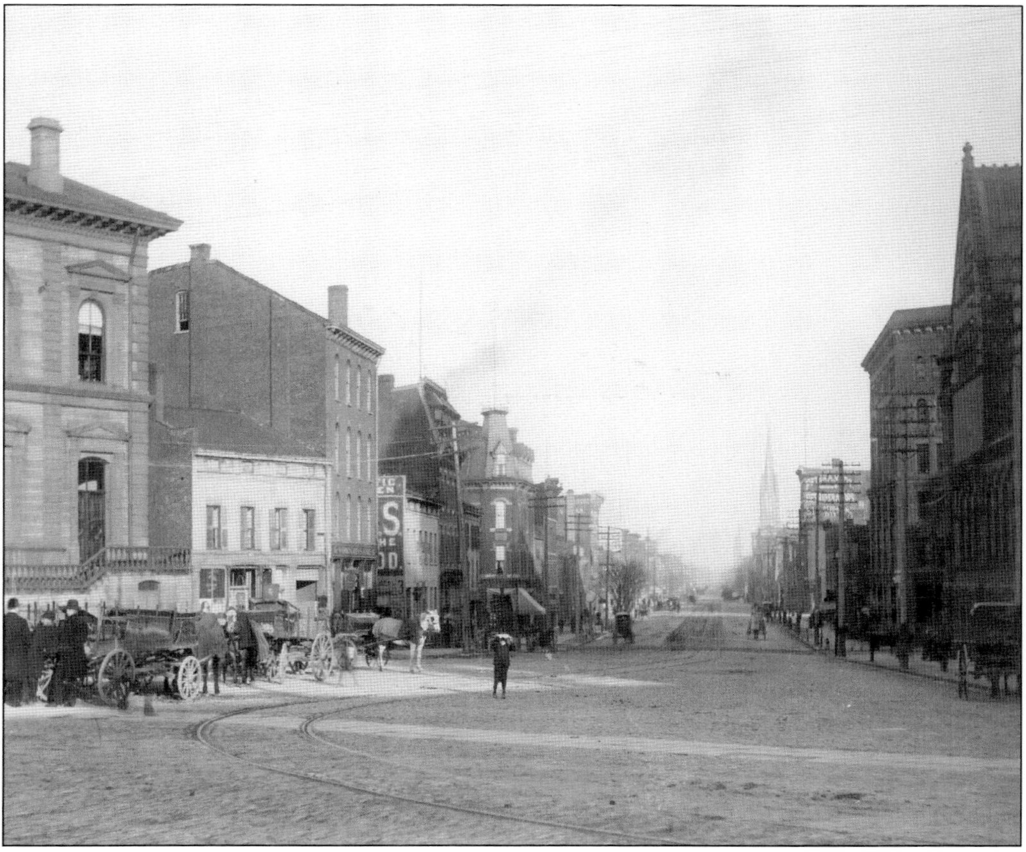

In this undated photograph, the grand scale of Broadway is shown while looking east from the intersection at Washington Street. To the far right is the magnificent Buffalo Library, and in the distance is the now demolished St. Mary's Church of the Redemptorists. In the background are the twin spires of St. Ann's Church, and down the middle of the thoroughfare is one cog in Buffalo's extensive streetcar system.

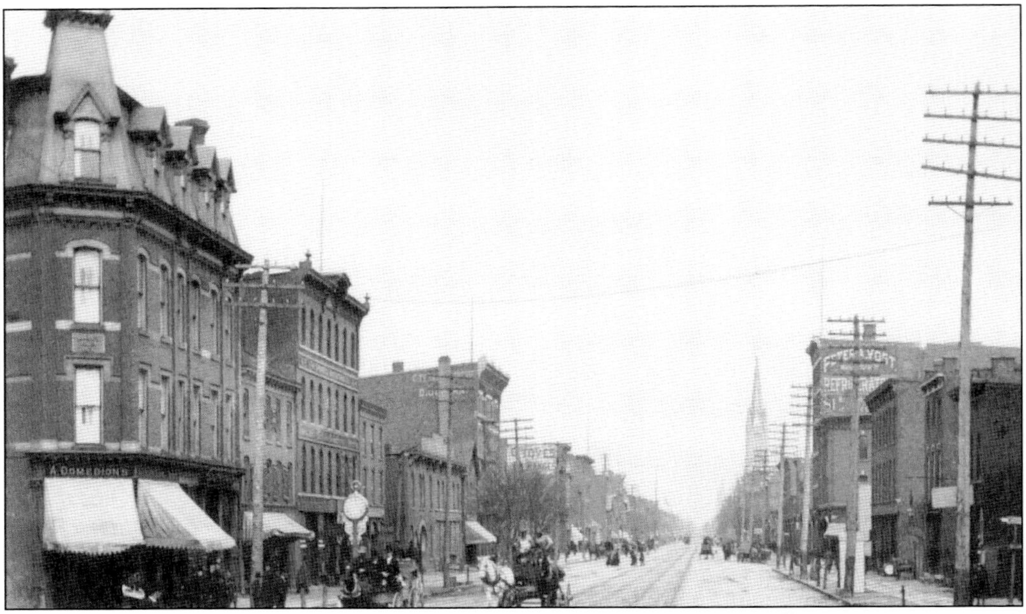

This photograph was taken in 1890 from the intersection of Broadway and Ellicott Street. St. Mary's Church of the Redemptorists is visible at right, along with the twin spires of St. Ann's Church in the distance. To the left is Andrew Domedian's Barber Supplies Store, and to the right is Peter A. Vogt's Manufacturing Company, which produced refrigeration and watercooler supplies.

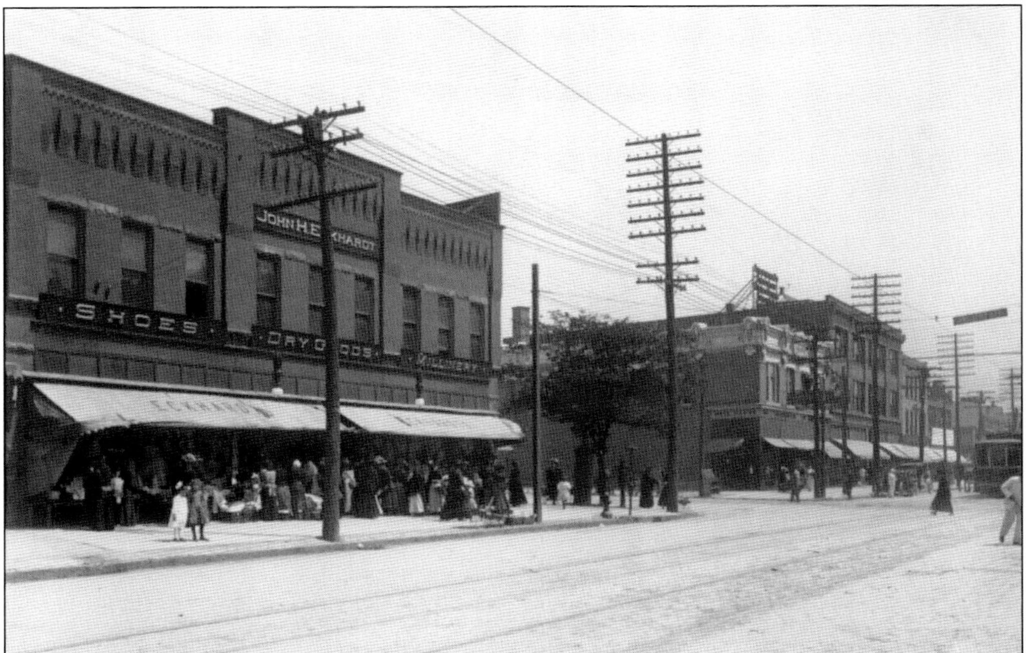

Here is the bustling intersection of Broadway and Fillmore Avenue in 1912. Most prominent is John H. Eckhardt's department store at left, which remained in that location until it closed in 1941. The signage on the building reads "Shoes—Dry Goods—Millinery." A newer building, constructed here in 1940, still stands and has had various tenants since 1941.

Carts, people, and cars dominate this picture taken at the corner of Mills Street and Broadway in 1930. This view looks west toward downtown. Businesses on the north (right) side of the street include Sattler's Department Store, the Lion Shoe Company, the R.G. Dun cigar shop, and the office of dentist Dr. Swados. The open-air, covered Broadway Market is across the street (at left).

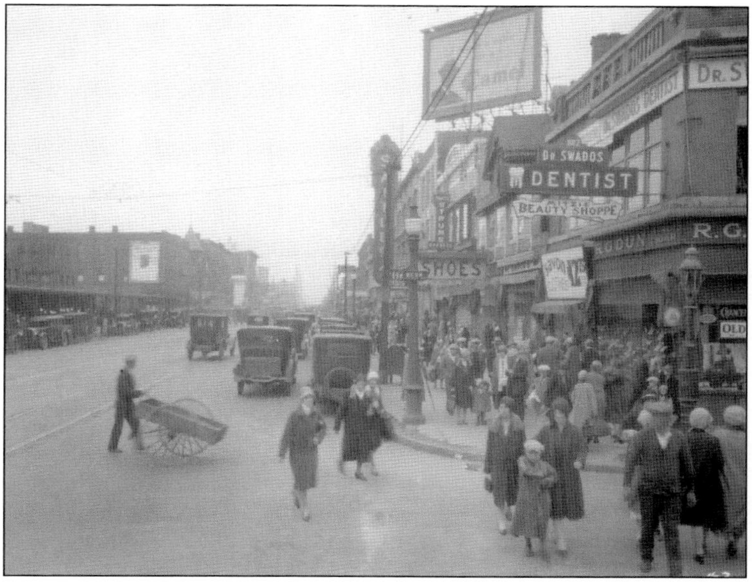

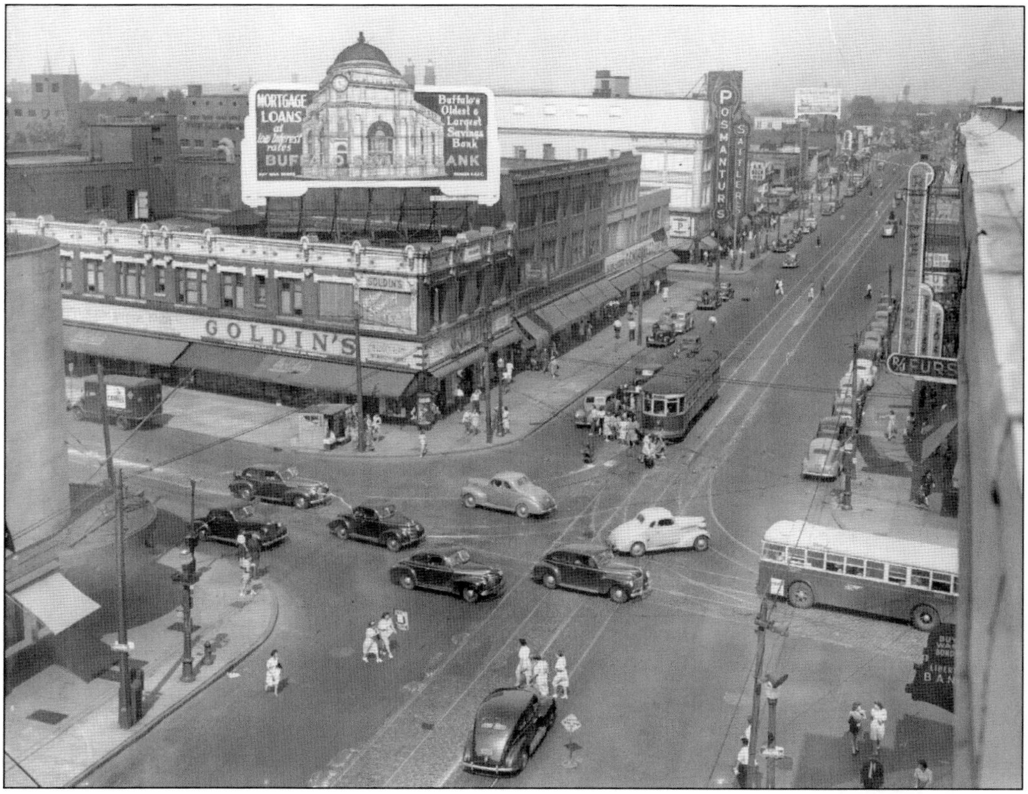

This 1948 photograph shows the intersection of Broadway and Fillmore Avenue. Although streetcars are still on their tracks, cars are beginning to control the streets. Two years later, streetcars were removed from the streets of Buffalo. The Goldome building is pictured on the Buffalo Savings Bank advertising board atop Goldin's Personal Finance Company.

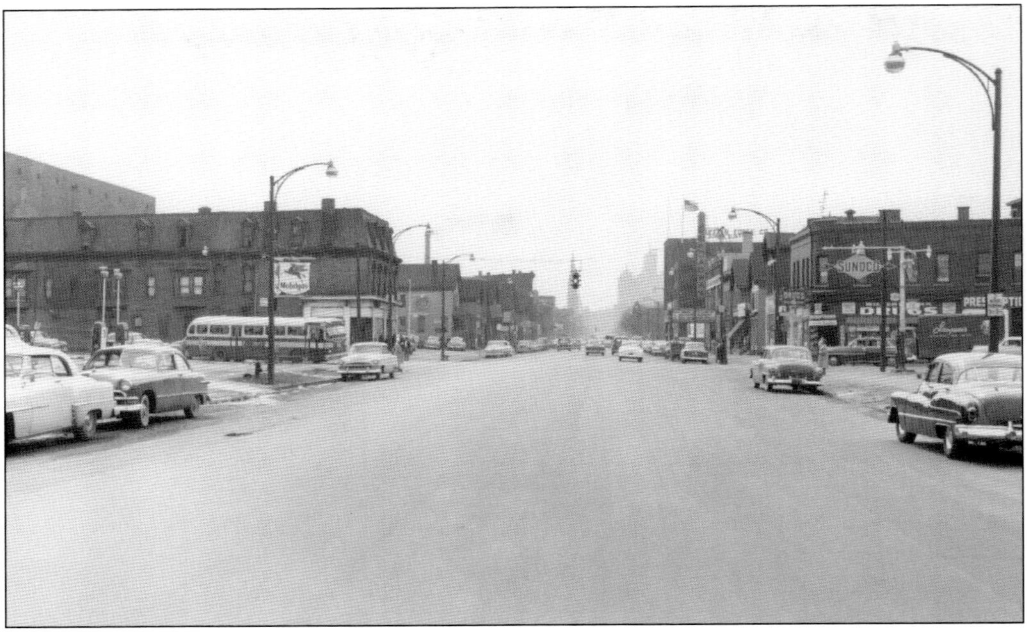

This is the intersection of Broadway and Fillmore Avenue in 1952. On the north (right) side of Broadway, the Buffalo Forge rooftop sign is visible, along with the marquee of the Broadway Theater (originally the Sattler Theater). Recent events regarding this theater include a partnership between Ellicott Development Company and Western New York Minority Media Professionals to rehabilitate the building.

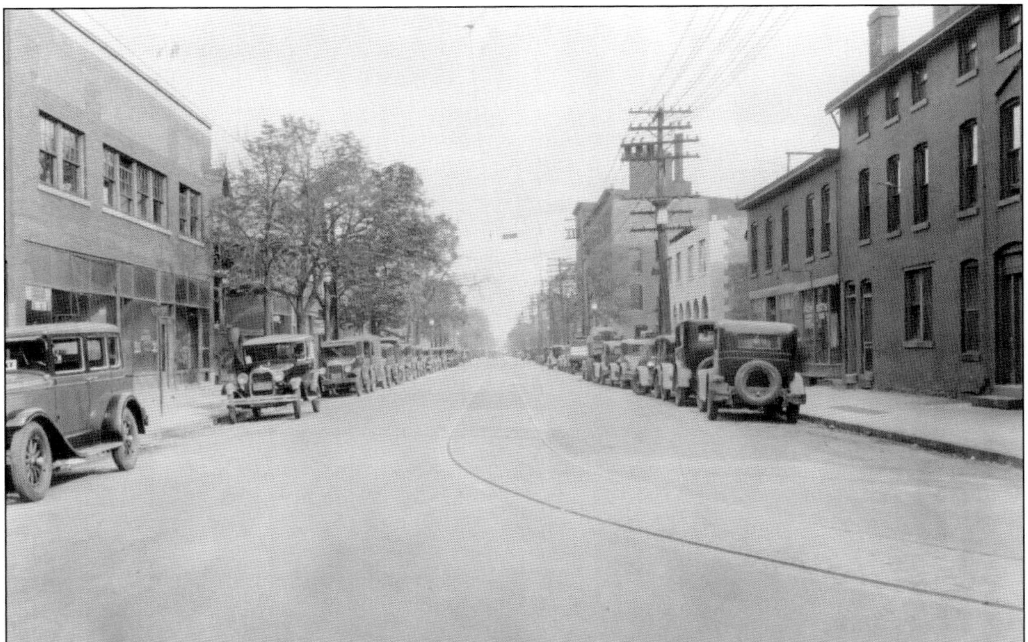

At the corner of Clinton Street and Michigan Avenue in 1928, there was a mixture of restaurants, residential homes, and apartments. Streetcar tracks run down the middle of the street and turn south on Michigan Avenue. The block at right is now the parking lot for Compass East, the development located at the former site of Sheehan Memorial Hospital.

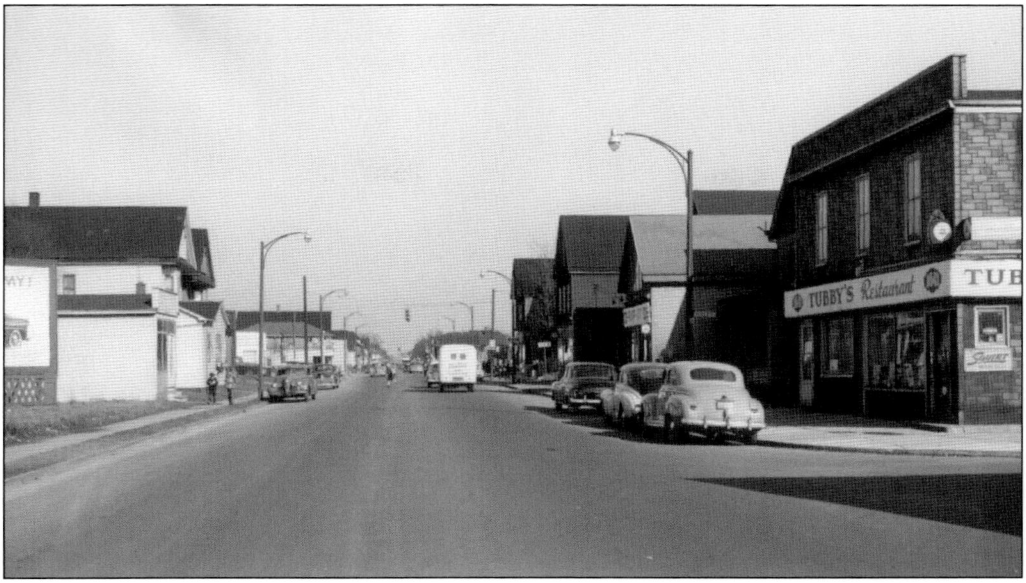

This 1953 image shows the intersection of Clinton Street and Roberts Avenue. Not many businesses are decipherable in this photograph except Tubby's Restaurant on the south side of the street. Construction of Interstate 190 was beginning at South Ogden Street; it would soon pass over Clinton Street at this intersection. At the time, the Worthington Pump Company–Buffalo Works Company Division was located farther down Roberts Avenue.

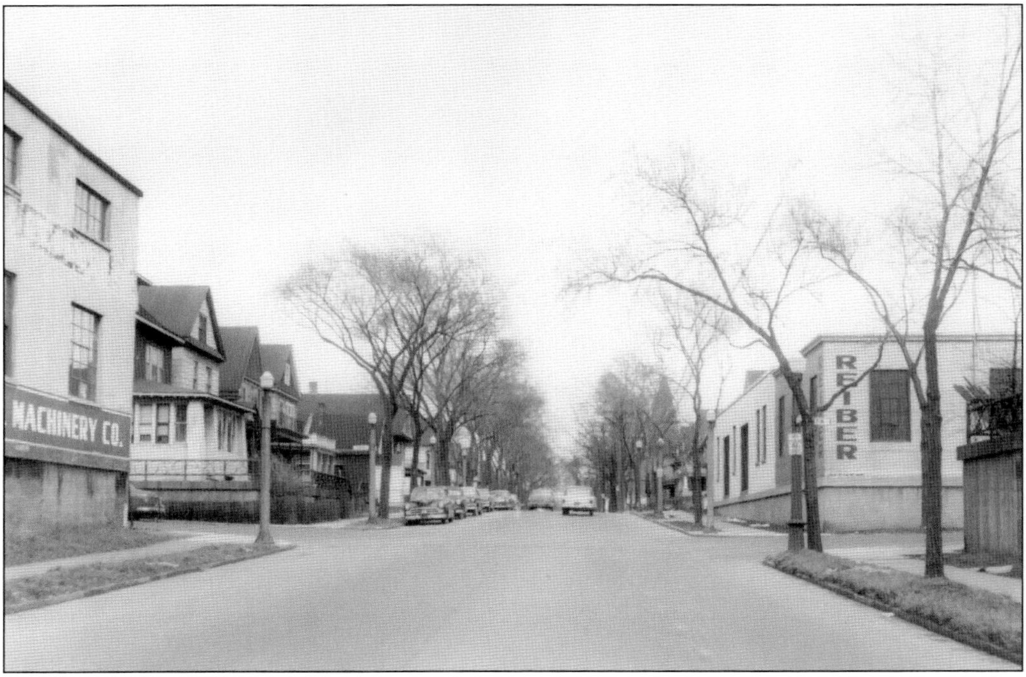

The corner of Doat Street and Rapin Place—pictured in 1957—looks much different today (see page 125). This image looking east shows the Mohawk Machinery Company at left and Reiber Roofing and Sheet Metal Works at right. Both buildings are still standing, although the Reiber structure has been refaced. All the houses at left have been demolished; only the concrete wall and iron fence remain.

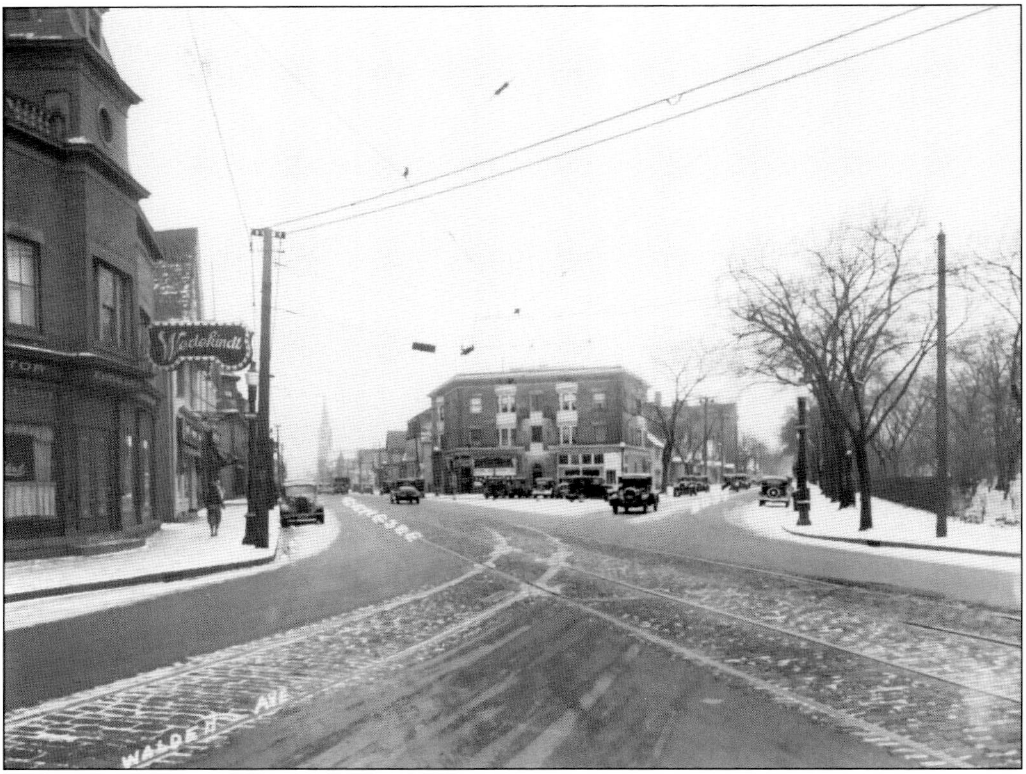

Best and Genesee Streets and Walden Avenue are pictured here in 1929. This photograph faces west, looking down both Genesee and Best Streets. Shown are Wedekindt Embalming Services, an x-ray production company, and the gate and trees of what is now Martin Luther King Jr. Park (which is managed by the Buffalo Olmsted Parks Conservancy). The steeple in the distance belongs to St. Mary of Sorrows Roman Catholic Church, which now houses the King Urban Life Center.

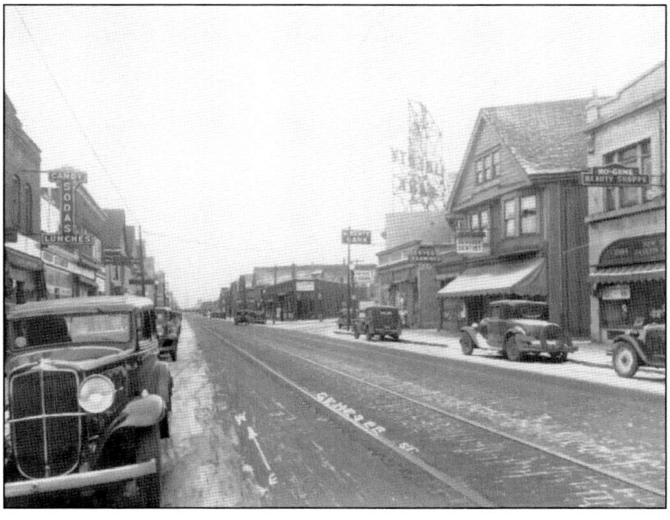

Looking west near the intersection of Genesee and Fougeron Streets in 1934 shows a plethora of businesses. On the south (left) side of the street are Swiss Cleaners, a lunch and soda shop, and R&S Shoes. On the north side are Mo-Gene and New York Beauty Shops, dentist Dr. Hager, an optician, and a Liberty Bank branch with a roof sign. The only buildings remaining are the Liberty Bank building and the brick building on the left anchoring the "Lunches" sign.

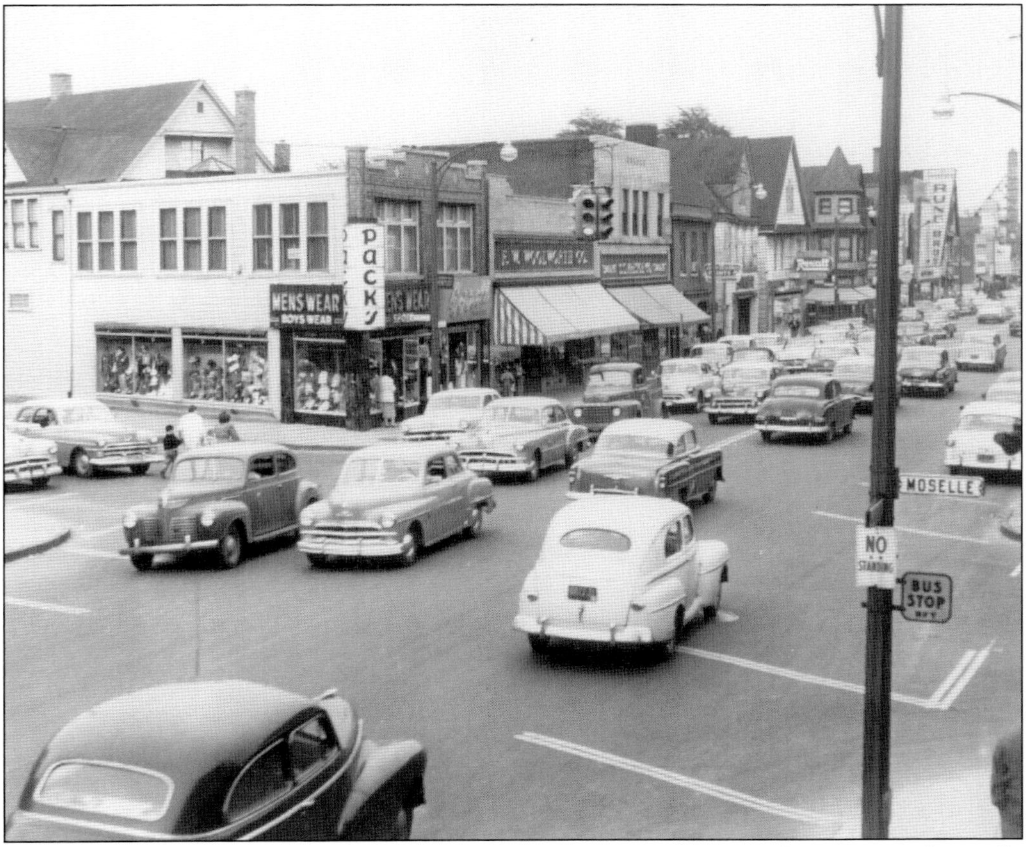

This image shows a neighborhood bustling with activity at the corner of Genesee and Moselle Streets. This looks east down Genesee Street, showing Pack's Boys' and Men's Wear, a Woolworth Company Five and Dime, Rexall Drugstore, Rung Bros. Furniture Store, and the Genesee Theatre (in the distance). Sadly, today's streetscape only includes the first four structures on the left; the rest of the block has been demolished.

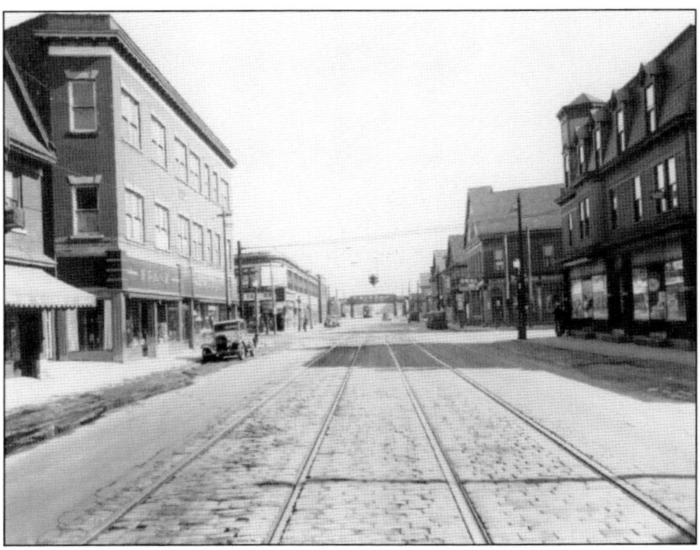

Franz Winegar's Hardware Store was the main business at the corner of Genesee Street and Bailey Avenue, as shown in this image looking east, away from the city. Opposite Winegar's is the Genesee-Bailey Drug Store, and in the distance is the overpass for the Lackawanna Railroad. This 1935 image also shows the streetcar system. A McDonald's currently occupies the corner where Winegar's once stood.

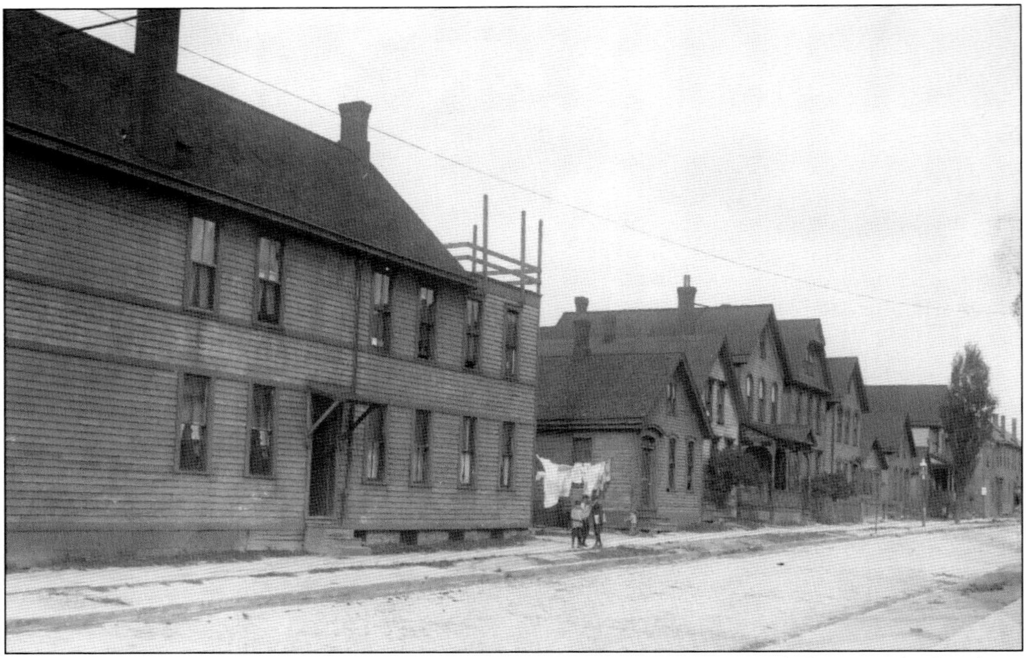

Peckham Street became a minor arterial in the East Side. In this undated photograph, four boys play together by a line of hanging laundry. Peckham Street cemented its place in East Side history as the home of St. Stanislaus Bishop and Martyr Church, one of the "big three" Polish churches on the East Side. It also is home to Wardynski Meats, founded in 1919.

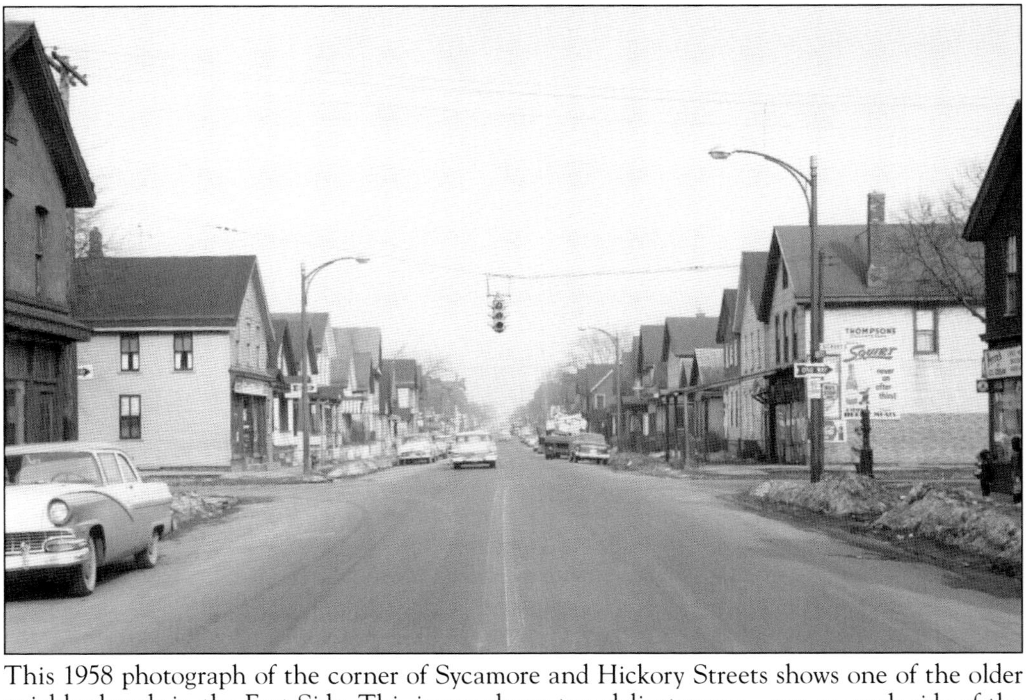

This 1958 photograph of the corner of Sycamore and Hickory Streets shows one of the older neighborhoods in the East Side. This image shows two delicatessens—one on each side of the street. Today, this corner features newer, suburban-style housing. The back of the Buffalo Forge Company is visible at right in the far distance.

This 1962 picture of Sycamore and Mortimer Streets shows Buffalo Forge Company dominating the intersection. The back of the plant is visible, along with the company's storage facility and "dust lab" across the street, built in 1911. Farther down at right is the Schenecker Iron Works Company. The only structure shown here that is still standing is the Buffalo Forge storage facility.

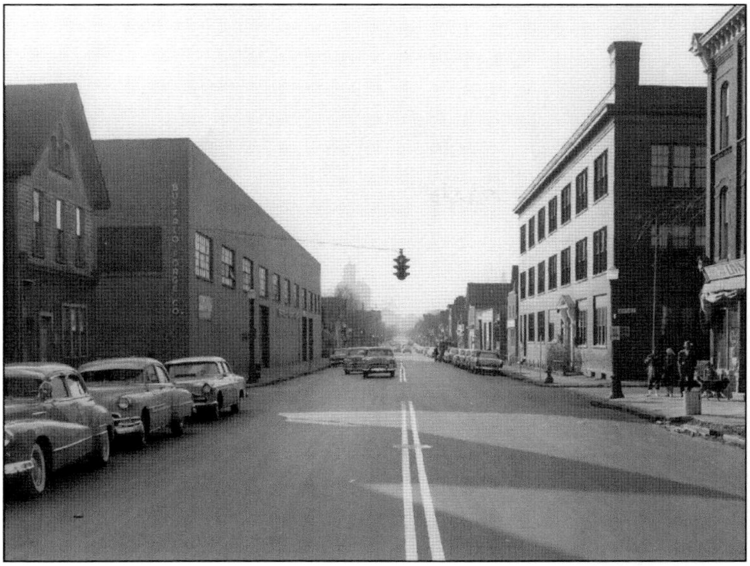

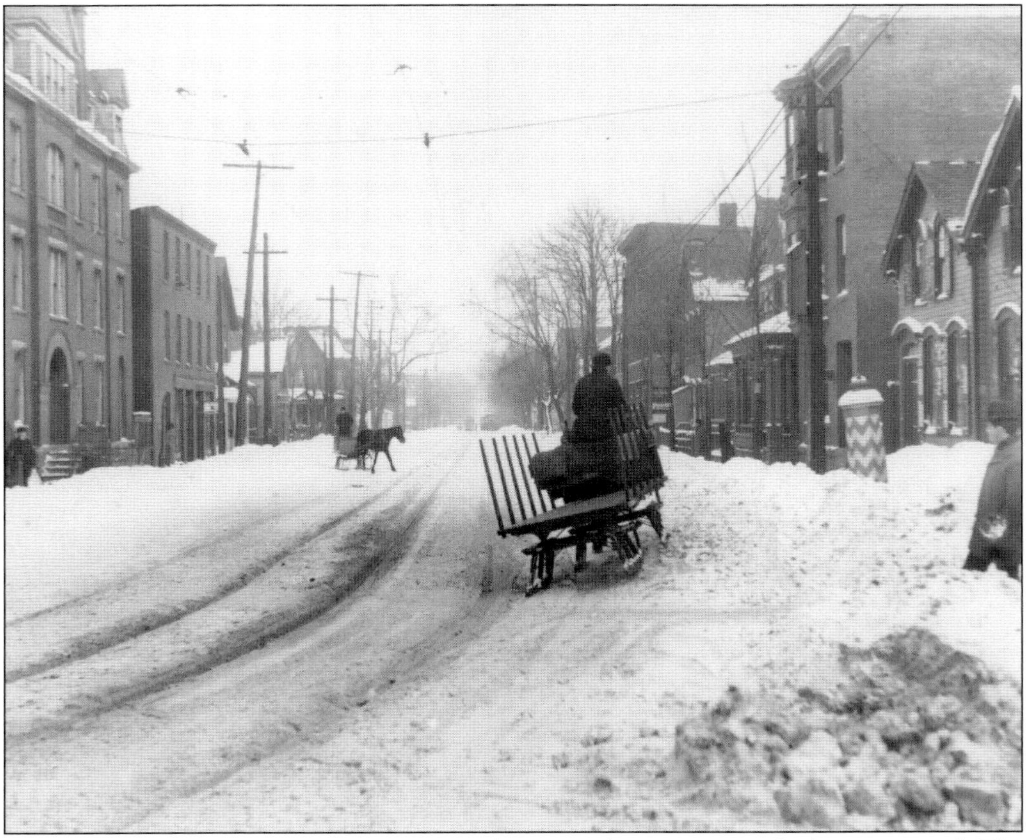

The familiar sights of Buffalo in winter are shown in this 1902 image looking eastward. The corner of Sycamore and Oak Streets is a little farther west (toward downtown), but this image reveals a nice contrast to current downtown blocks. Behind the photographer is E. Huron Street, which ends at the beginning of Sycamore Street. A workman's cottage is at right, a shoemaker's is at left, and streetcar tracks run through the street.

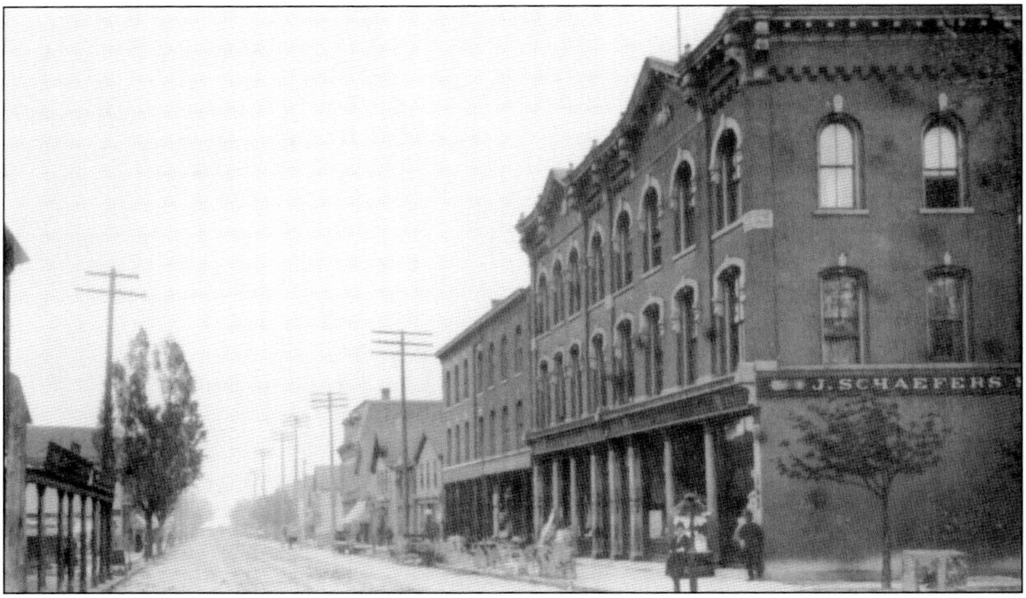

The wilderness beyond William Street is apparent in this 1890 image that features the corner of William and Cedar Streets. Most dominant is J. Schaefers Dry Goods store, and farther down the street, the three-story building near the center of the photograph is likely Conrad Machemer's Dry Goods. At the time this photograph was taken, Buffalo had 76 dry goods stores, and 51 were located on the East Side.

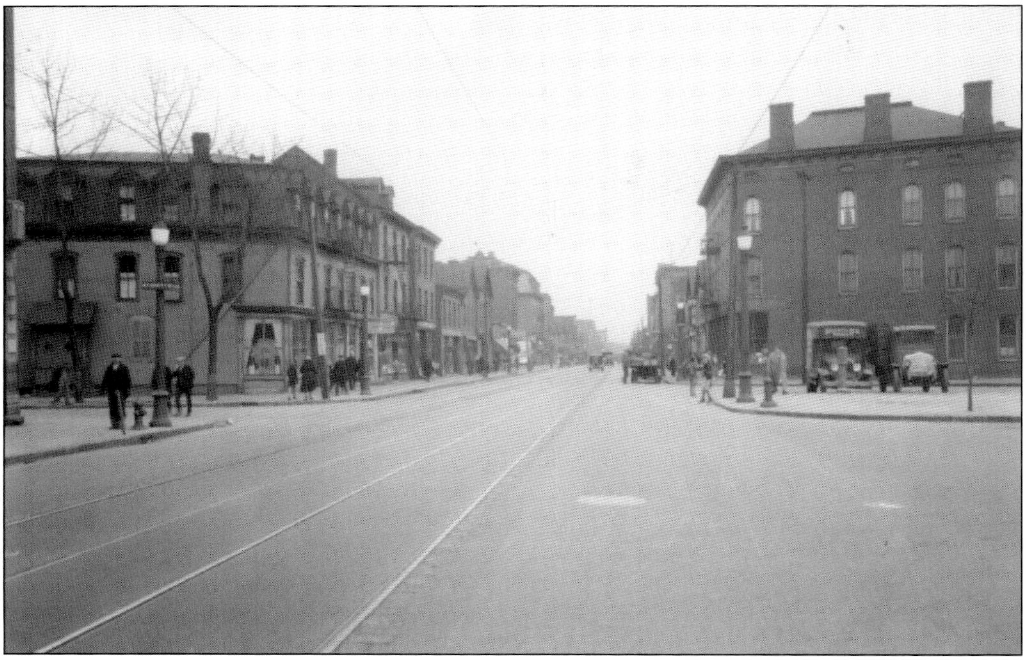

An industrial cluster, which included restaurants and small businesses, is pictured at the intersection of William and Bennett Streets in 1930. Bennett Street (on the right) had a large common area, which was once home to the Clinton Bailey Market. A large public bathhouse was built there in 1927, and eventually, most of the street was used for the playground of Bennett Park Public School No. 32. This intersection is near the current location of the JFK Recreation Center.

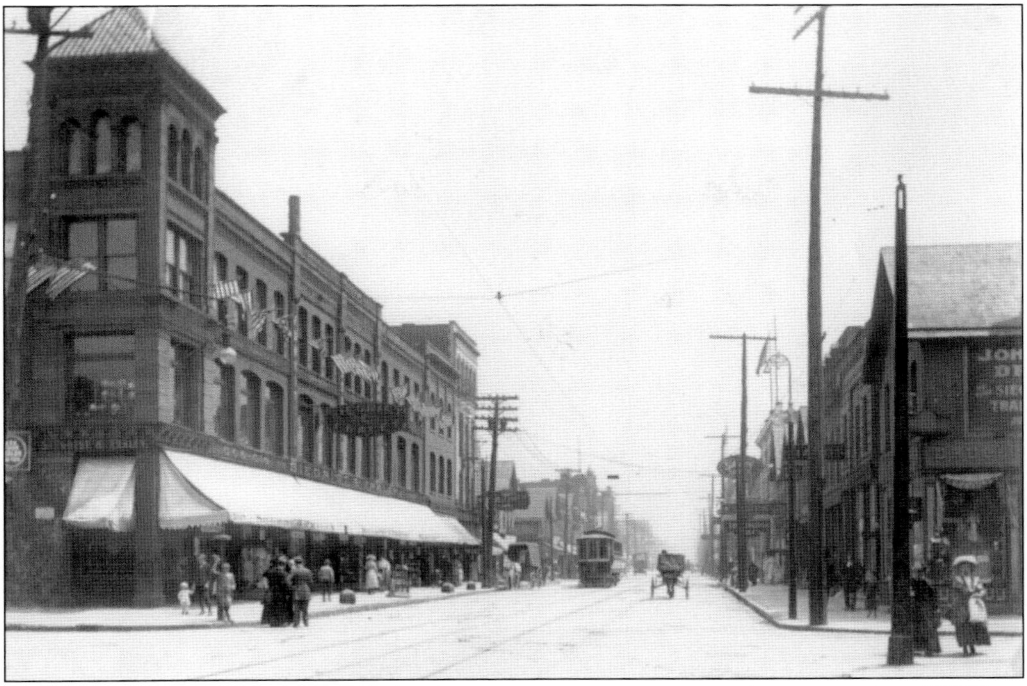

The patriotic facade of Seigrist & Fraley department store towers over the intersection of William and Emslie Streets. When this photograph was taken in 1912, Seigrist & Fraley had two stores; the other was located at 1018 Broadway. Across the street is the Abraham Slotkin Cloak and Millinery Shop. The Slotkins owned three millinery and clothing shops on William Street. Also shown is the Savoy Theater, which was an early "moving picture" theater.

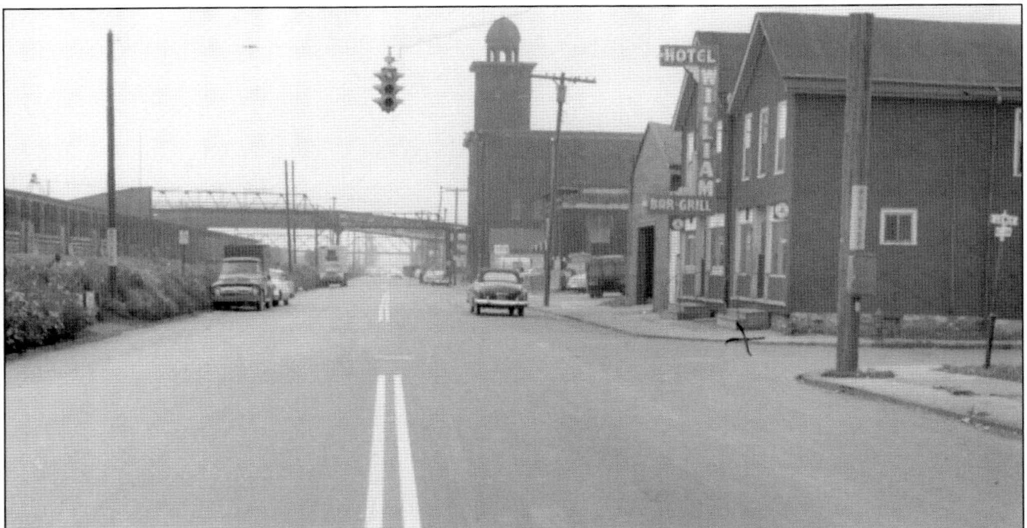

The Livestock Exchange Building, which included a walkable bridge over William Street to the stockyards, was designed by Louise Bethune. This 1956 photograph shows a clear image of the bridge and the domed tower at 1167 William Street. The Buffalo stockyards were removed in 1964 and replaced with the William Street Post Office. The Livestock Exchange Building was also torn down in 1964, and the Buffalo Community Federal Credit Union is currently located near the exchange building's former site.

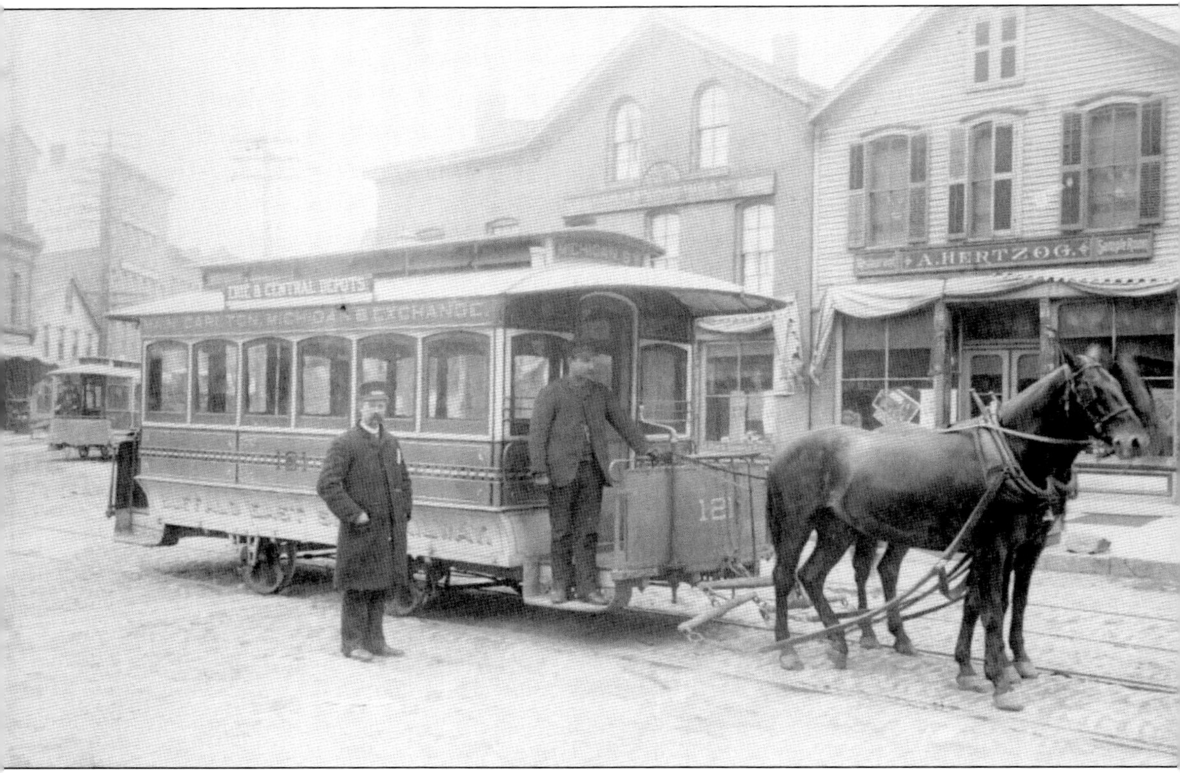

Pictured is Car No. 121 of the Buffalo East Side Railway, a part of the extensive streetcar system in Buffalo. Although a horse-drawn car is pictured here, electric streetcars were introduced to various lines over the course of 20 to 30 years beginning in the early 1880s. This is the Main, Carlton, Michigan, and Exchange Line, which ran between those streets. In the background is the German-American Brewing Company, which made its first appearance in the city directory in 1886. Judging from the location of the brewing company, this may be the corner of Main and High Streets, though it is difficult to verify because A. Hertzog's restaurant and sample room (next to the brewery) cannot be confirmed in city directories. Research reveals that an Albert Hertzog ran a saloon beginning in 1887, but the address is listed as 690 Michigan Avenue, leading to the possibility of this being the intersection of Michigan Avenue and Exchange Street. Between 1889 and 1899, the saloon moved to 160 Exchange Street; it later became the Buffalo Hotel, where Hertzog served as proprietor.

Two

BROADWAY
THE GRANDDADDY OF BUFFALO STREETS

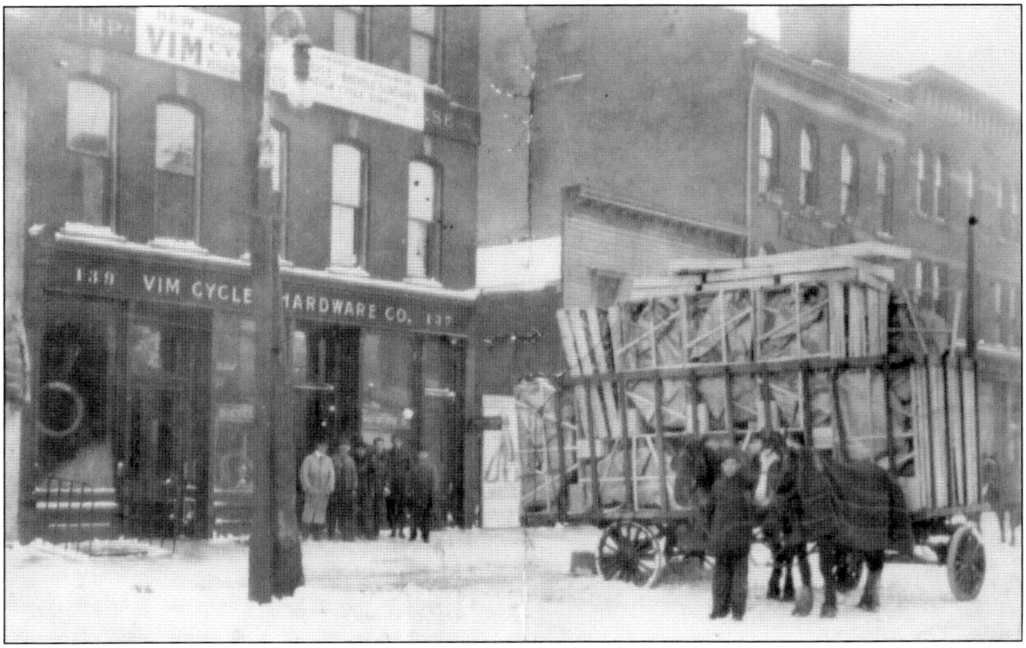

Winter was obviously not a slow time for the Vim Cycle Hardware Company, located at 137–139 Broadway between Elm Street and Michigan Avenue. Employees of the company are shown sending off a shipment of bicycles headed to waiting customers. The company opened in 1899 and was located at 224–226 Broadway until 1909; in 1910, it moved to its "new home," as shown on the sign above the second floor.

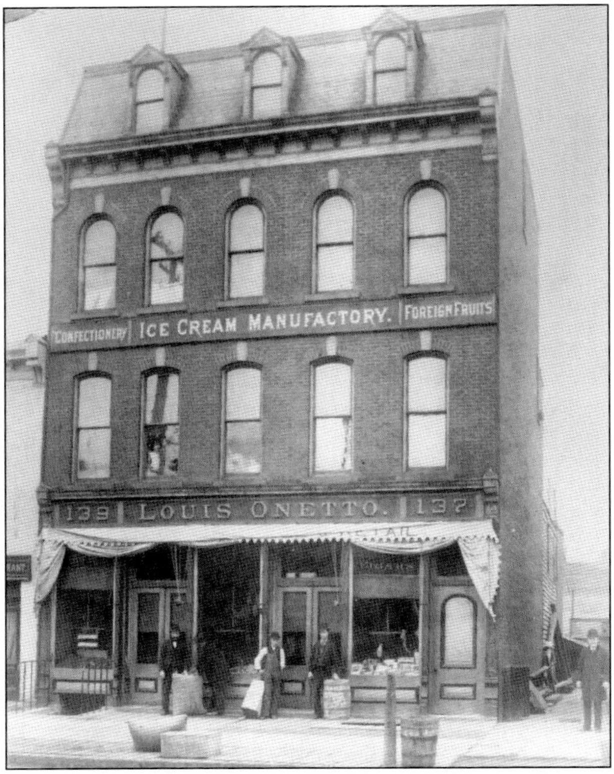

In a unique twist, Louis Onetto's "ice cream manufactory" (pictured in 1884) was the tenant at 137–139 Broadway before the Vim Cycle Hardware Company moved into the structure in 1910. Onetto had a long and fruitful business career and is pictured here with his hand on a barrel. His business opened in 1878 and lasted until 1975, when O-Nut-Tos Nut Shops, Inc., opened. In 1979, Nut-Tos Peanut and Popcorn Supply Company bought O-Nut-Tos out of bankruptcy and moved the business to West Seneca, New York, where it is still in operation today.

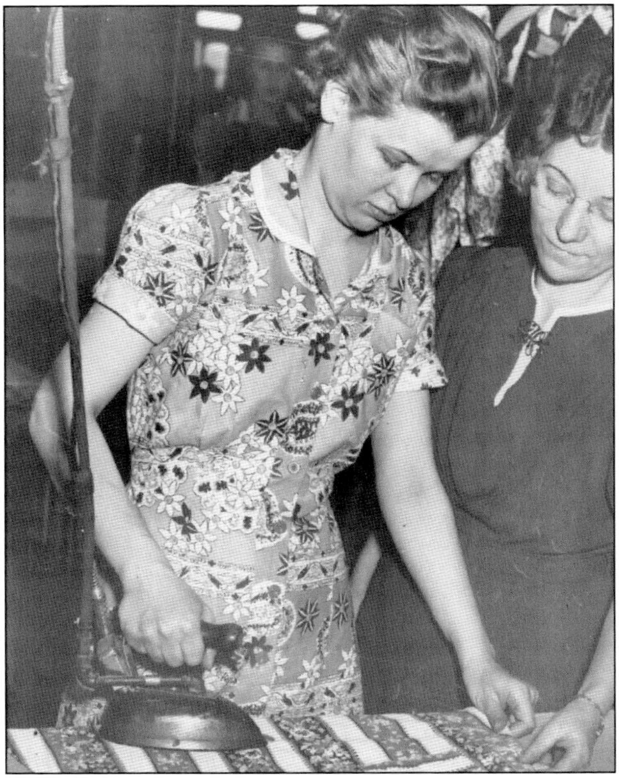

The Bernard Dress Manufacturing Company did not last long. In the 1930 city directory, the American Slicing Machine Company carried the address 144–148 Broadway, with no mention of Bernard. In the mid-1930s, the company was located at the Broadway address, but by 1940, the building was vacant. The building was located between Elm Street and Michigan Avenue and is now demolished.

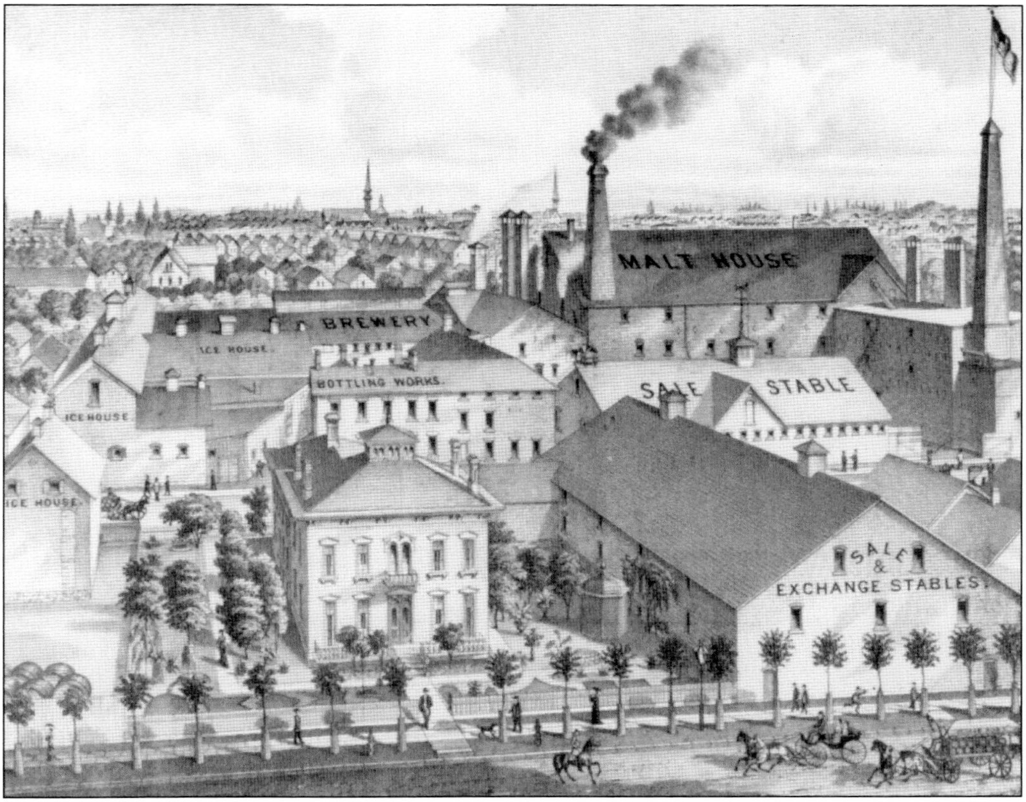

The George Roos Brewery on Broadway between Hickory and Pratt Streets is shown in this 1880 lithograph from the *Atlas of Erie County*. Successor to Jacob Roos, George Roos, ran the business as Roos Cooperative Brewing Company. The business was sold in the early 1890s to what would be become Iroquois Brewing Company, which remained open until 1971. These two breweries constituted the second-longest-running brewery operations in Buffalo.

The George F. Stein Brewery is being demolished in this 1959 photograph. Located at the corner of Broadway and Smith Street, it lasted a little over 100 years in various forms. Opened in 1852 by Albert Albrecht, it had various names, such as Julius Binz and Broadway Brewing and Malting Company. Facing stiff competition from national brewing companies, Stein Brewery closed in 1958 and was summarily demolished.

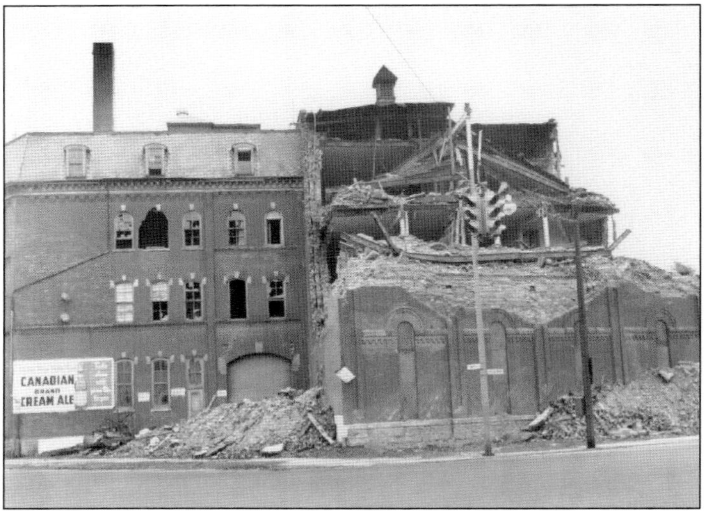

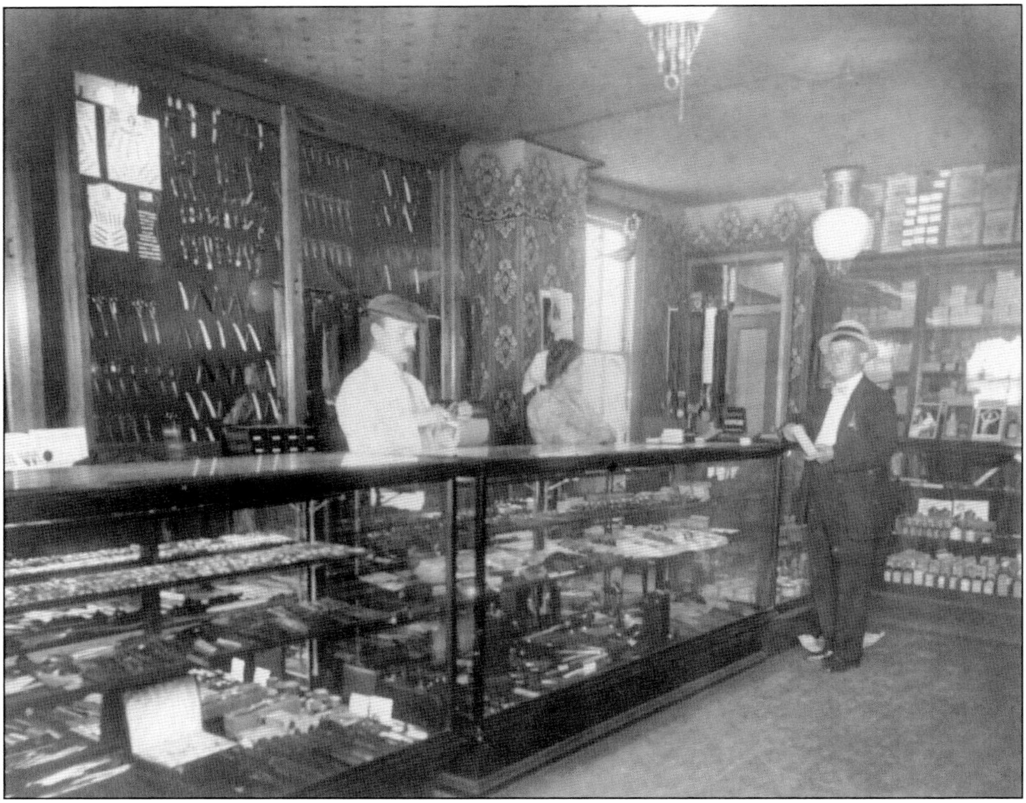

Otto Reuters' Barber Supplies Shop, located at 505 Broadway between Mortimer Street and Jefferson Avenue, sold various barber devices (as shown in the display cases), along with elixirs and ointments. Reuters is behind the counter at left, with his wife, Pauline, standing next to him. When this photograph was taken in 1920, there were ten barber supply stores in the city, and seven of them were located in the East Side. Reuters's first store was located at 358 William Street.

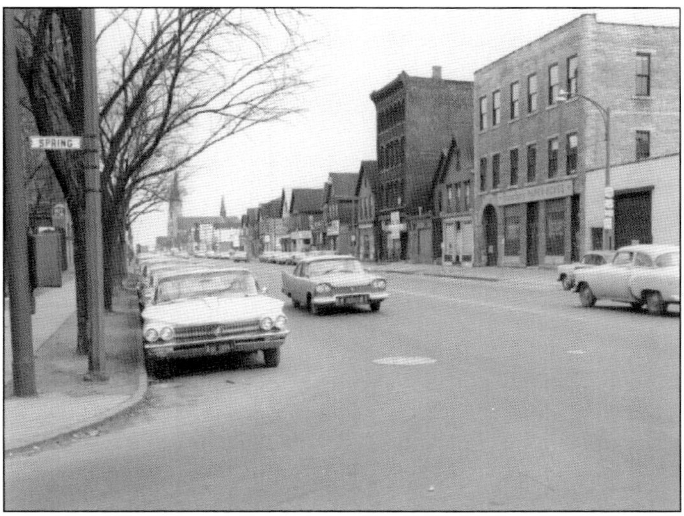

Drescher Paper Box, Inc., is shown at right in this photograph taken from Spring Street. The company was and is currently located at 459 Broadway. This 1960 photograph shows one of the original buildings that is still in use today, although an expansion led to the demolition of the houses and structures to its immediate right. The company, called Charles A. Drescher & Son's when it opened in 1867, is currently owned by the Langworthy family.

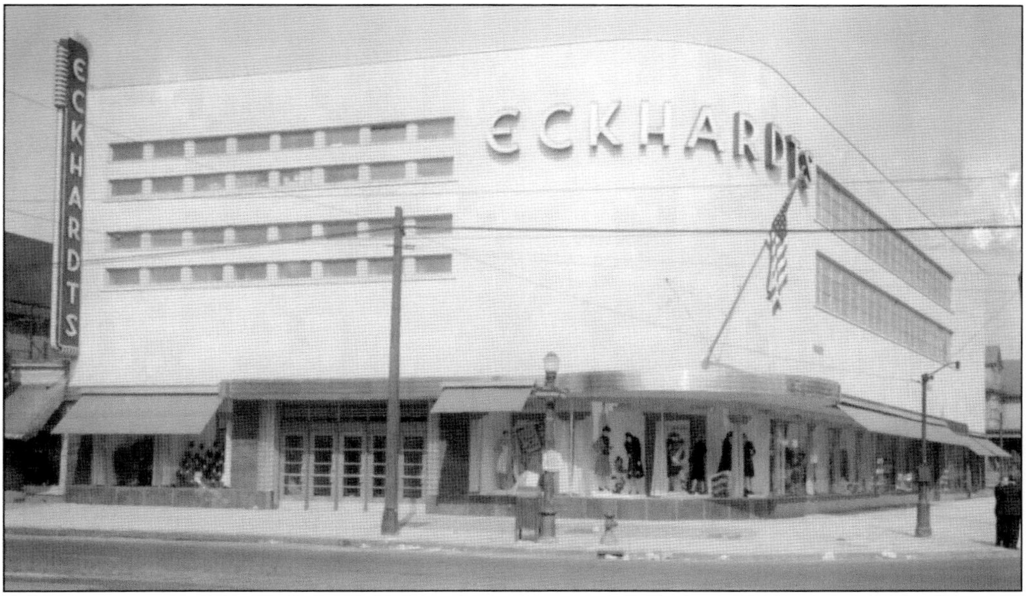

Eckhardt's Department Store has a long—if disjointed—history at the corner of Broadway and Fillmore Avenue. John Eckhardt worked as a clerk for his family, who owned a dry goods store at 514 William Street. In 1892, Eckhardt and his son opened a new dry goods store at 950 Broadway, which remained in the family until 1941. This building is still standing and was also home to a Sears and Kobacker's Department Store.

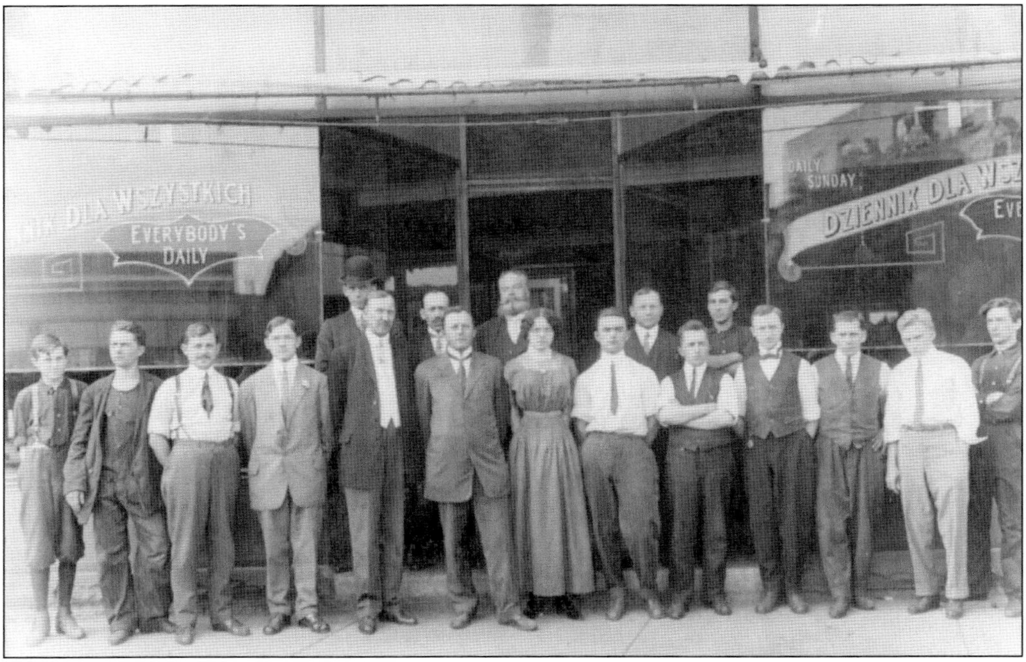

Dziennik Dla Wszystkich, also known as *Everybody's Daily*, began in 1907 and was the preeminent Polish newspaper for the growing population that developed around the Broadway and Fillmore Avenue intersection. The paper's office, located at 928 Broadway, is shown in this c. 1910 employee photograph. After the paper closed in 1957, community leader Matthew W. Pelczynski felt the loss; three years later, he became publisher and editor of the *Am-Pol Eagle*.

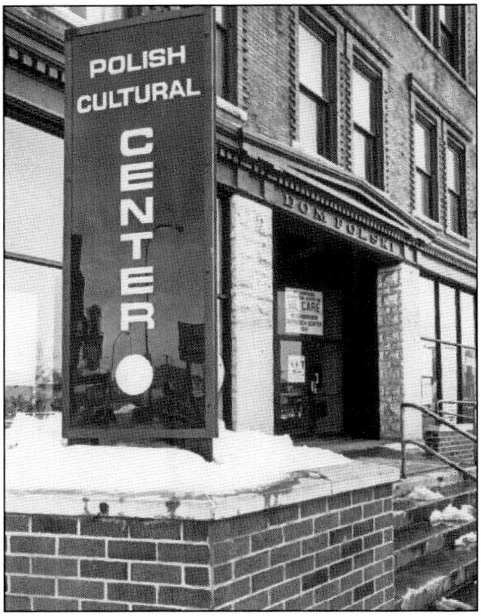

The Dom Polski building at 1081 Broadway was built in 1905 as a gathering place for the burgeoning Polish community in the Broadway–Fillmore Avenue area. In 1976, the building became the Polish Community and Cultural Center, and in 2000, the name was changed to the Lt. Col. Matt Urban Human Services Center of Western New York. Currently, the center offers housing and senior, youth, family, and homeless services.

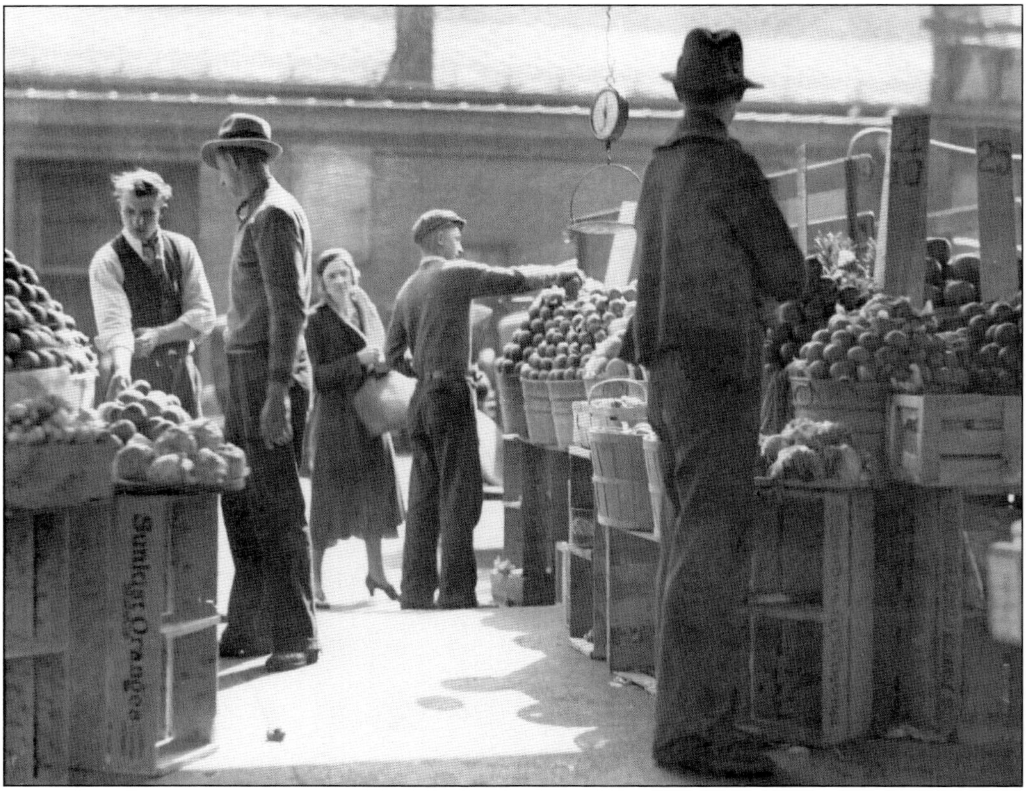

The famous Broadway Market is pictured around 1930. It was first established as an outdoor gathering place to mimic the old-town marketplaces of the immigrants landing in Buffalo. Residents of all ethnic backgrounds founded the market in 1888 to bring some of their traditions to the New World. It became a place for the purchase of goods, food, and wares—but also for socialization. Broadway Market is considered one of the oldest public markets in America.

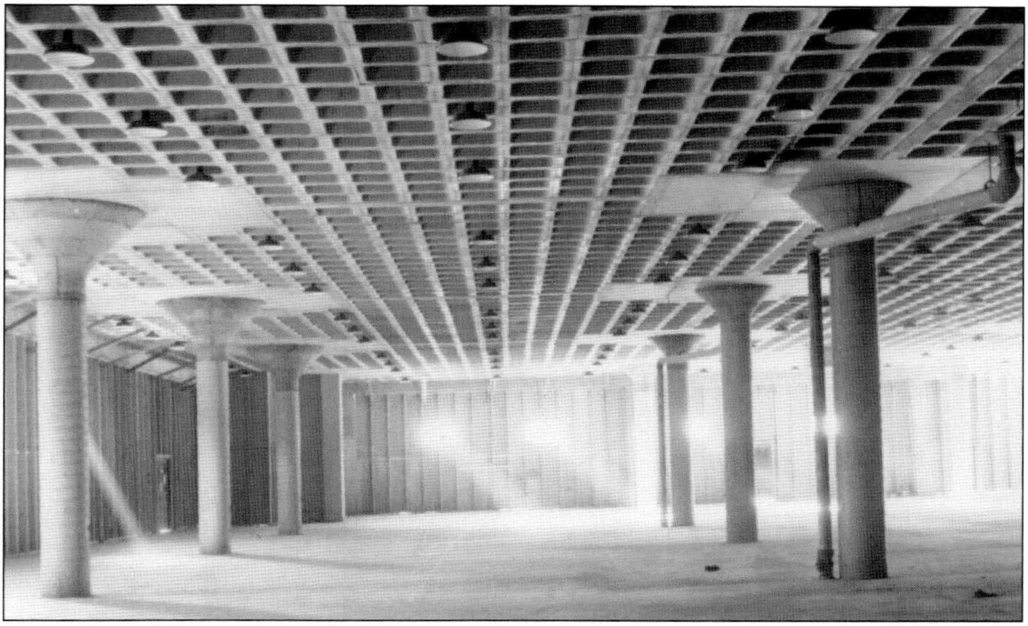

The Broadway Market is pictured in 1954 during its third and final construction phase. What started as a fully open-air market with vendor carts became an indoor-outdoor market architecturally similar to the Washington (Chippewa) Market, and it eventually morphed into the structure that is still in use today.

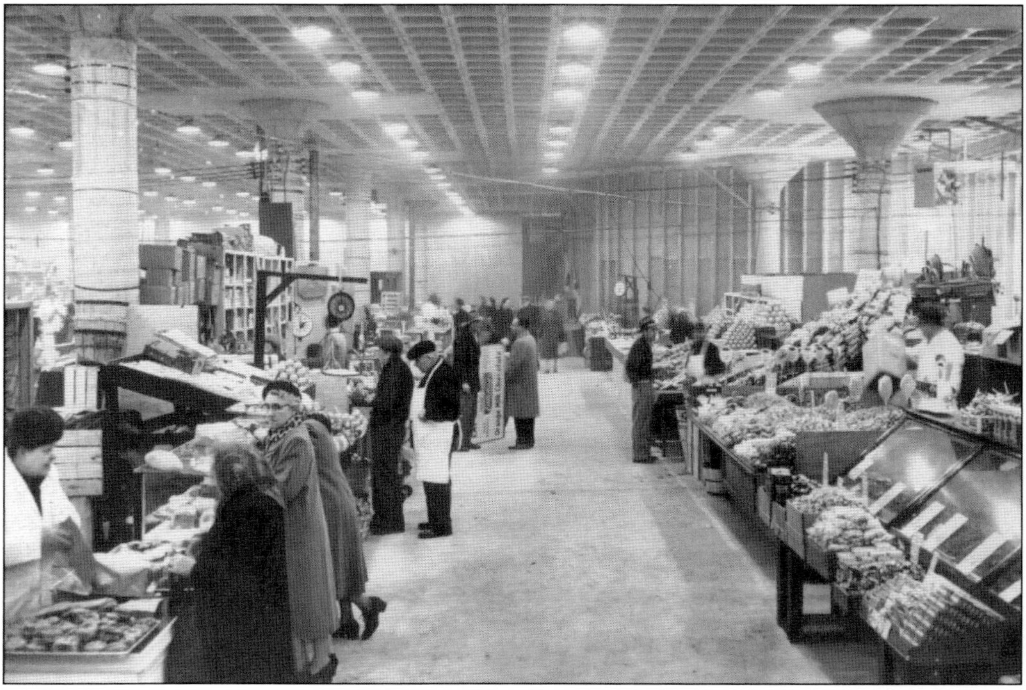

The Broadway Market is pictured here in 1955 during a soft opening. Shown are temporary vendor booths and shoppers eager to support them. The building was not yet fully completed, but the demand was high enough that construction crews worked around the vendors' schedules. This is the first floor of the building, and rows like this were set up throughout the floor.

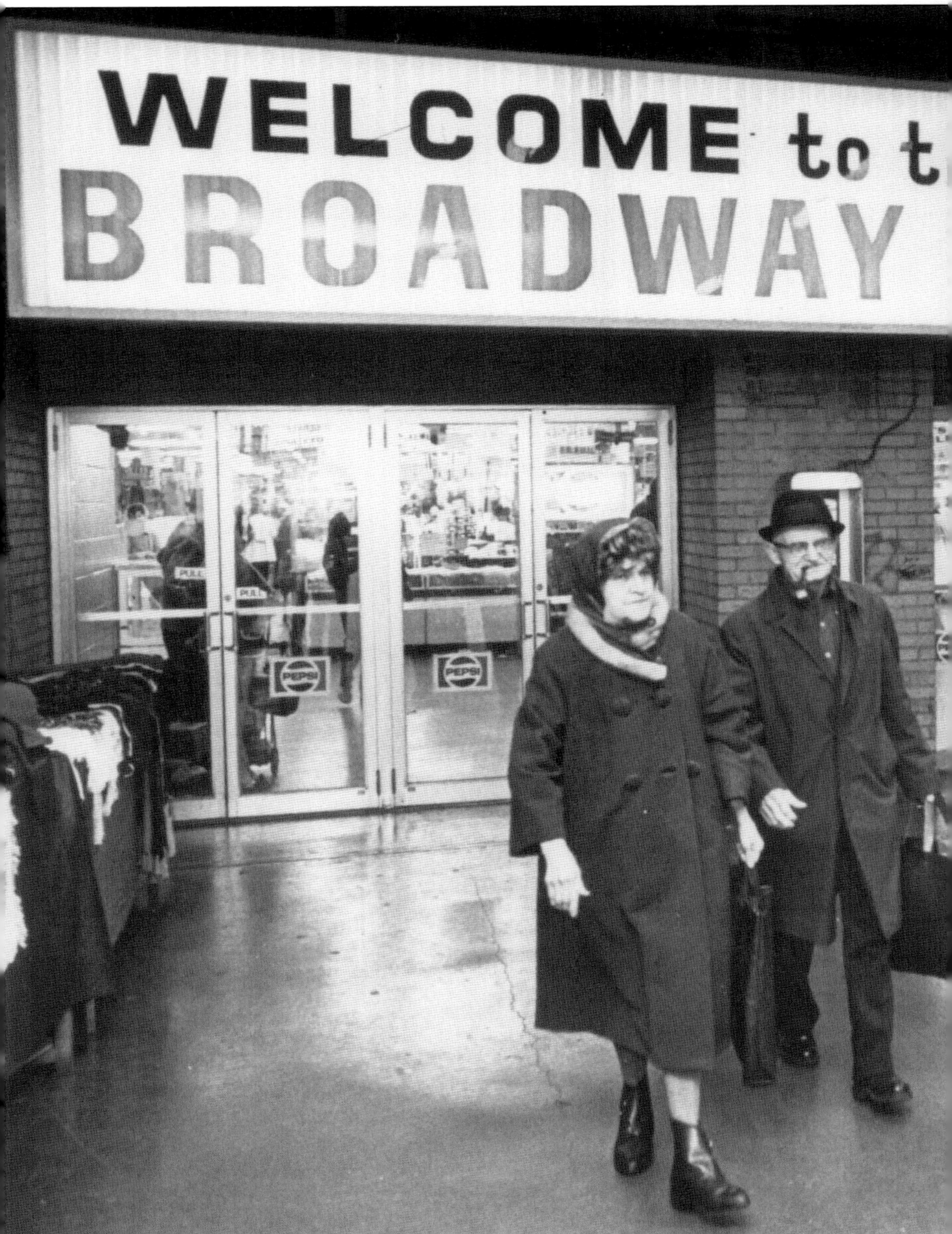
WELCOME to t
BROADWAY
PULL
PULL
PEPSI
PEPSI

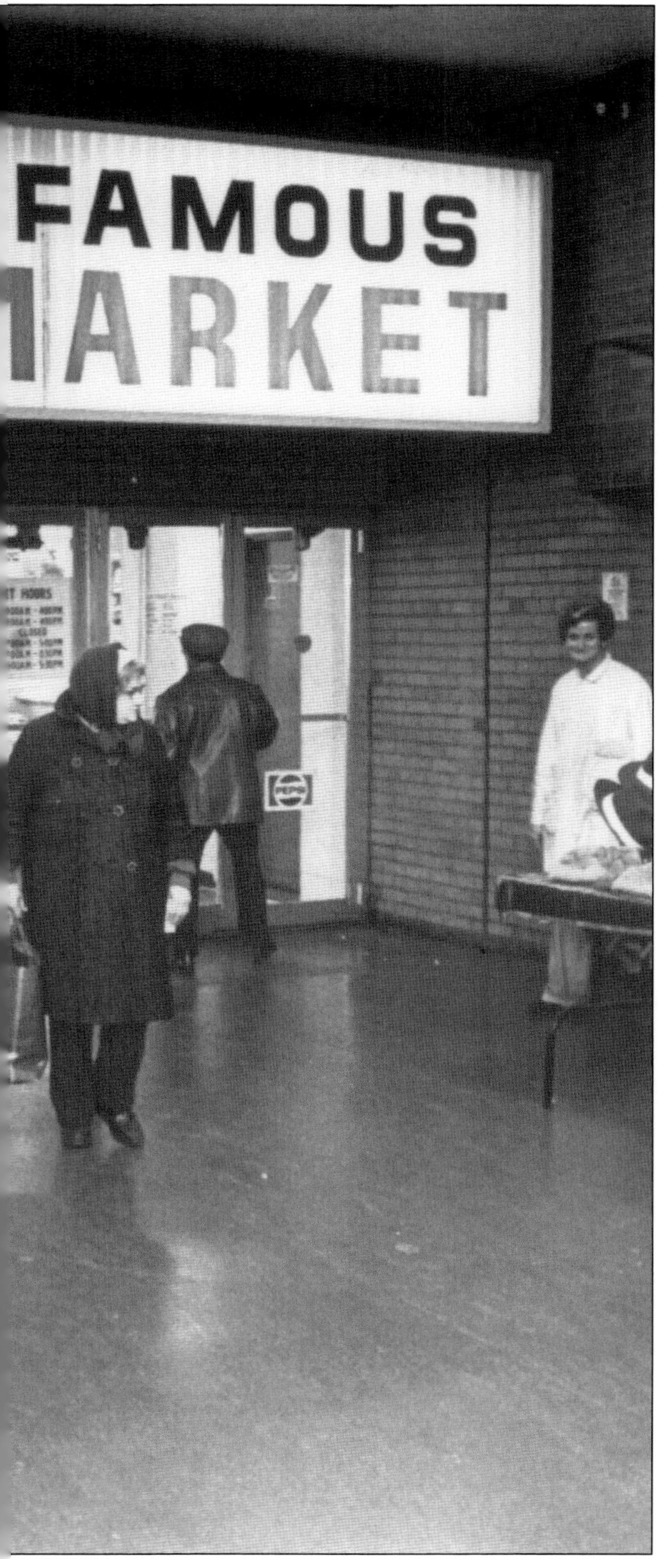

Patrons leave the world-famous Broadway Market in this c. 1963 photograph. The market has had its share of hard times, with 50 percent of the population in the surrounding neighborhoods leaving over the last 50 years. However, customers now return by the thousands in the weeks leading up to Easter. With bakeries such as Chrusciki Bakery, Melanie's Sweets, and White Eagle; a fish market; four meat-market stands; and restaurants like the East-West Café and the Soul Food Shack, the market is again on solid footing as a place for shoppers to find diverse cuisine. In addition to the events of Easter week, the market has year-round programs and events such as the Senior Center, Mother's Day and Dyngus Day festivities, and a community rooftop garden. The Broadway Market has undergone tremendous changes over its 128-year history, but it has not lost its place in the hearts of those who value tradition.

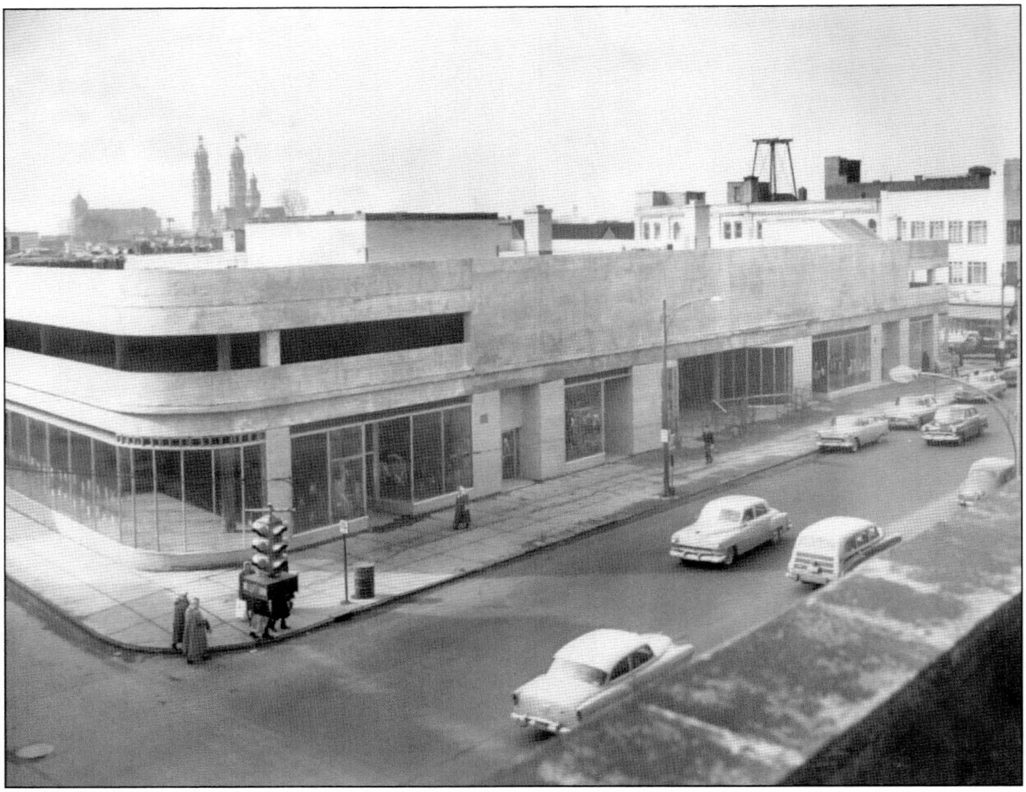

The Broadway Market needed to be fully indoors in order to accommodate patrons year-round. The market's exterior is pictured here in 1955. The building was fully completed in 1956, but in this photograph, is still a concrete shell waiting to be filled. At far right is Charles's Clothing Shop, and in the distance is St. Stanislaus Bishop and Martyr Church.

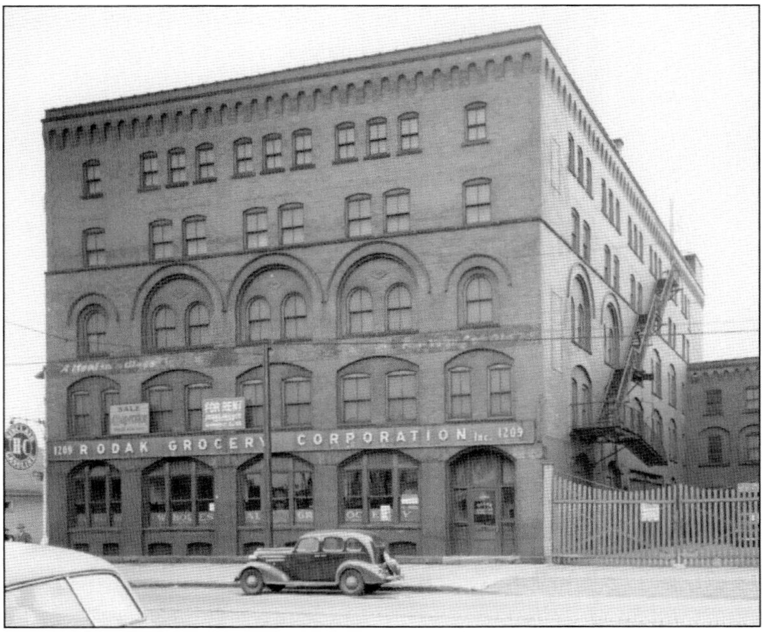

The Rodak Grocery Corporation, located at 1209 Broadway, is pictured in 1945, when the building was for sale. This building was connected to the three-story building at 1199 Broadway (to the right; see page 35). For at least 50 years, various wholesale grocery companies—including Rodak and Stanislaus Lipowicz—occupied both 1199 and 1209 Broadway.

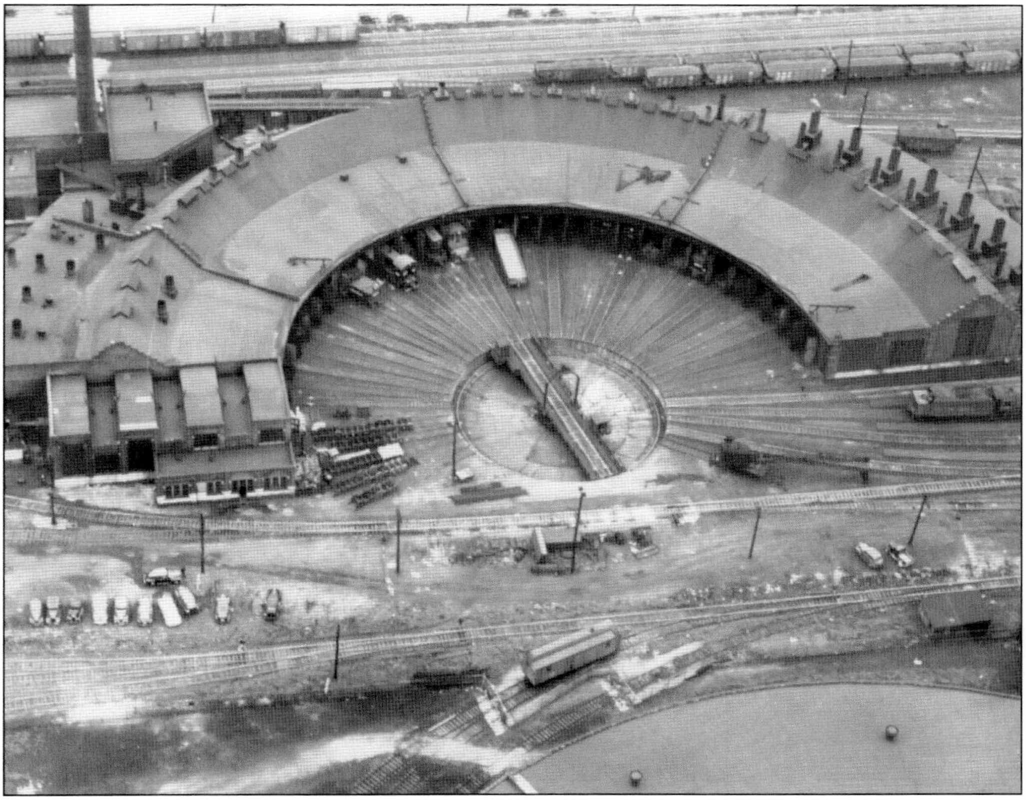

The Broadway Bailey Roundhouse was part of a larger complex that included the New York Central and West Shore Railroads, the Wagner Palace Car Company, and, later, the Pullman Car Company. Roundhouses incorporated turntables for the easy repair and/or storage of locomotives. When newer locomotive technology allowed trains to more easily move in forward or reverse, roundhouses were put to other uses.

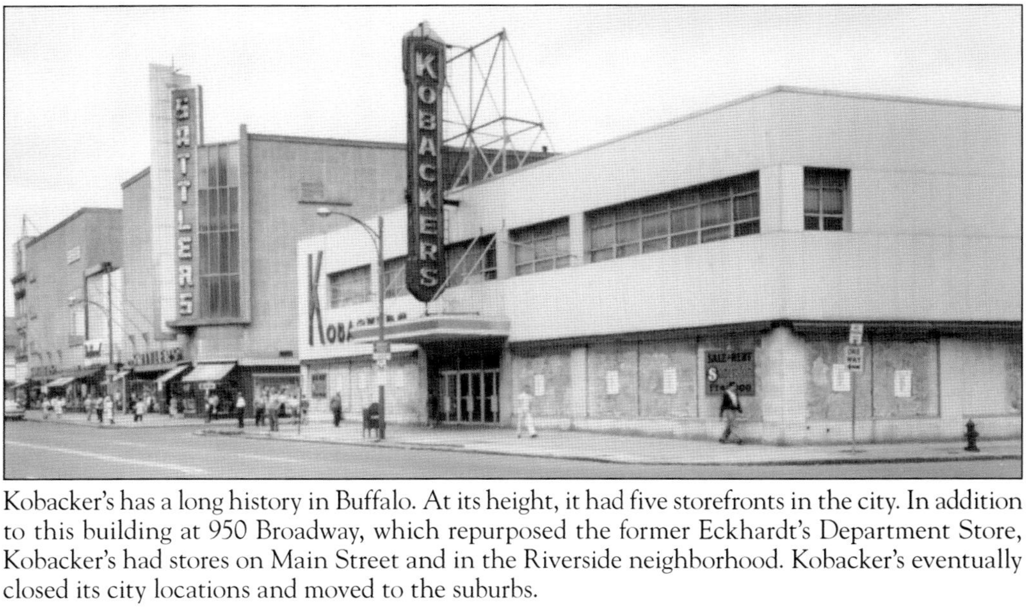

Kobacker's has a long history in Buffalo. At its height, it had five storefronts in the city. In addition to this building at 950 Broadway, which repurposed the former Eckhardt's Department Store, Kobacker's had stores on Main Street and in the Riverside neighborhood. Kobacker's eventually closed its city locations and moved to the suburbs.

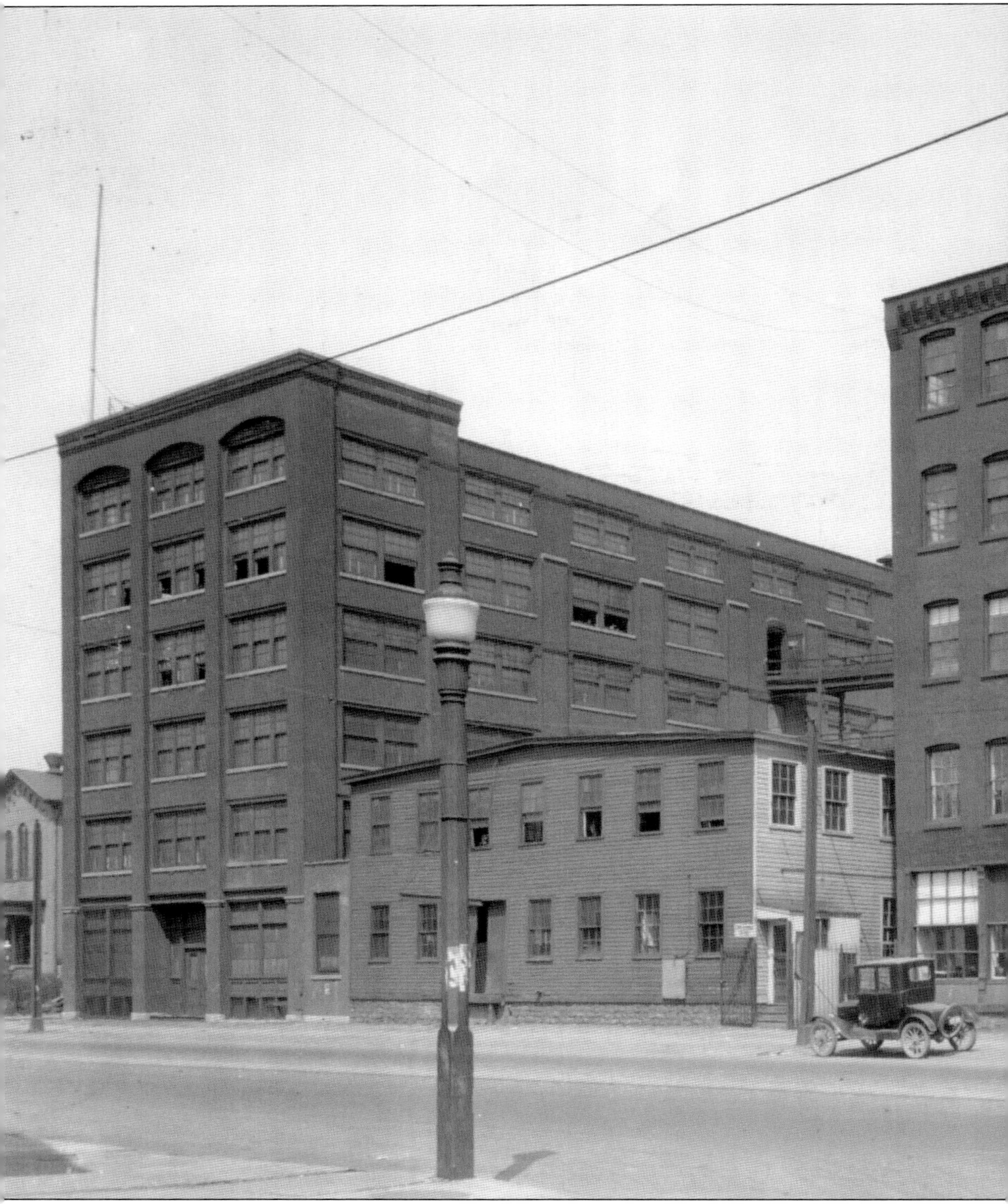

One of the most successful businesses founded in Buffalo is the Buffalo Forge Company. In this undated photograph, the mammoth building sits at 490 Broadway on a whole city block bounded by Broadway, Sycamore Street, Mortimer Street, and Spring Street. The company, founded by William Wendt in 1878, produced forges and exhausters for blacksmiths, along with an independent air pump to stoke the fire and exhaust piping to carry away the smoke. It diversified its product

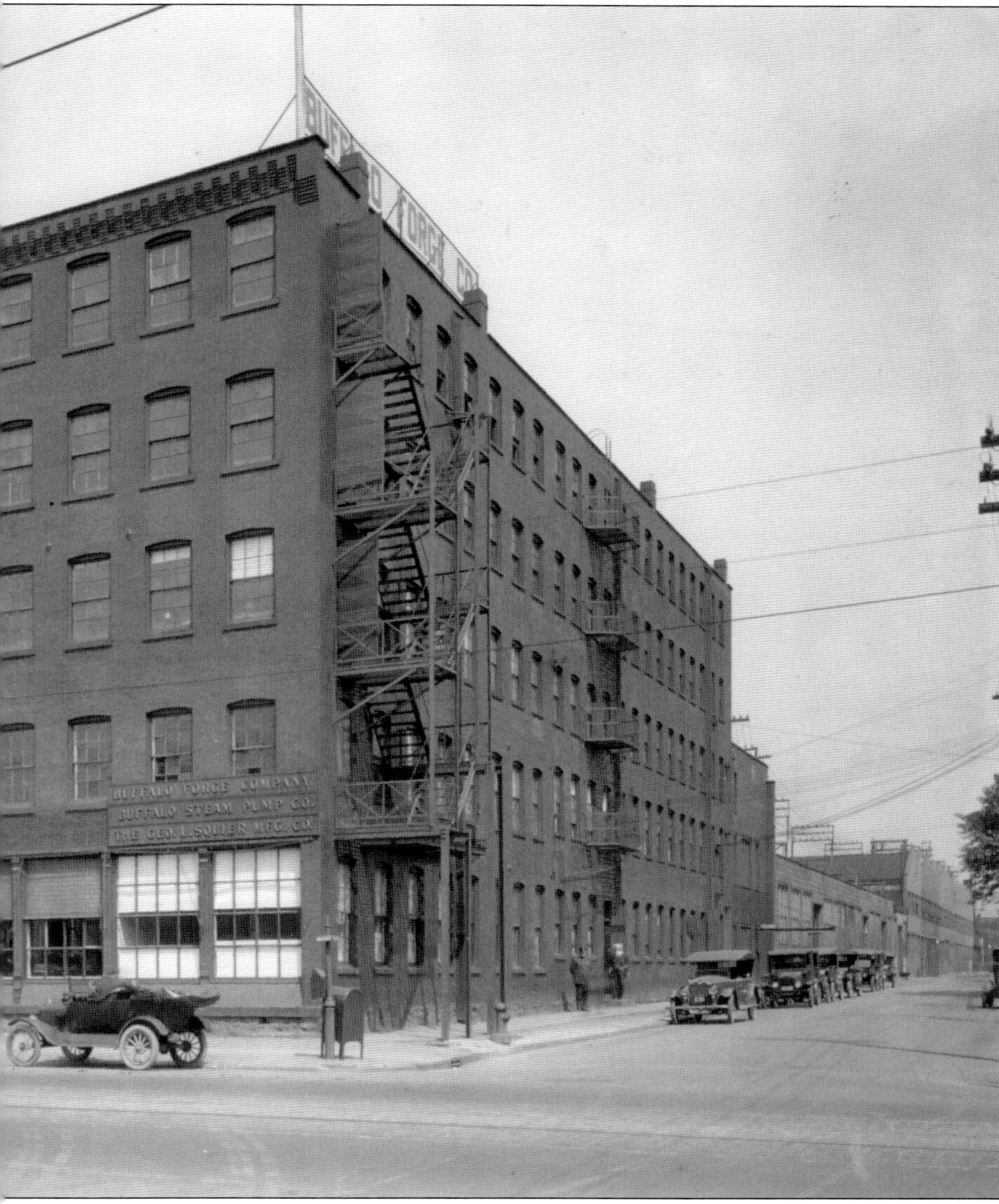

base to include air blowers and machinery. In 1914, Buffalo Forge engineers wrote the industry standard guidelines in "Fan Engineering," a manual on gas and air movement. The company moved into heating and cooling products; it is known as the birthplace of air conditioning because Buffalo Forge employee Willis H. Carrier designed and developed the first modern air conditioning system.

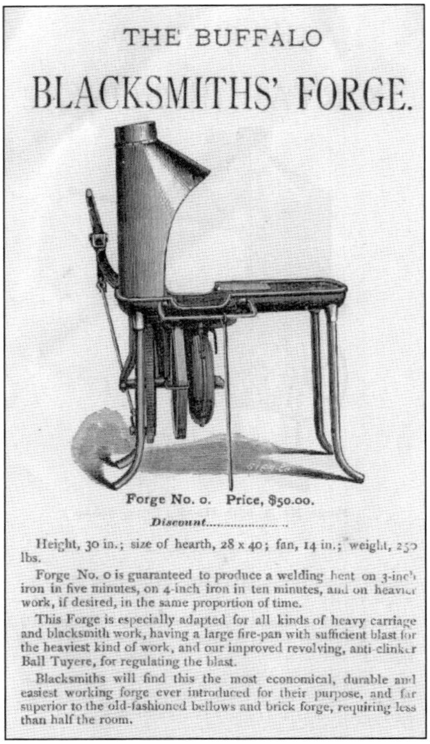

Pictured at left is an advertisement for Buffalo Forge Company's Forge No. 0, the first forge the company produced. Buffalo Forge made its name in products that produced "blast," or airflow, to keep fires stoked. These products also released exhaust and smoke away from the blacksmith, making for a cleaner work environment. The sale price for Forge No. 0 was $50, and—as the ad mentions—the forge was "far superior to the old-fashioned bellows and brick forge, requiring less than half the room." Below is a 1936 photograph of a Buffalo Forge employee working on an industrial cutter-grinder machine in the machine shop. In 1993, James Howden and Company (headquartered in Glasgow, Scotland) purchased Buffalo Forge, but the craftsmanship and pride of thousands of Buffalo Forge employees lives on in Howden North America, Inc., which has numerous offices across the continent, including one in nearby Depew, New York.

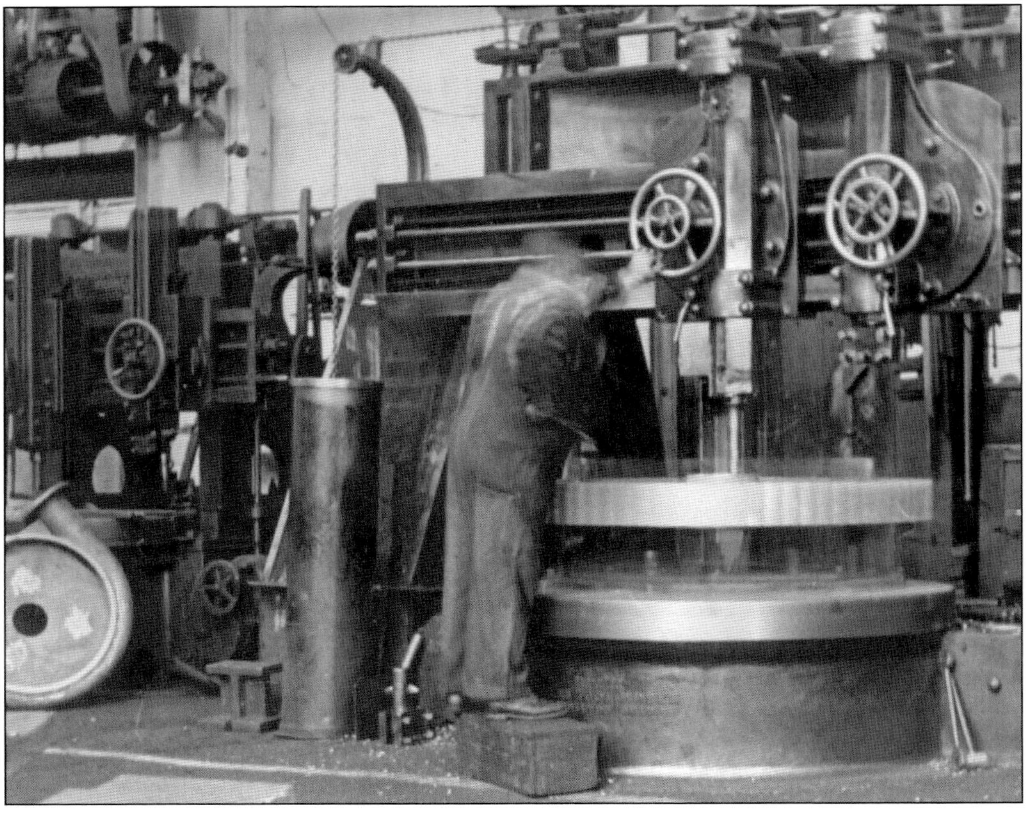

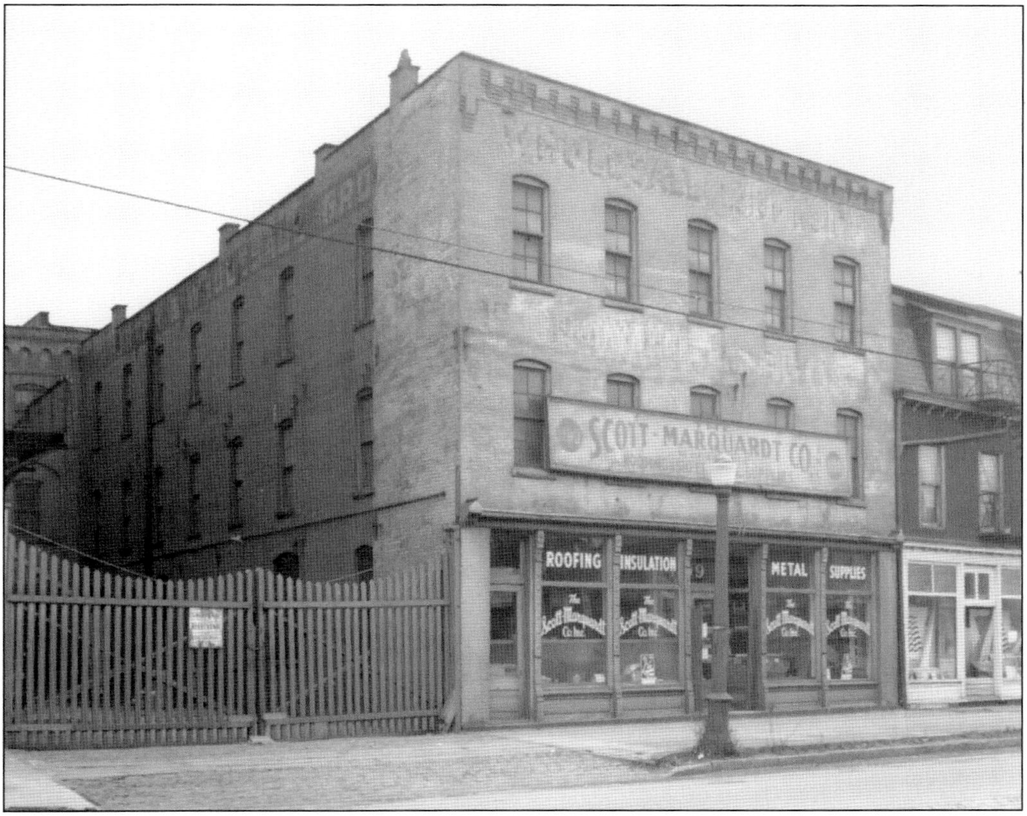

Stanislaus Lipowicz Wholesale Grocers was housed in the pictured building from 1890 until 1921. The Scott-Marquardt Company, which produced roofing and sheet metal supplies, moved into the building in 1938 and operated there until 1964. There are numerous faded painted signs and company names on the building, such as "Brownie and Bros." and an incomplete "Wholesale Grocer."

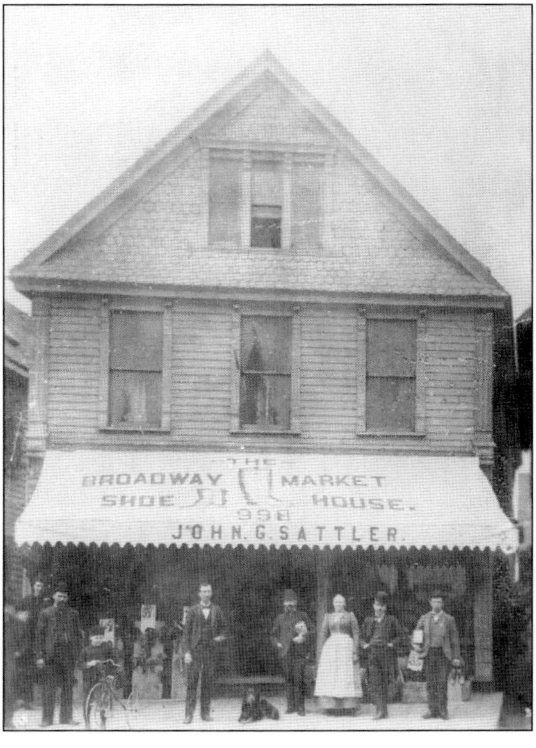

Sattler's Department Store is synonymous with a bustling East Side. John G. Sattler's shoe store, located directly across from the open-air Broadway Market, is pictured here in 1898. Sattler is standing to the left of the doorway. This store was initially located in the front section of Sattler's mother's house but outgrew the storefront and occupied the entire first floor just two years later.

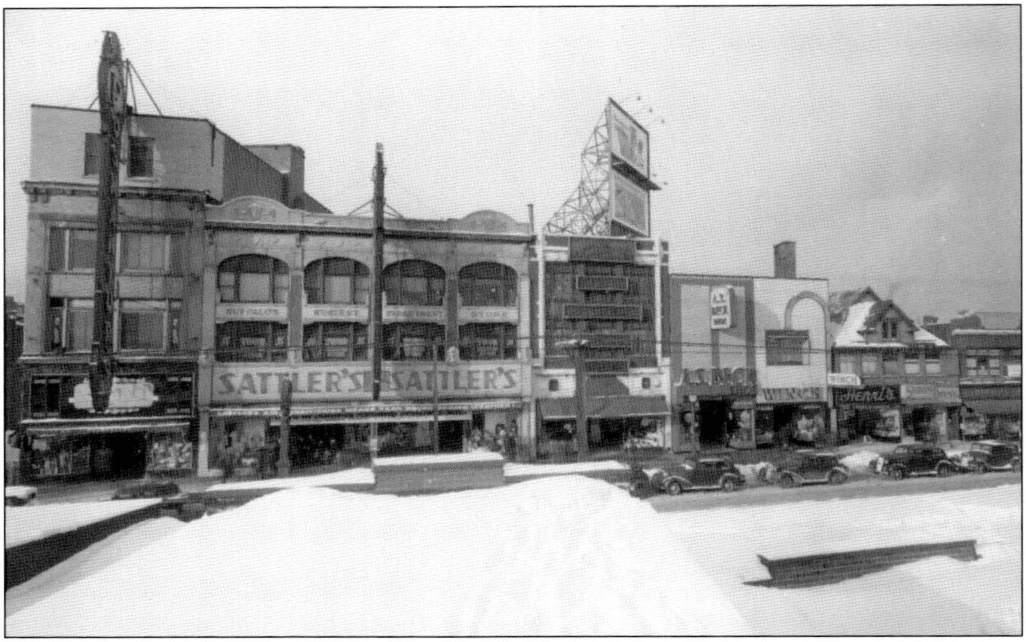

By 1925, John G. Sattler had one of the largest shoe stores in Buffalo and brought new executives to the ownership table. Charles Hahn Jr., Sattler's son-in-law, and Aaron Rabow, who diversified the sales floor and brought on women's ready-to-wear clothing items, were two such executives. The above photograph, taken around 1930, shows Sattler's offering air-conditioning for "year 'round spring weather." Also shown here are Posmantur's Men's Clothing store, Adler's, A.S. Beck, Winch's, and Henri's. This block was the center of clothing and retail shopping in Buffalo. Through the 1930s and 1940s, Sattler's continued to expand back from the street, and the store had two acres of sale floors by 1946. Sattler passed away in 1941, but in 1946, the cornerstone was laid for a new 106,000-square-foot addition and refurbishment. Sattler's is pictured below during a snowfall on December 22, 1961.

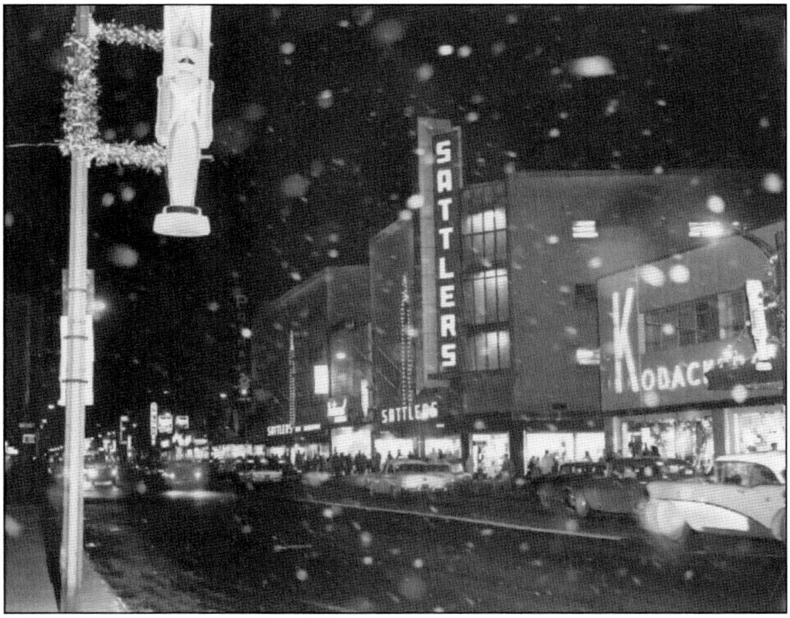

Three

Clinton and William
Localities of Commerce

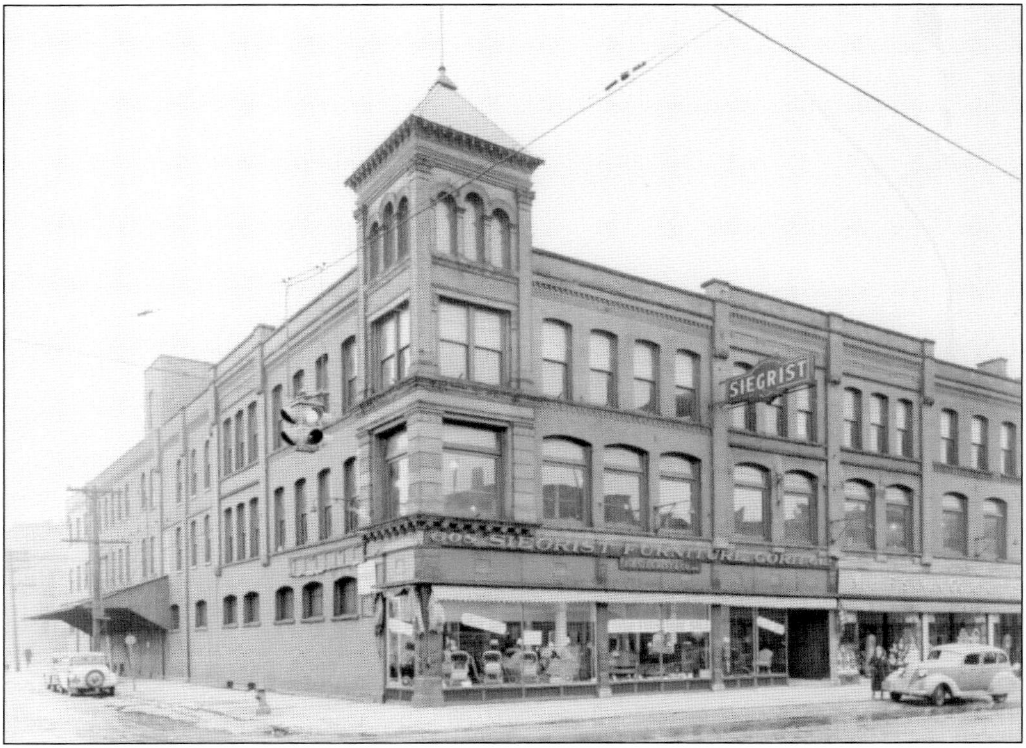

Siegrist and Fraley is pictured here around 1935, after the business became Siegrist Furniture Store. When the company opened in 1891, it was a general department store and warehouse. After 35 years, the company began selling only furniture, and by 1947, the store and warehouse were closed. Currently, this is the location of the Sherman L. Walker Human Services Center and the Jesse E. Nash Health Center.

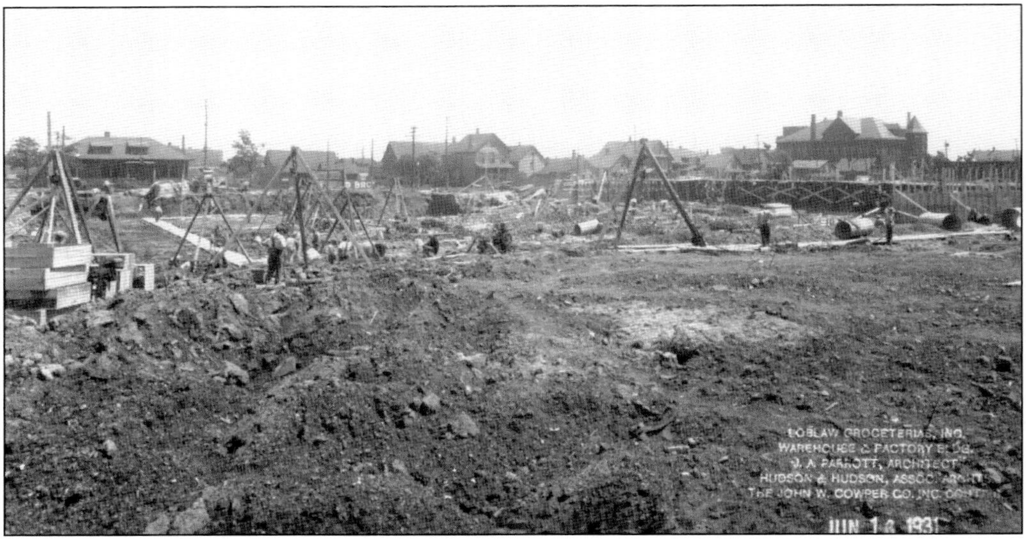

Various agricultural concerns of Western New York conceived the Niagara Frontier Growers Cooperative Market in 1930. The structures that remain today were constructed in 1931, as evidenced by the above image labeled "Loblaw Grocerterias, Inc." by the John Cowper Corporation. The photograph shows the equipment and machinery used to lay the building foundations, and the south side of Clinton Street is visible in the background. In 1933, the market became the Niagara Frontier Food Terminal, as shown by the signage on the building in the below photograph, which was taken in 1940. Thanks to this terminal and the Buffalo Stockyards, the East Side began taking shape as a major distribution center both locally and nationally.

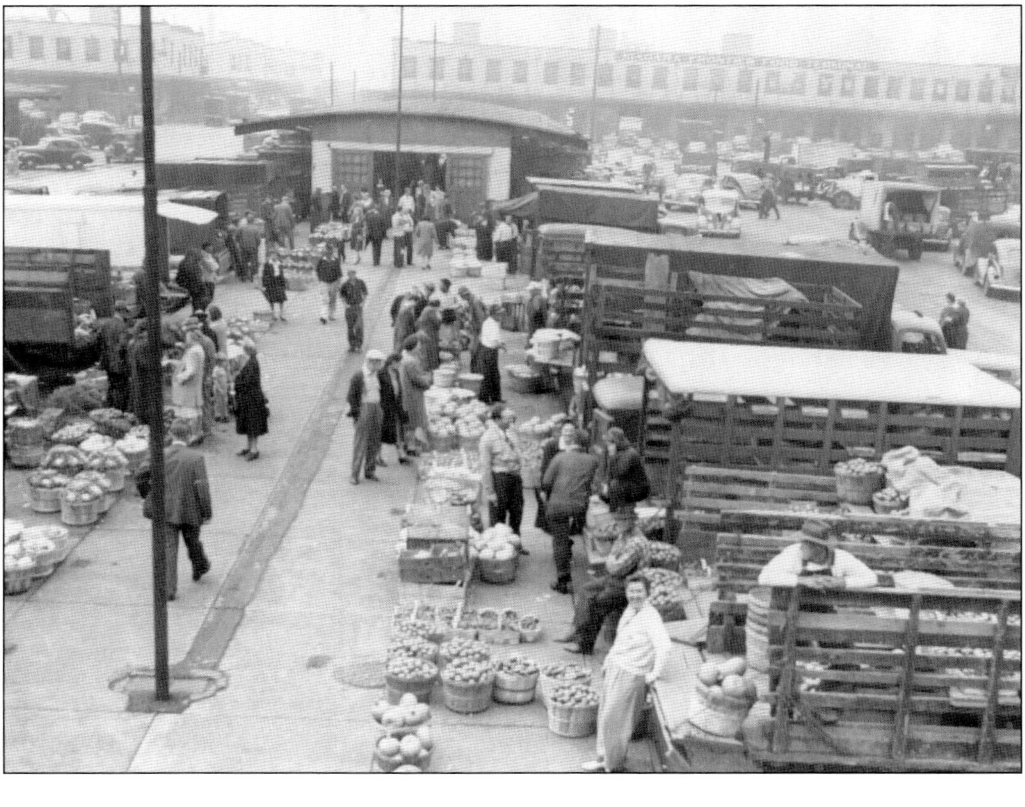

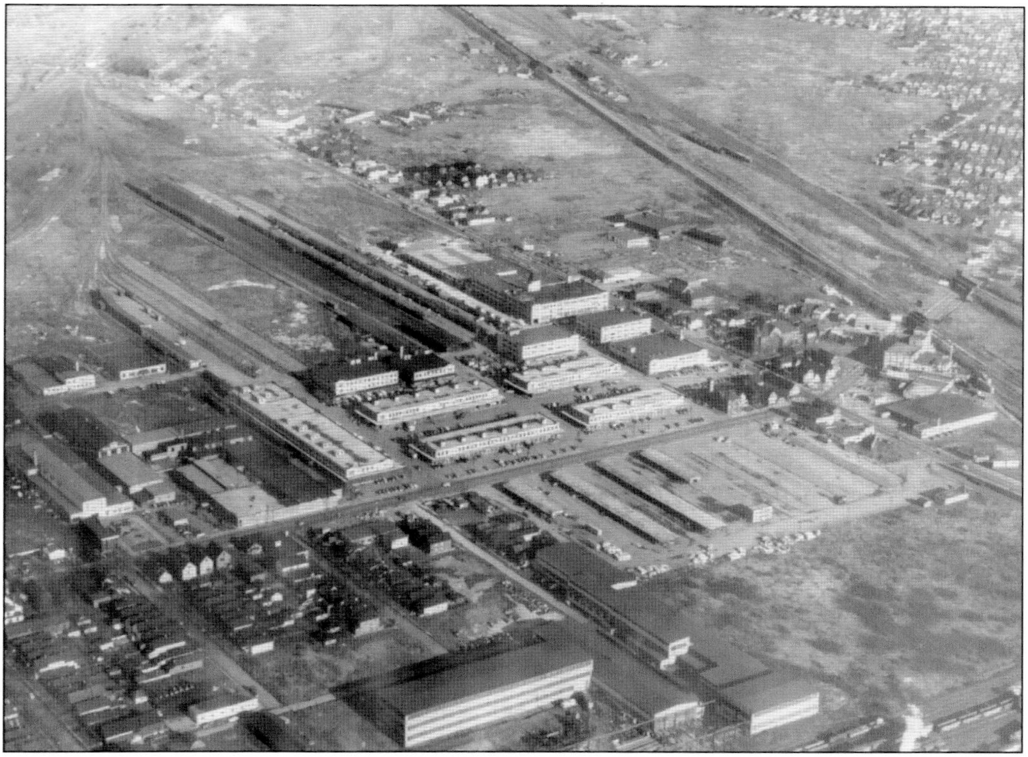

According to the Clinton Bailey Farmers Market website, the terminal was created to "promote, foster and encourage the intelligent and orderly marketing of agricultural products between producer and consumer." The above aerial photograph, taken in 1947, shows the expansive terminal campus, its proximity to rail lines, and the various open-walled structures designed to foster a connection between producer and consumer. The photograph also shows the rural landscape that surrounded Bailey Avenue, which cuts across the image vertically. The 1970 photograph below shows the diversity of products. The Clinton Bailey Farmers Market has recently enjoyed an awakening via the "eat local" movement. The growth and number of farmers markets currently in Buffalo and the surrounding suburbs owes a debt of gratitude to the "granddaddy" of them all.

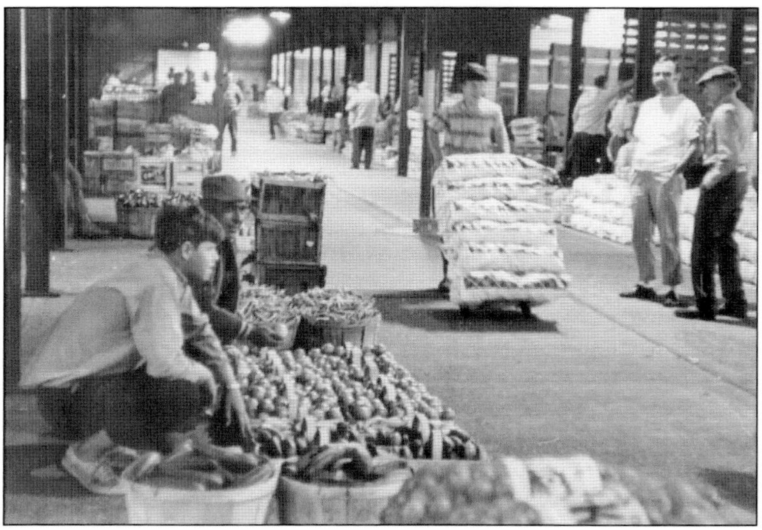

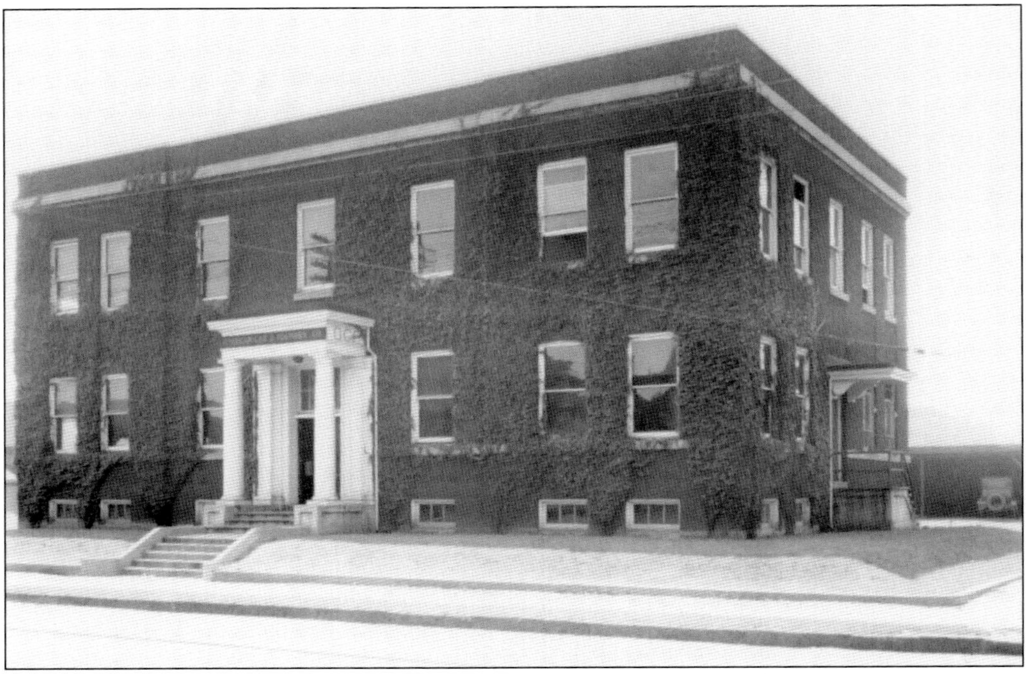

The American Car & Foundry, located near the corner of Clinton and Babcock Streets, created a diverse product line. Commencing operations in 1899 as a plant that constructed train cars, the company was defunct by 1932. After the plant was scuttled for 10 years, it reopened in 1942 as a producer of Army shells and served as the nation's principal source of large howitzer shells for England. Pictured above is the main office, which was located directly on the corner of Clinton and Babcock Streets, and below is the plant. Before its shutdown, the plant employed between 900 and 1,000 workers. The American Car & Foundry office building is still standing.

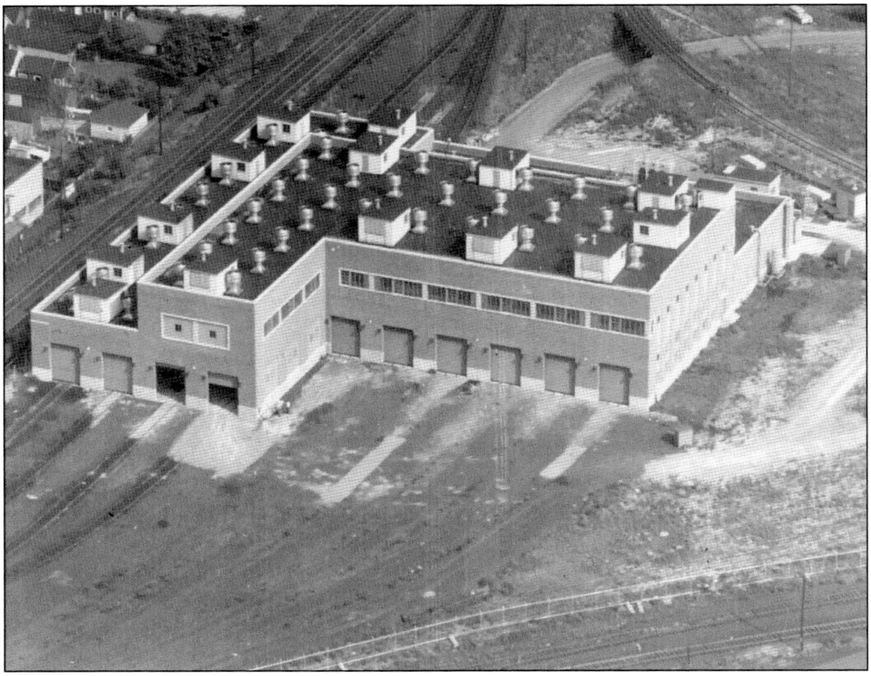

American Lubricants, now incorporated as Battenfeld-American, Inc., and still in existence at 1575 Clinton Street, produces various oils, greases, and lubricants for automotive companies. This 1936 photograph shows an employee filling Tru-Penn oxygenated oil containers for shipment. At the time of the photograph, American Lubricants had about 37 employees. The facility now operates under the parent company, Battenfeld-Grease & Oil Corporation of New York, located in North Tonawanda.

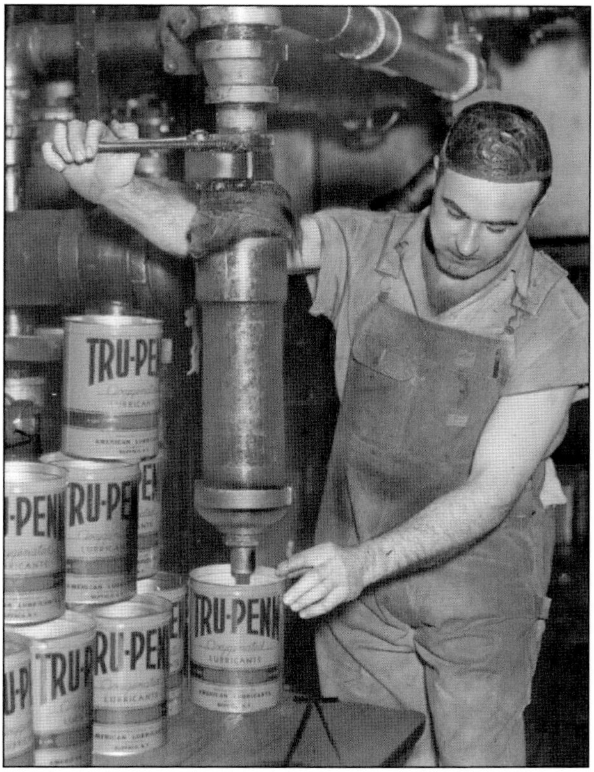

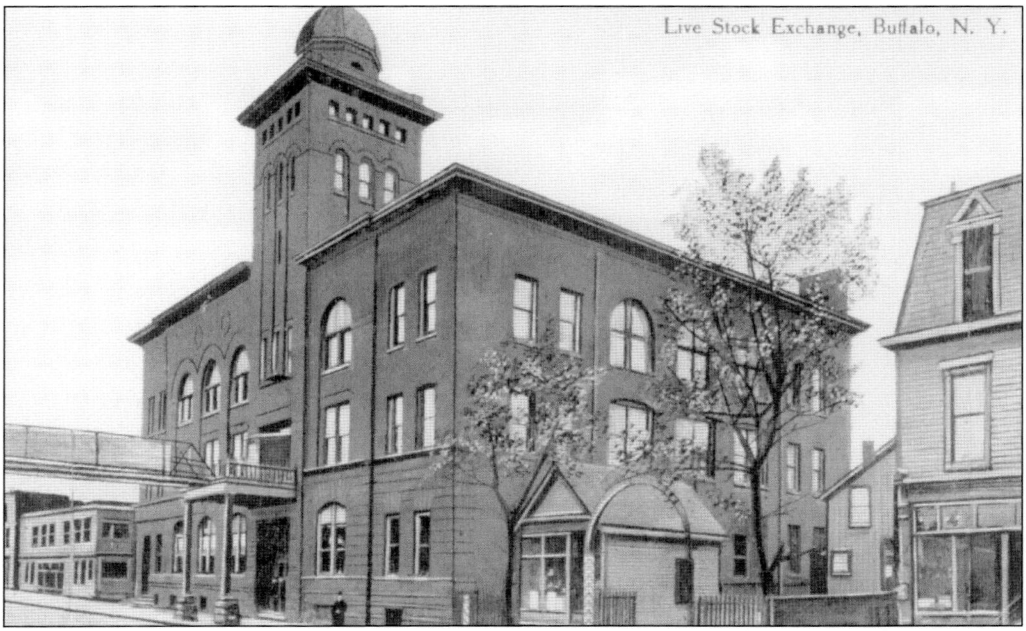

This postcard shows the Buffalo Stockyards Livestock Exchange Building at the corner of William and Depot Streets. Louise Bethune designed the structure in 1892, and this image shows part of the bridge that connected the building to the rest of the stockyards. Bethune was the first woman architect acknowledged by the American Institute of Architects. The Livestock Exchange Building was demolished in 1964.

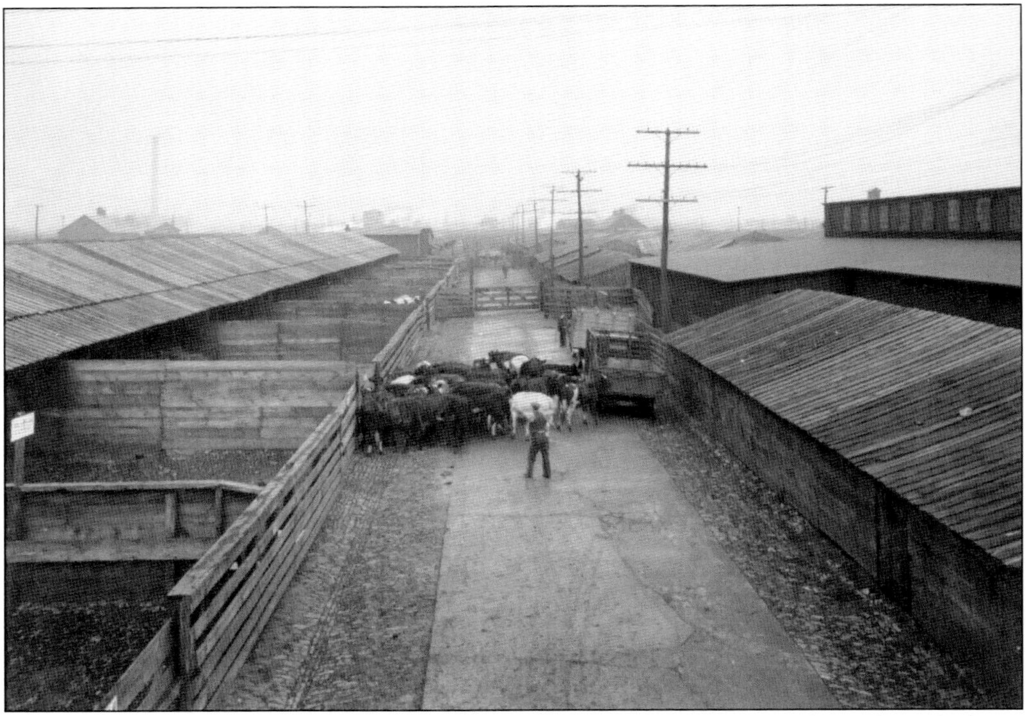

The East Buffalo Stockyards opened in December 1863. The stockyards housed cattle, hogs, and sheep and were marketed as the "ideal housing facilities for livestock." The Lake Shore & Michigan Southern Railway acted as the shipping train for livestock from the west, and the New York Central & Hudson River Railroad served as the receiving train for livestock headed to points east. The stockyards had a total capacity of 100 acres and, at its height, could handle 100,000 animals at a time—15,000 cattle, 50,000 sheep, and 35,000 hogs. In the above photograph, cattle are maneuvered before being loaded onto waiting trains or placed in a holding pen. The below image shows a bird's-eye view of the yards, with a Lake Shore & Michigan Southern Railway train in the foreground.

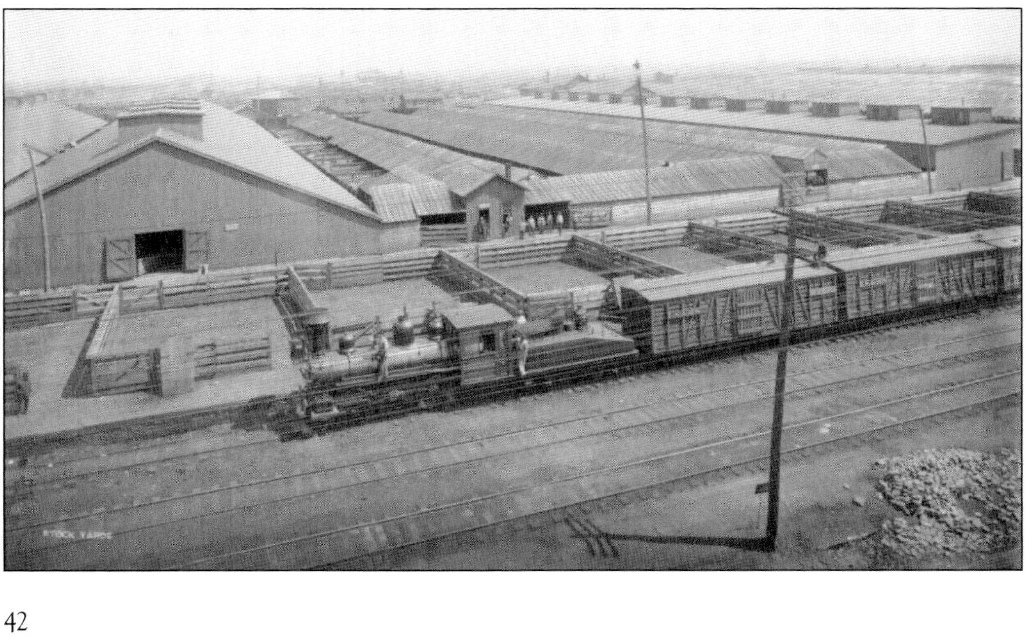

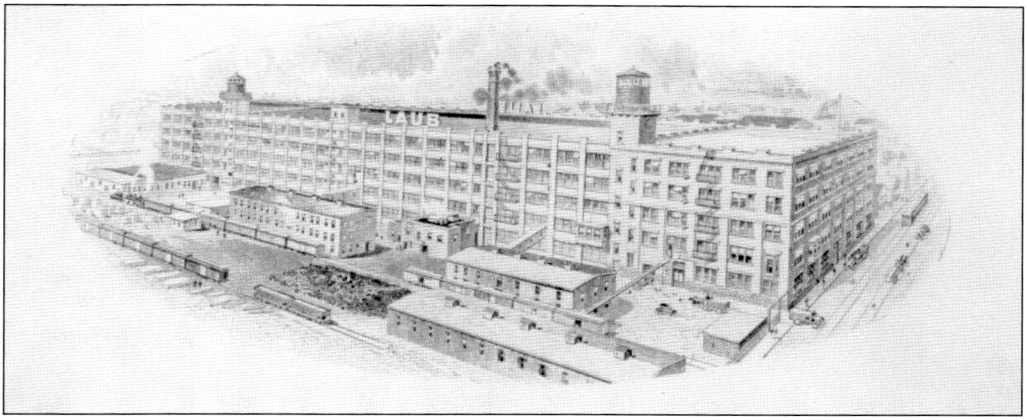

The colossal structure with the iconic Laub sign still stands at 1051 Clinton Street. It was built in 1890 and used as the primary facility of George Laub & Sons Tannery until 1935. The Laubs' long history in the leather tannery business dates back to 1847, when George Laub owned a leather tannery in Hamburg, New York. In 1858, he and business partner G. Frederick Zeller moved to Buffalo and opened Laub & Zeller, and in the 1880s, the partners amicably split and the company became the George Laub & Sons Tannery. The building is currently in use as Laub Warehouse, Inc., which was established by the family in 1979. The warehouse provides distribution and storage services for Canadian and American companies. Above is a sketch of the building, and below is an image taken during its construction.

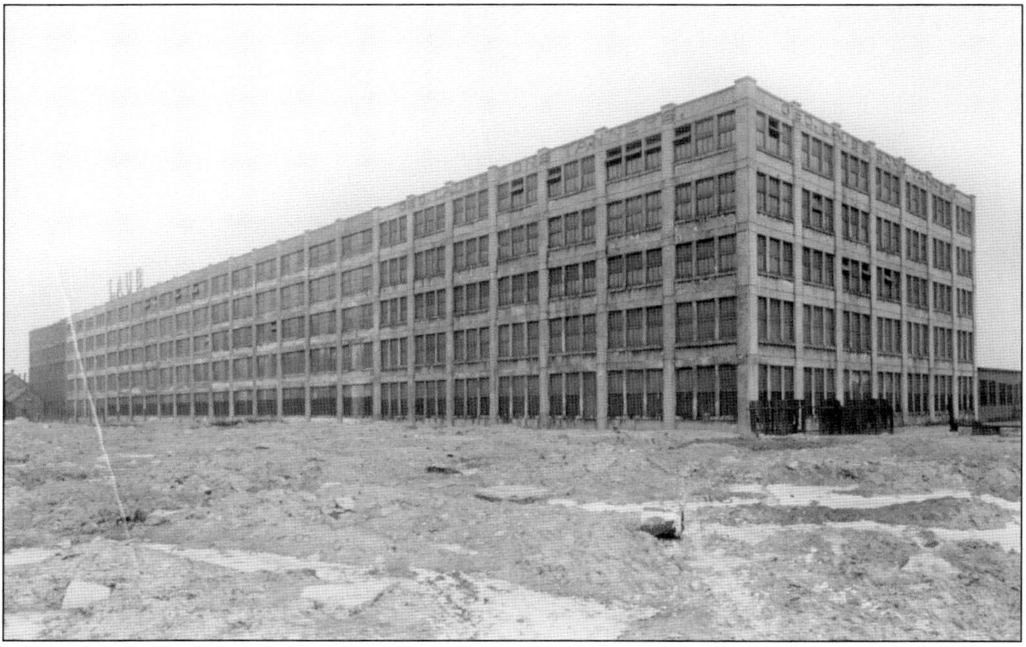

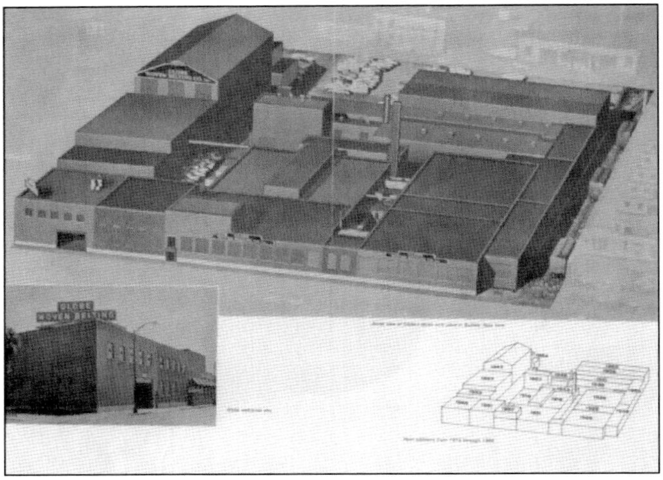

Irish-born Michael Beecher started the Globe Woven Belt Company in 1916. This depiction shows its explosive growth through the years as the company expanded from inhabiting one acre to seven acres at 1396 Clinton Street. The company manufactured conveyor belts for the food-processing industry. Albany International purchased Globe in the 1960s, but the company was repurchased in 1983 by local management and became Globe International Company.

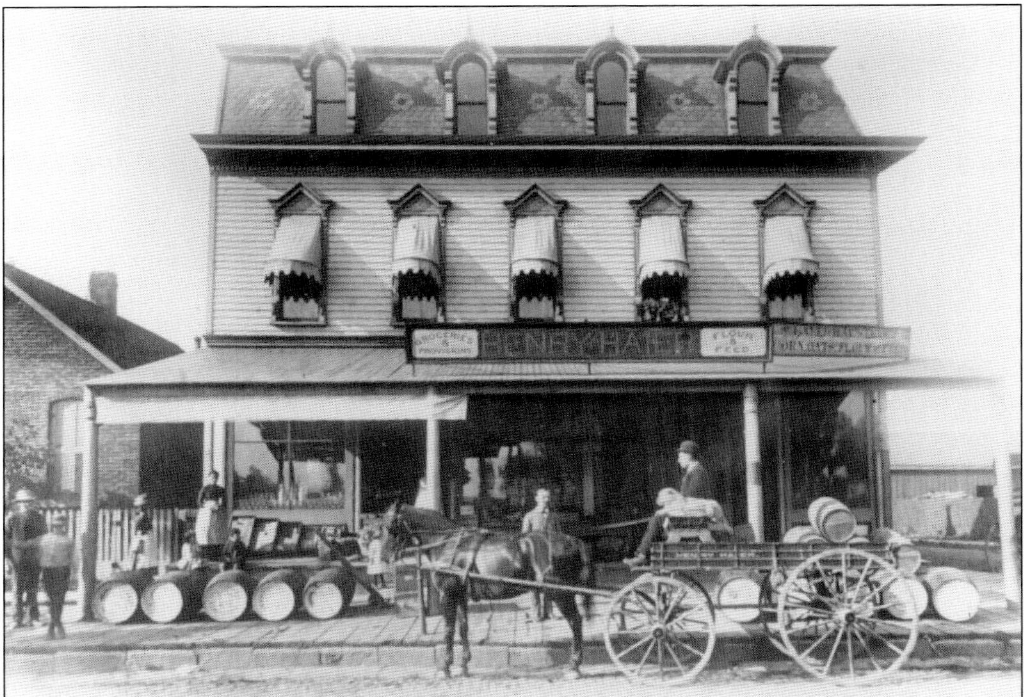

In 1887, Henry Haier opened a grocery store at 852 Clinton Street with Conrad Kleinfelder. For a year, the store was named Haier and Kleinfelder, but in 1888, Kleinfelder left the partnership and opened his own grocery store at 893 Clinton Street. Haier Grocers remained open until 1908. Henry's two sons worked in the business, and his older son, John, opened his own grocery store at 2188 Seneca Street.

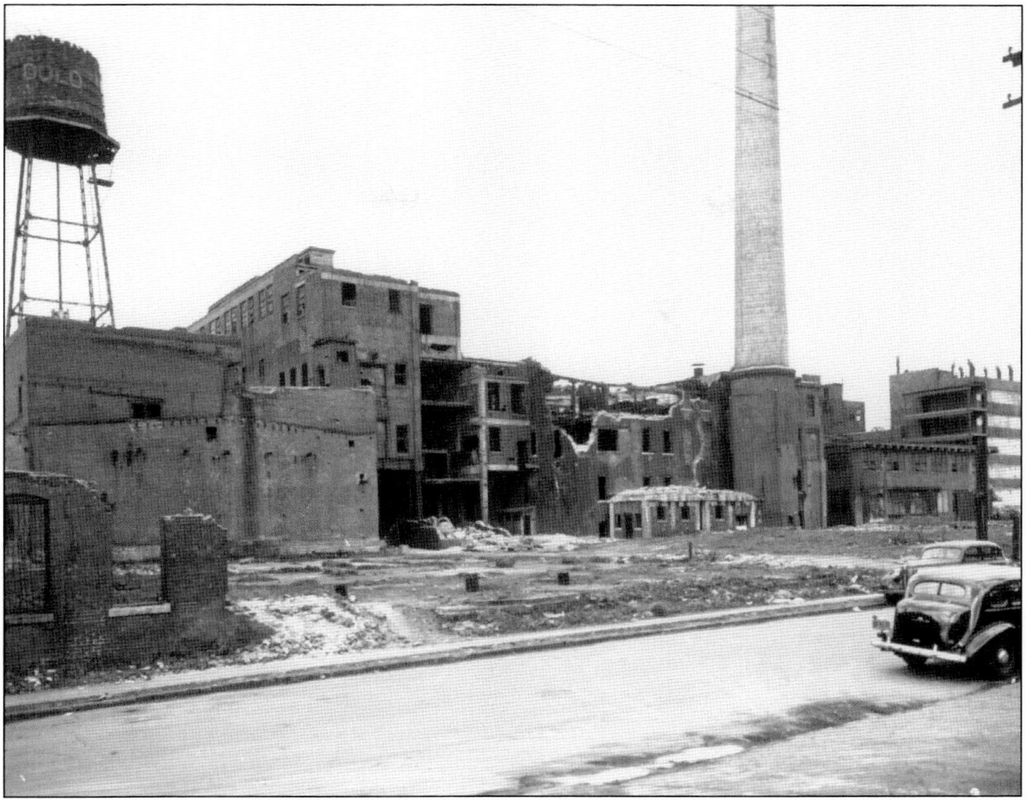

This c. 1944 photograph shows the demolition of the Jacob Dold Meatpacking Company building at 845 William Street at the corner of Fillmore Avenue. At its height, Jacob Dold had five meatpacking houses—two in Kansas; one in Washington, DC; one in Nebraska; and one in Buffalo. Dold came from Germany to Buffalo in 1848, and by 1860, he had opened his company's first plant. In 1938, the company was sold to Hygrade Food Products, which liquidated the company in 1943.

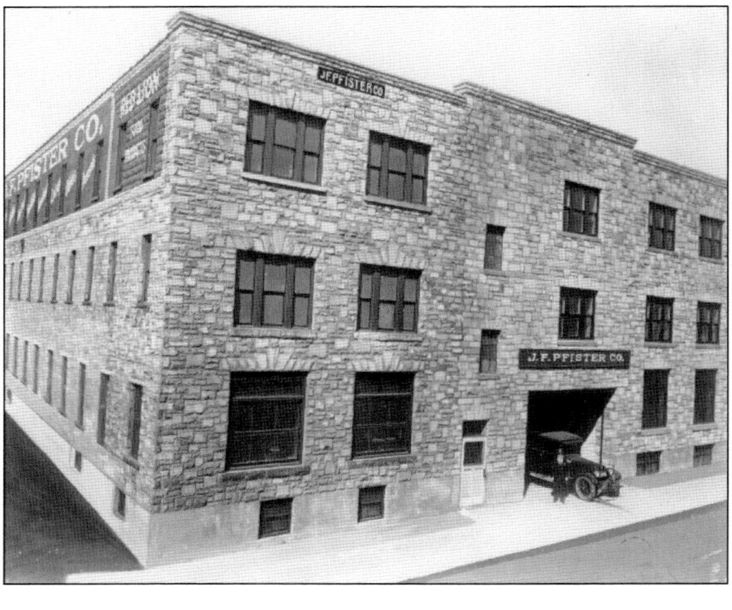

The J.F. Pfister Company, Inc., located at 22–26 Metcalfe Street near the corner of William Street, manufactured condiments such as pickles, vinegars, and ketchups. John F. Pfister worked as a manager at W&G Klipfel Vinegars on Michigan Avenue. He opened his shop at 225 Walnut Street in 1896 and moved to this location in 1911. By the 1950s, the company had closed and this building was a junk warehouse.

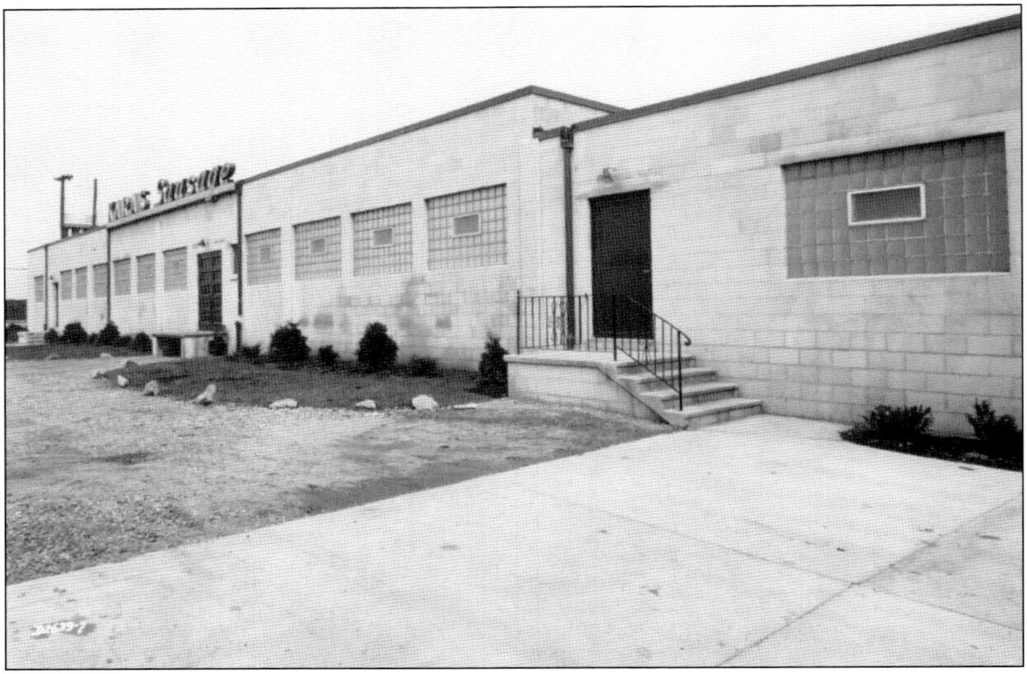

Karas Sausage Meat Company was located at 1490 William Street, close to the hub of butchers and meatpacking plants and the Buffalo Stockyards. Located near the corner of William Street and Central Avenue, Karas Sausage used the tagline "Aristocracy of Meats" in their advertising. By 1954, it had been bought and incorporated by the Armour & Company meatpacking business based in Chicago. The facility was next to the Erie Railroad and had a long loading and unloading dock by the railroad tracks. These two photographs show the facade of the facility and the front elevation of the building with a fleet of new delivery vehicles. This site is currently part of the Tripifoods complex at William Street and Central Avenue.

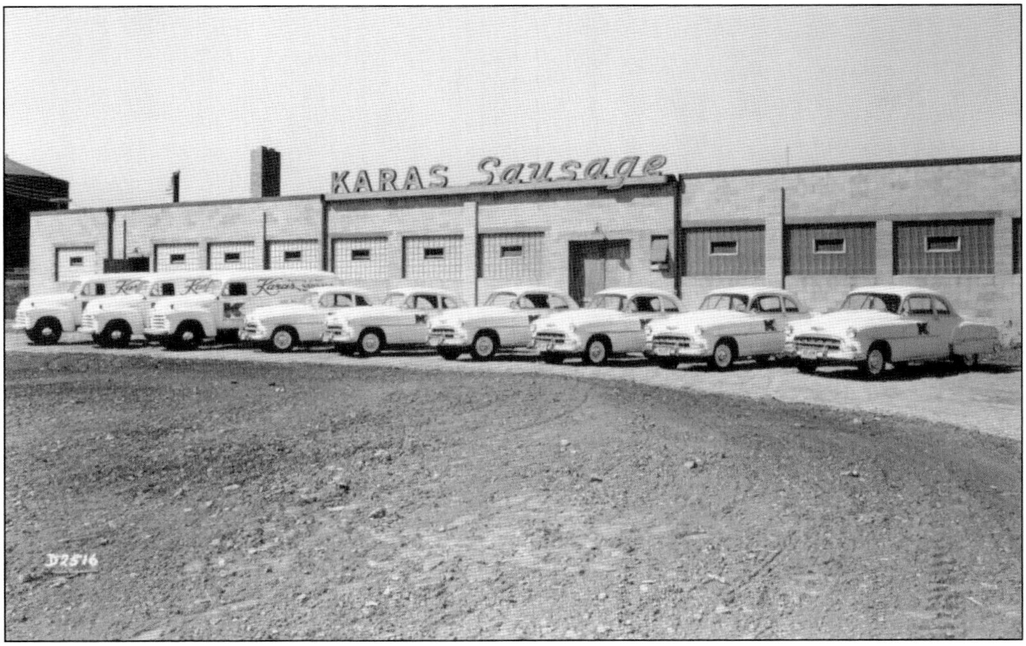

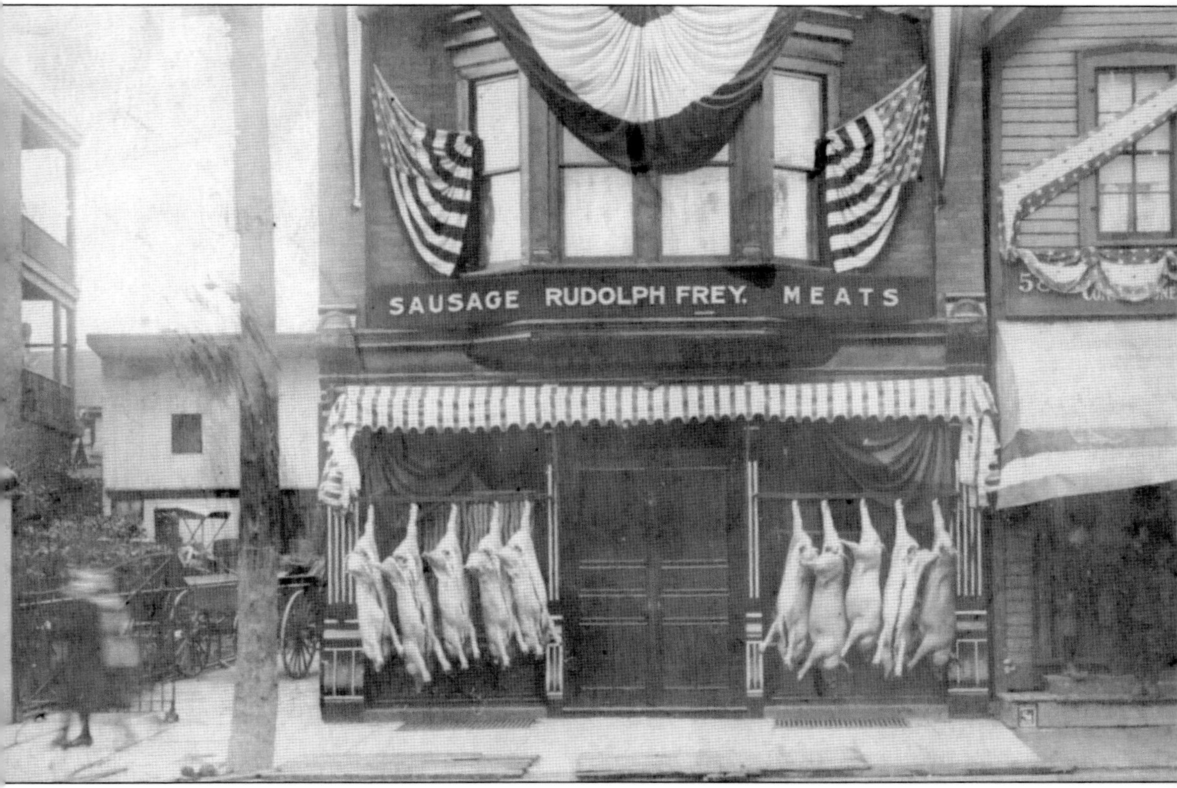

The Rudolph Frey Sausage and Meat Company, which opened in 1896 at 576 William Street, is featured in this undated photograph. Frey, like many butchers and sausage-makers, came to Buffalo from Germany. Throughout the years, Frey expanded his business, and by 1945, his two sons, Harold and Rudolph Jr., were running the shop. In the 1970s, the business had 25 employees, but by 1993, Russer Foods had purchased and merged the business. The William Street Corridor, centered around the Buffalo Stockyards, became the core for meatpacking and its secondary industries, which used the by-products of animals. Howard, Lewis, Newell, Depot, Thomas, and Metcalfe Streets became home to a variety of butchers and meat dealers. The Danahy Brothers, Sahlen and Roland, Malecki, Pasco Sausage Company, Klink Brothers, Oswald Brothers, and Horlein and Sons, Inc., all were located in these few blocks.

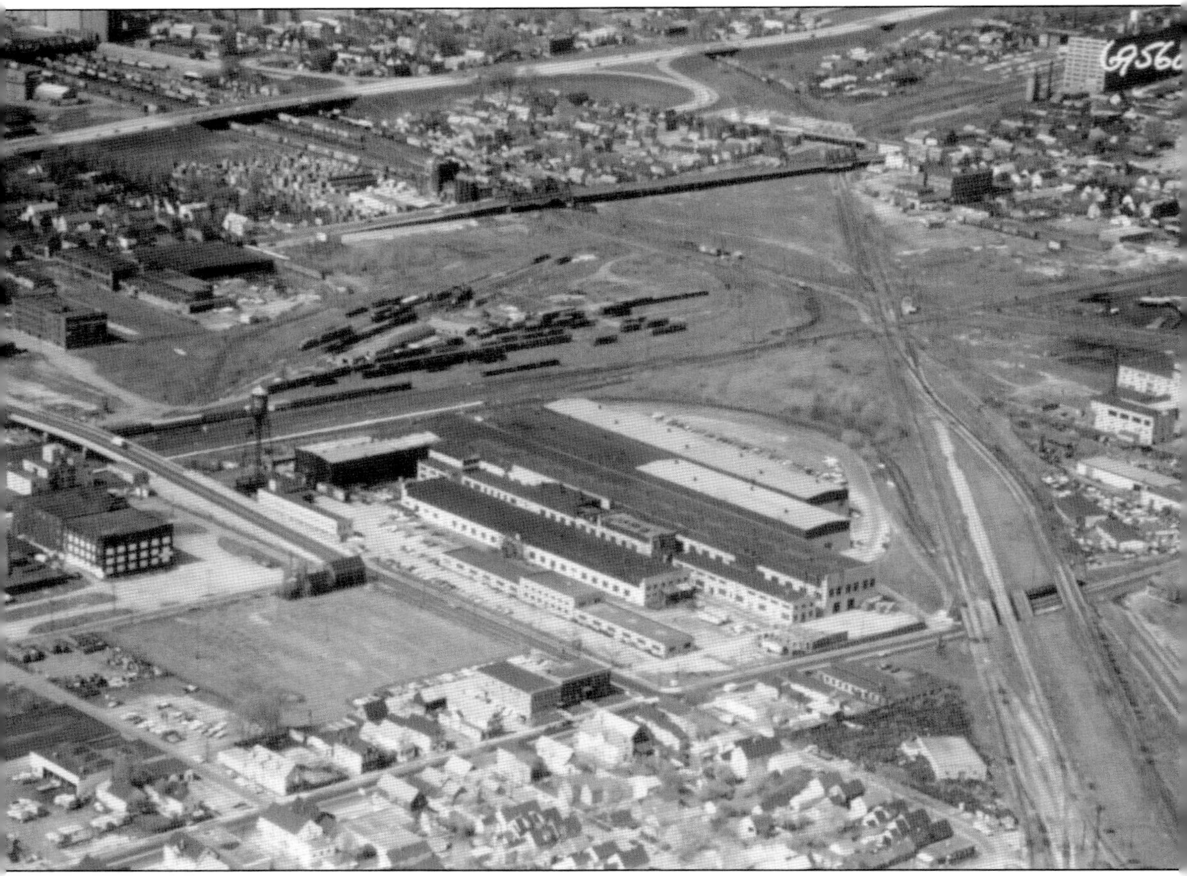

The Lisk-Savoy Headquarters, located at Clinton and Babcock Streets, is shown in this undated photograph. In 1944, the company was created as the result of a merger between the Lisk Manufacturing Company—based in Clifton Springs and then Canandaigua, New York—and the Savoy Corporation of Buffalo, New York. Both companies produced enamel, copper, and tinwares such as basins, utensils, and pans. After the merger, the Lisk-Savoy Company continued to expand, and four divisions are pictured—Allan Herschell, Kelley Machine, Farnham Division, and Wiesner-Rapp. The Allan Herschell Company, a producer of carousels in North Tonawanda, New York, was purchased wholesale by the Wiesner-Rapp Corporation and relocated to this corner. Wiesner-Rapp, in turn, was bought by the Lisk-Savoy Company in 1963 and remained on-site. American Car & Foundry was also near this site. The Larkin at Exchange Building is visible at upper right.

Four

Genesee and Sycamore
Interior Arterials

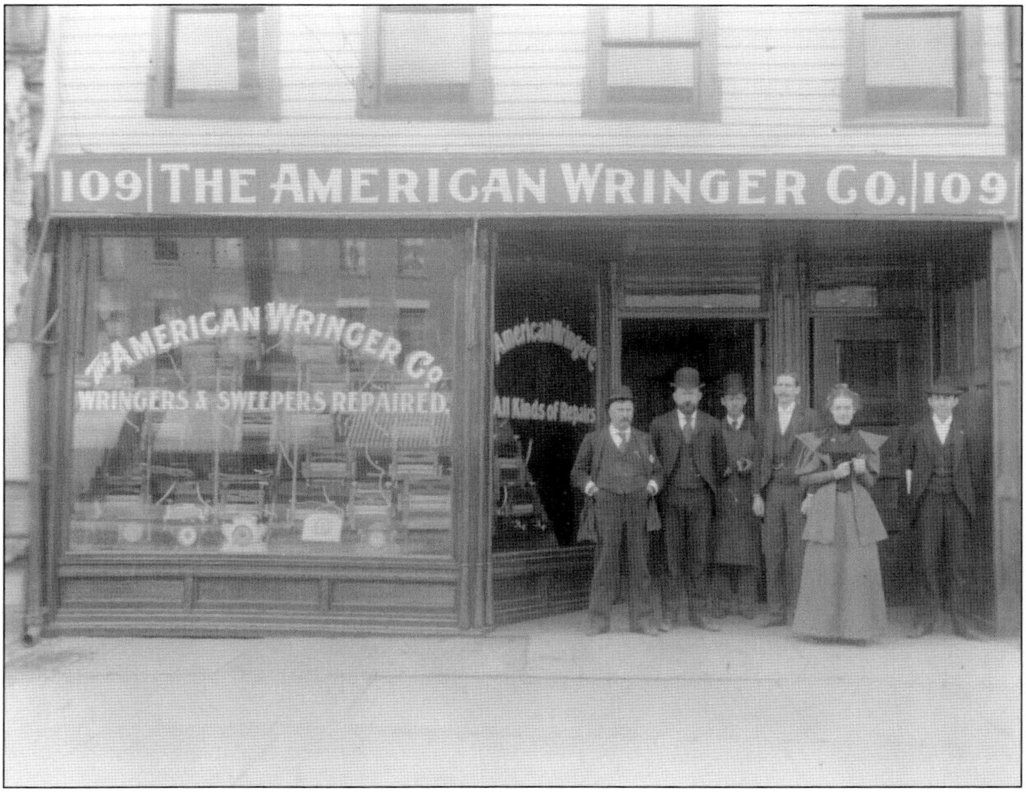

The American Wringer Company was located at 109 Genesee Street from 1896 until 1900. This company repaired sweepers and "wringers"—early vacuum cleaners. The store was managed by James R. Baldwin, and in 1901, he renamed it the Baldwin Specialty Company. In 1903, Baldwin moved the company to 290 Main Street and opened a men's furnishings store. Baldwin is believed to be in this image, but unfortunately, there is no indication of which man is which.

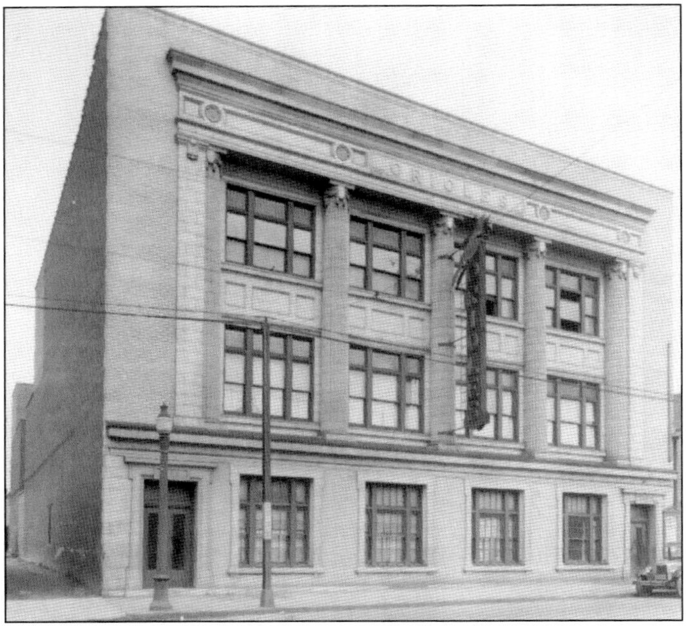

This is the Orioles Building located at 556 Genesee Street. In this c. 1925 photograph, the building housed the Fraternal Order of Orioles, which was a charitable and social organization founded in 1910 in Rochester, New York. Each local chapter was called a "Nest," state chapters were "Grand Nests," and the national structure was the "Supreme Nest." In the early 1920s, the Supreme Nest was headquartered in this building, where it remained until the 1970s.

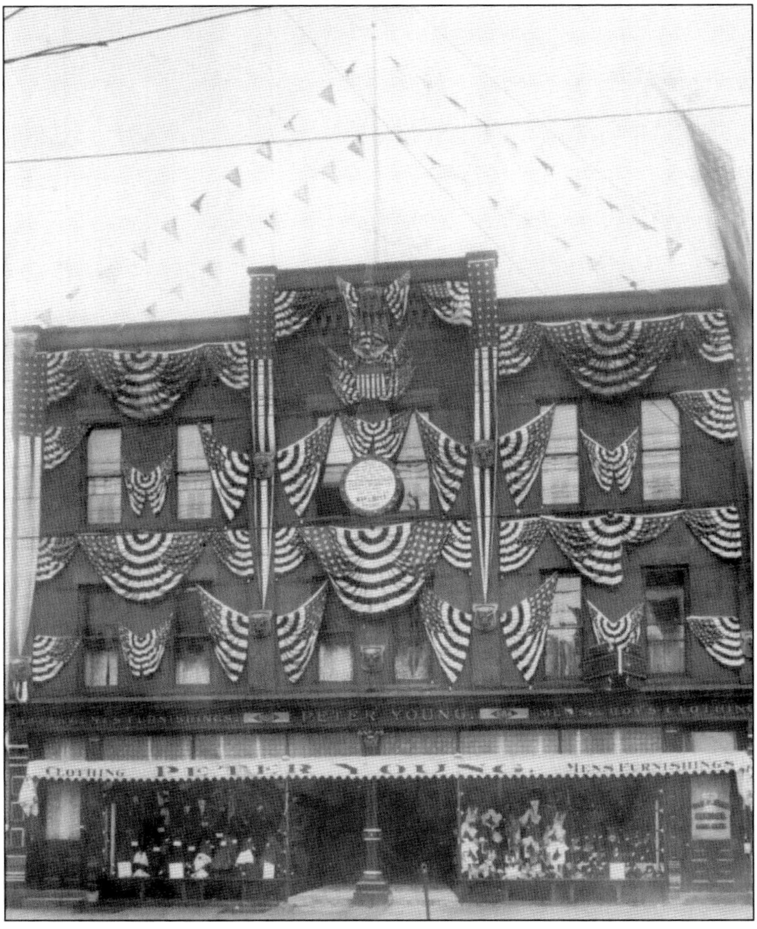

Peter Young's men's and boys' department store was located at 582–584 Genesee Street between Jefferson Avenue and Davis Street. The facade is decorated for the Genesee Street Carnival, which celebrated businesses and industry on Genesee Street from Main Street to Jefferson Avenue. Attended by roughly 20,000 people, the carnival featured parades, floats, high-wire acts, and other attractions along the street, renamed "Carnival Lane." Young's store opened in 1882 and remained at this address until 1974.

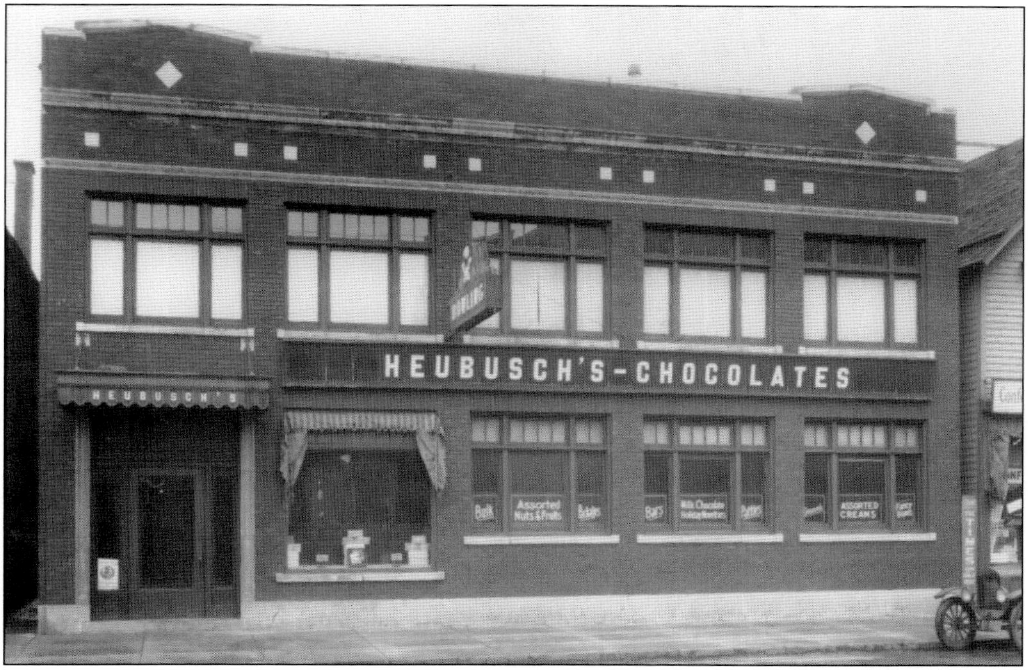

In 1930, Heubusch's Chocolates was located at 656 Genesee Street near the intersection of Genesee and Monroe Streets. Henry Heubusch owned the company, which produced wholesale confections. Heubusch's first opened as a store on William Street (in 1905), then as a factory at 30 Krettner Street (in the early 1920s), then in this location (in 1929). The shop remained in business until 1971. The Monroe Bowling Academy—and, later, Genesee Lanes—was located above Heubusch's Chocolates from 1929 until Heubusch's closed in 1971.

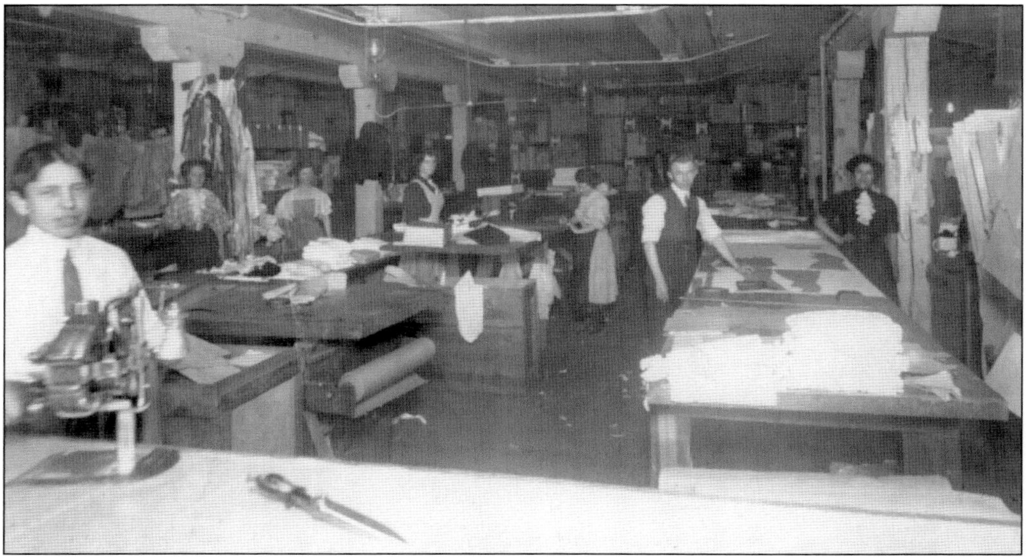

This is an interior photograph of Berman Bros., Inc, a clothing and textile manufacturer located at 1234 Genesee Street, between Spiess and Marshall Streets. Not much is known about the company, but in the 1870s and 1880s, there was an Abraham Berman who was a tailor in the area, and he or his offspring could have opened the clothing manufactory. The 1889 Sanborn Map shows a vacant parcel of land at this address, meaning this building had not yet been constructed.

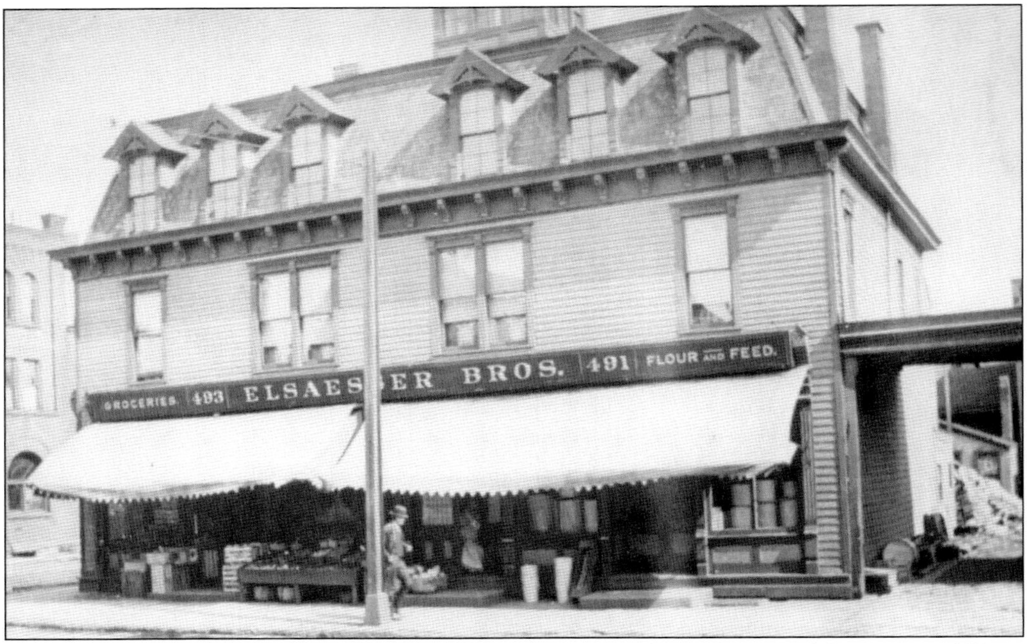

Elsaesser Bros. Grocery and Feed Store operated at the southwest corner of Genesee and Kane Streets. The store opened in 1860 and was in operation until 1935, when the building was demolished. This 1913 photograph looks south across Genesee Street. When the store opened, there were 486 grocers in Buffalo. Like many grocers, in later years, the Elsaesser brothers moved away from animal feed.

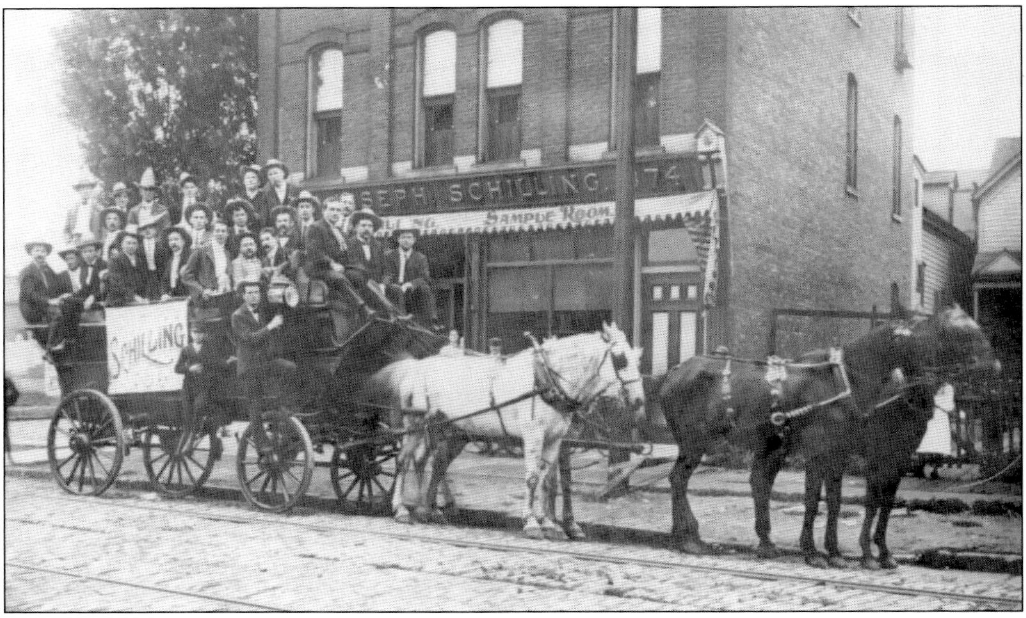

The Schilling Tavern was located at 374 Sycamore Street near the corner of Mortimer Street. City directories show that many Schillings in that block of Sycamore Street ran various stores in addition to this tavern. Joseph Schilling opened the tavern in 1895, but by 1919, he had switched to selling soft drinks—no doubt due to Prohibition. Whether he was selling or manufacturing the drinks is unclear. In 1928, the business was closed.

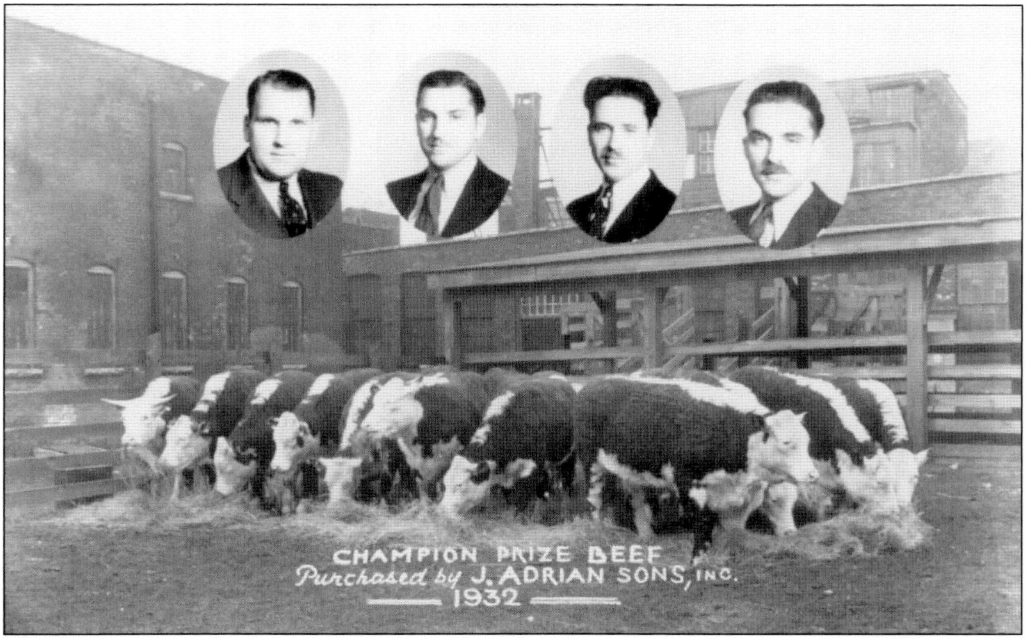

The J. Adrian Sons, Inc., wholesale meat business opened at 1750 Genesee Street in 1889. In later years, with the expansion of the suburbs, the company opened another store at 2256 Genesee Street in the Pine Ridge neighborhood. The company sold many products made from a variety of animals, including hogs, cattle, and sheep. A slaughterhouse and smoke room were operated in the back of the storefront. John Adrian opened the business in 1889, and it was carried on by his sons and grandchildren until the early 1990s, when the wholesale business closed. Throughout its existence, the company supplied hot dogs to the stadiums of the three Buffalo sports teams. In the below image, the 1750 storefront is ready to sell "Easter Meats," while the above image shows a promotional advertisement handed out at meatpacking association events.

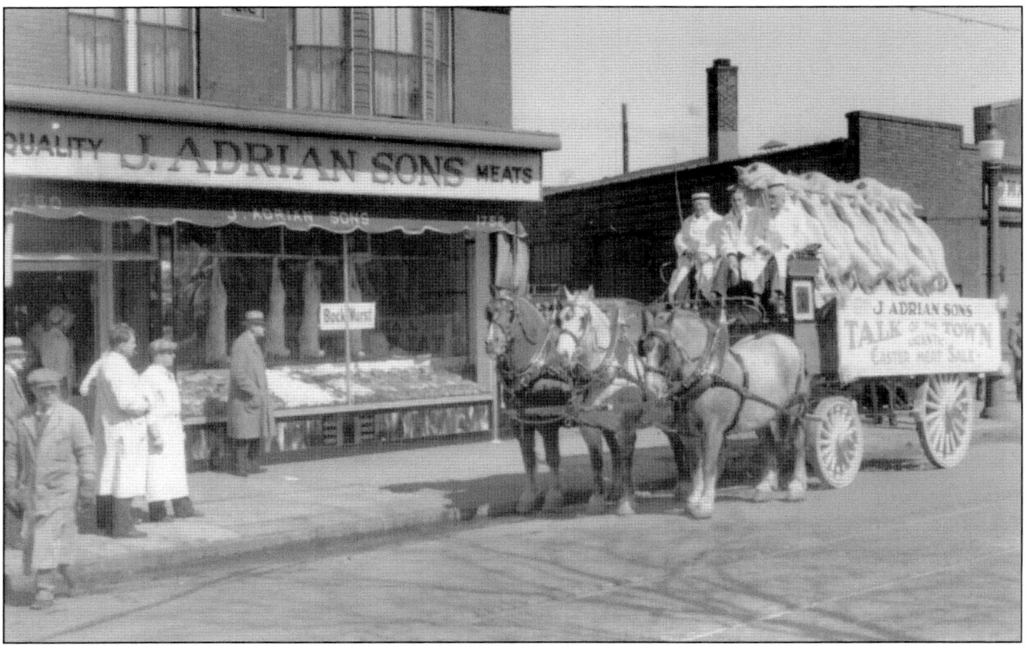

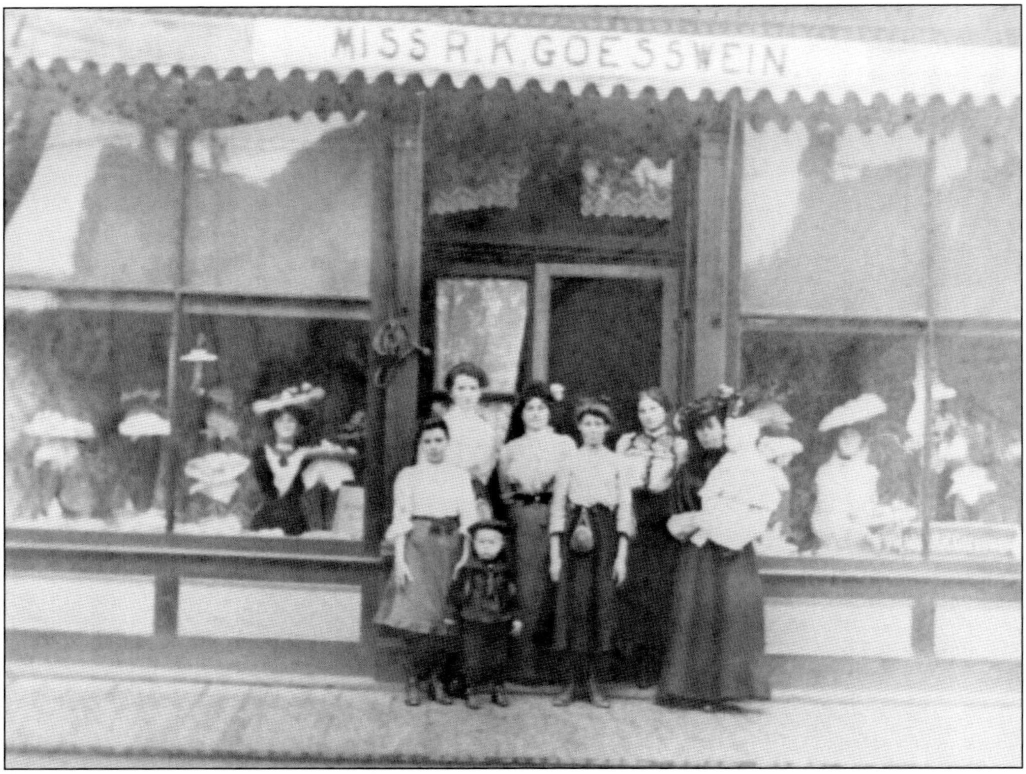

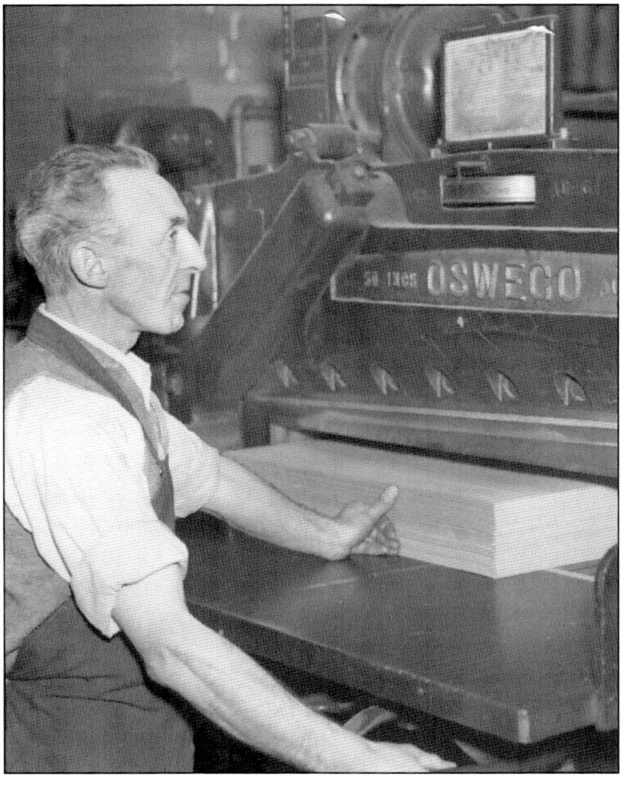

Pictured is Rose Goesswein's millinery. City directory records reveal that the millinery was established at 947 Genesee Street in 1902, and the store was moved to 975 Genesee Street in 1904. By 1906, the store disappears from the directory.

The Cooper Paper Box Company was founded in 1881 on Washington Street and was fully established by 1910 at Sycamore and Mortimer Streets, across from the Buffalo Forge Company. It was acquired by Astronics Corporation in 1972 and eventually became Mod-Pac, which is currently located on Elmwood Avenue. The company had great success and was awarded patents for its methods of converting raw materials into a wide variety of folding cartons. The building was repurposed as the Buffalo Forge Company storage facility and "dust lab" and remains on this corner.

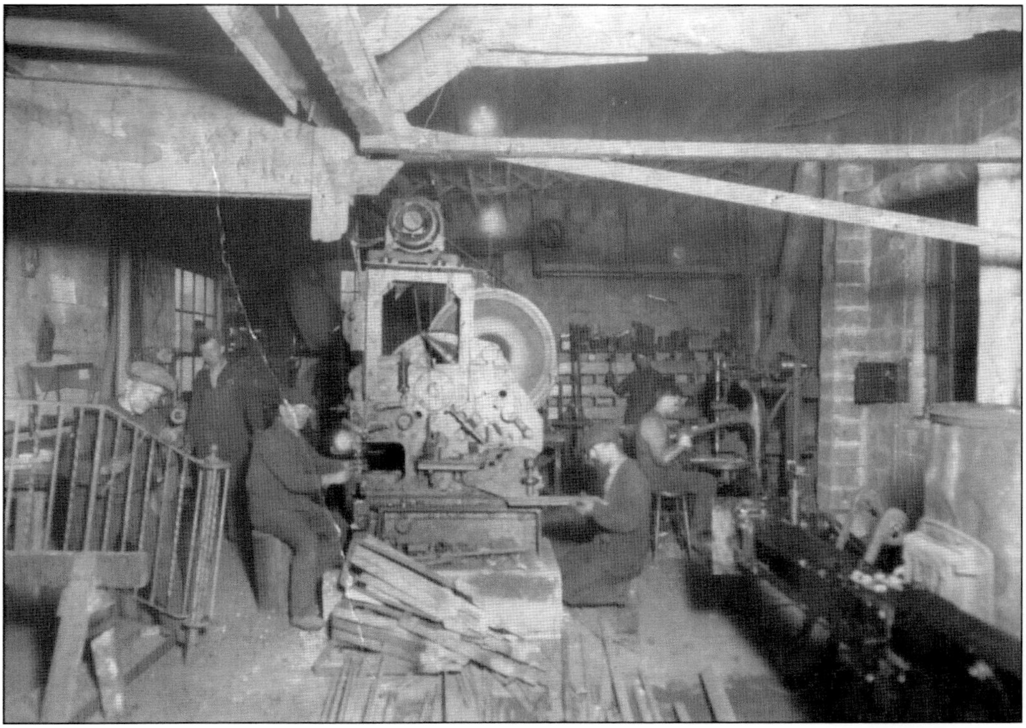

This is an interior photograph of the newly created Eberl Iron Works at 128 Sycamore Street. Pictured here—although not identified—are Frank J. and George Eberl, two brothers who operated the business along with other siblings. Frank and George entered into business in 1923, and their first products consisted of railings, fiberscopes, gates, and other iron products. The company is still located at its original address, though it expanded across the road to 103 Sycamore Street in 2014. (Courtesy of the Eberl family.)

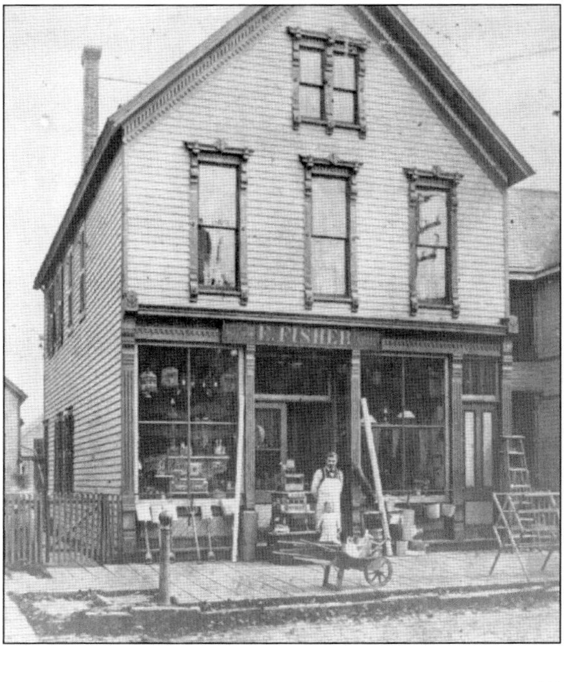

Egidius Fisher Hardware Store, located at 203 Sycamore Street, remained in business for over 30 years. Fisher started as a tinsmith on Elm Street in 1884, and in 1885, he opened this store between Walnut and Spruce Streets. He sold a variety of household and garden items, plus cutlery and sheet iron. Fisher is pictured here with his daughter around 1890.

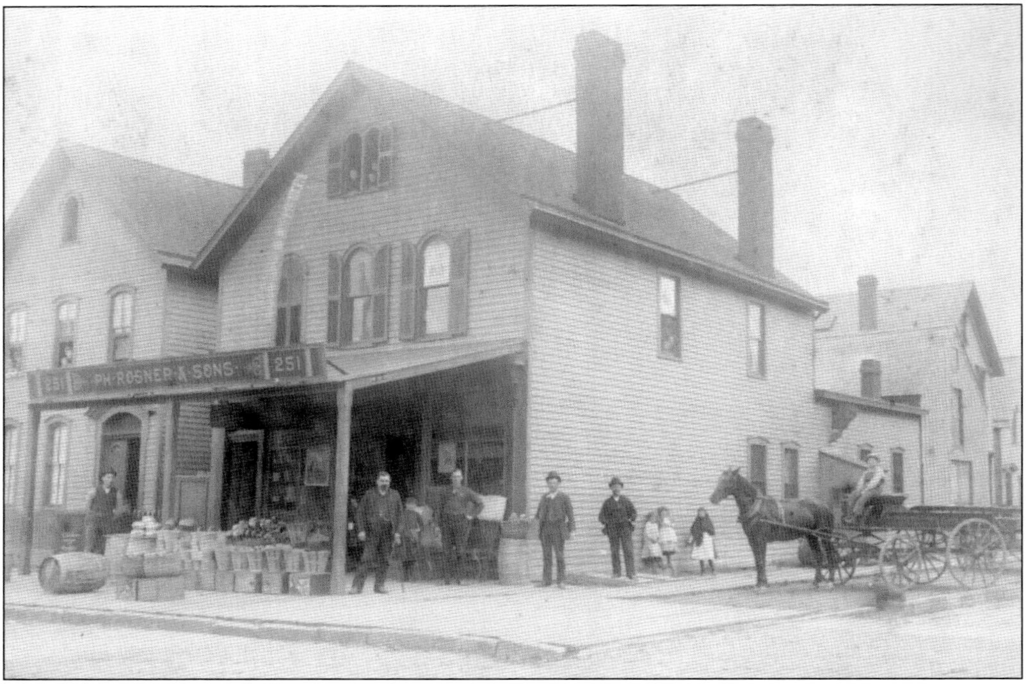

This is P.H. Rosner and Sons Grocery, located at 251 Sycamore Street at the corner of Hickory Street. Philip Rosner (standing by the support beam) started out in 1873 as a peddler of fruits, tobacco, and candies at 23 Central Wharf and ran a saloon at 251 Sycamore Street. In 1882, he left Central Wharf and converted the saloon on Sycamore Street into a fruit market. He gradually expanded and remained in business until 1950.

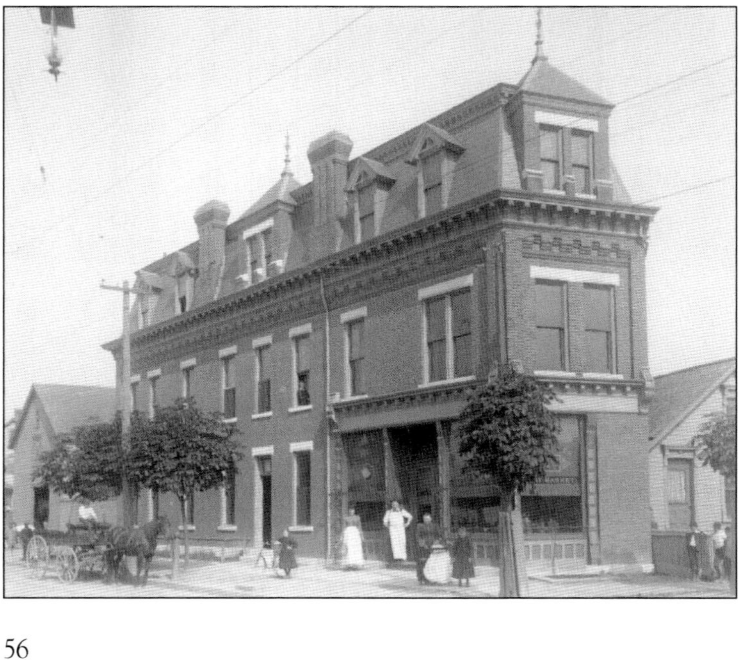

Galster's Meat Market was located at 495 Sycamore Street, where Madison and Beckwith Streets converge to form a triangle on the south side of Sycamore Street. This 1889 photograph shows the storefront and the household of the Galsters, who lived upstairs. Henry Galster opened his first meat market in 1880 at 373 Sycamore Street. In 1884, he moved to 495 Sycamore, where his business remained open for another 74 years.

Five

Michigan and Bailey
The East-West Borders

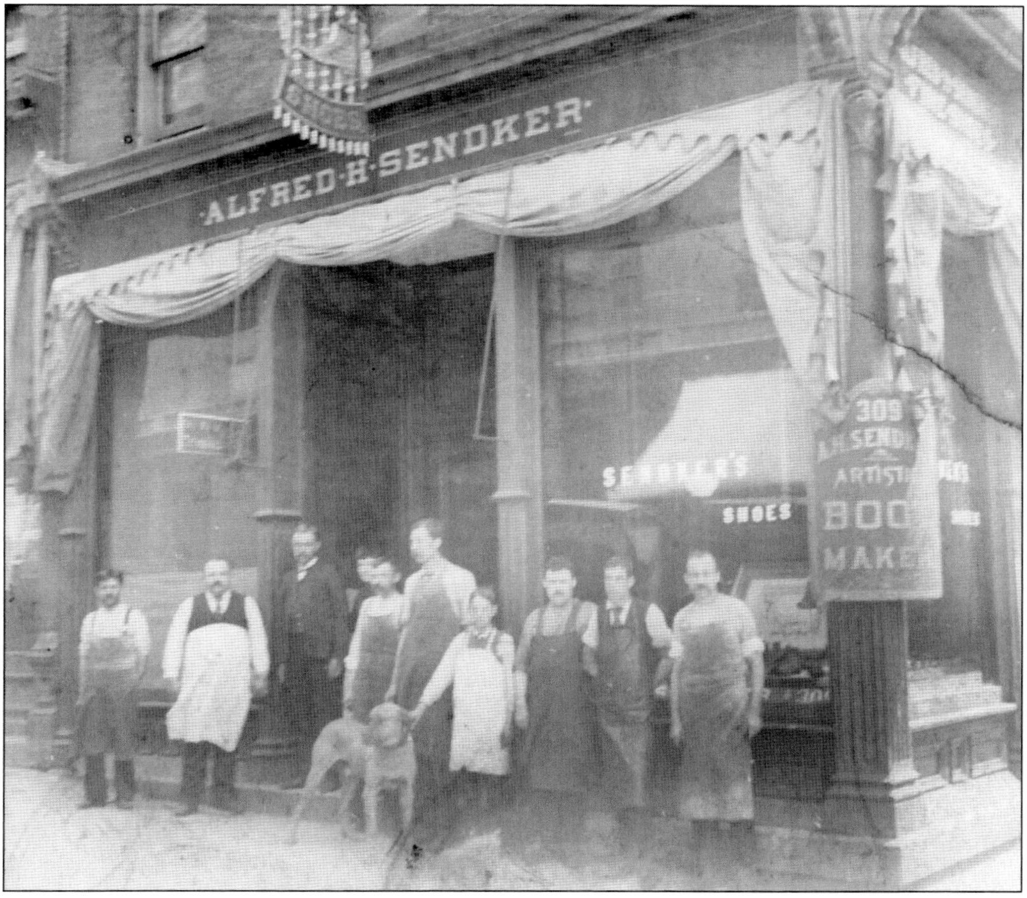

This c. 1893 photograph shows the Alfred Sendker shoe store at 309 Michigan Avenue between Myrtle Avenue and Swan Street. In 1864, Sendker appears in the Buffalo City Directory as a shoemaker but not as owning his own business. By 1870, he had opened a storefront at 245 Michigan Avenue at the corner of Exchange Street. In 1889, Sendker was firmly entrenched at 309 Michigan Avenue, where he remained until 1895, when he opened a saloon in the same location.

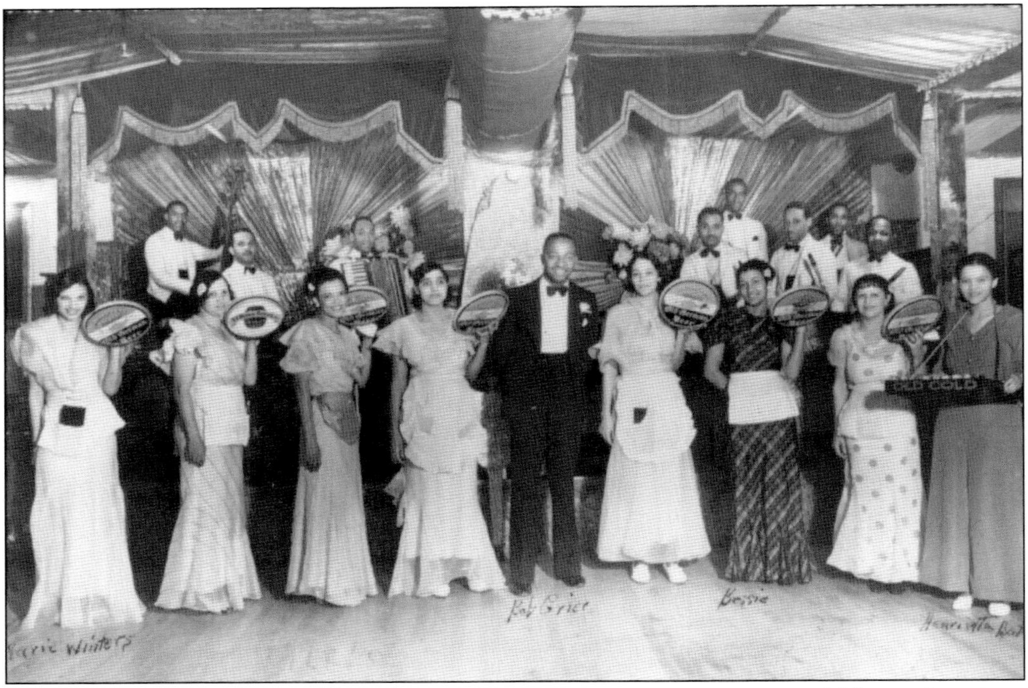

The famous Little Harlem Hotel, run by Ann Montgomery, was a centerpiece of African American cultural and musical life. The venue, located at 496 Michigan Avenue, was destroyed by fire in 1993. Many famous entertainers and leaders passed through its doors while the hotel was open, including Cab Calloway, Billie Holiday, and Billy Eckstine. Lil Hardin Armstrong, the ex-wife of Louis Armstrong, ran the house orchestra. Opened around 1920 as an ice cream parlor, it was not until after Prohibition that the building housed a nightclub. The Montgomerys started in the industry by running a saloon at 158 Exchange Street. Daniel, Ann's husband, continued to run the saloon while Ann bought and operated the hotel at 496 Michigan Avenue. The Moon-Glo, the Colored Musicians Club, and the Little Harlem Hotel formed Buffalo's "Jazz Triangle." There is now a historic marker located where the hotel once stood.

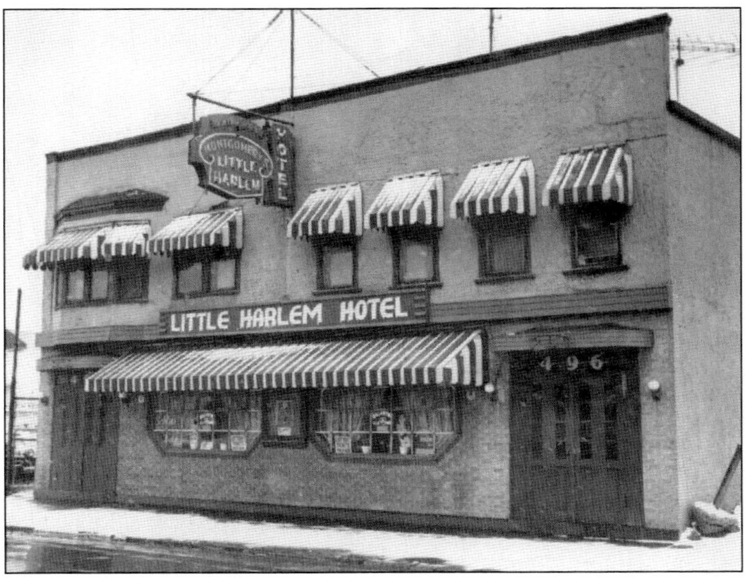

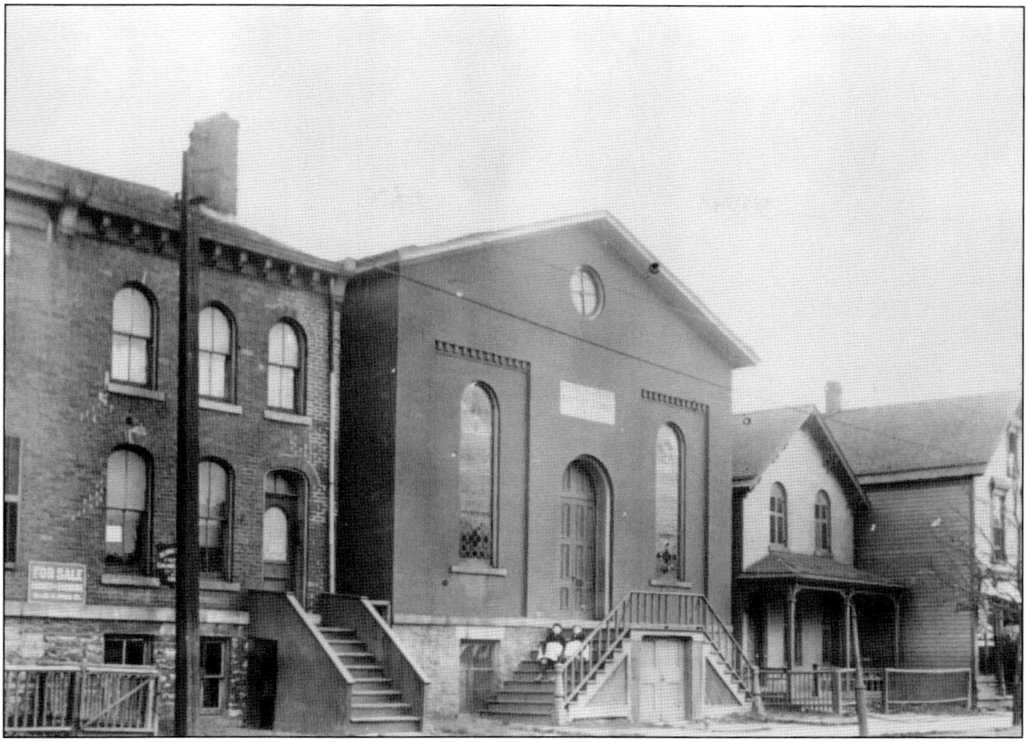

The Michigan Avenue Baptist Church and Mary Talbert are forever linked to Buffalo's African American community. The church, pictured above around 1898, became the core institution for equal rights—not only in New York State but across the county. The church opened in 1845 and centered around the African American neighborhood established in the Michigan Avenue Corridor. When it opened, there were roughly 350 free African Americans living in Buffalo. The religious doctrines of the mid- to late-19th century focused on hope and optimism for African Americans living in the north, which was still a relatively hostile region at that time. By 1900, Mary B. Talbert (pictured at right) had become a national leading advocate for social reform and equality, and the church had become a meeting place for other leaders, including W.E.B. Du Bois and Booker T. Washington. Meetings held at the church planted the seeds of the Niagara Movement, a precursor to the National Association for the Advancement of Colored People (NAACP).

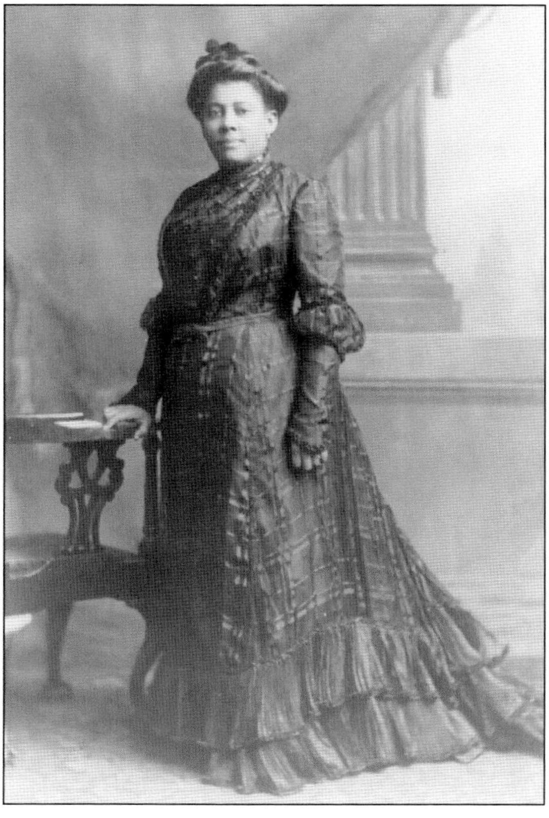

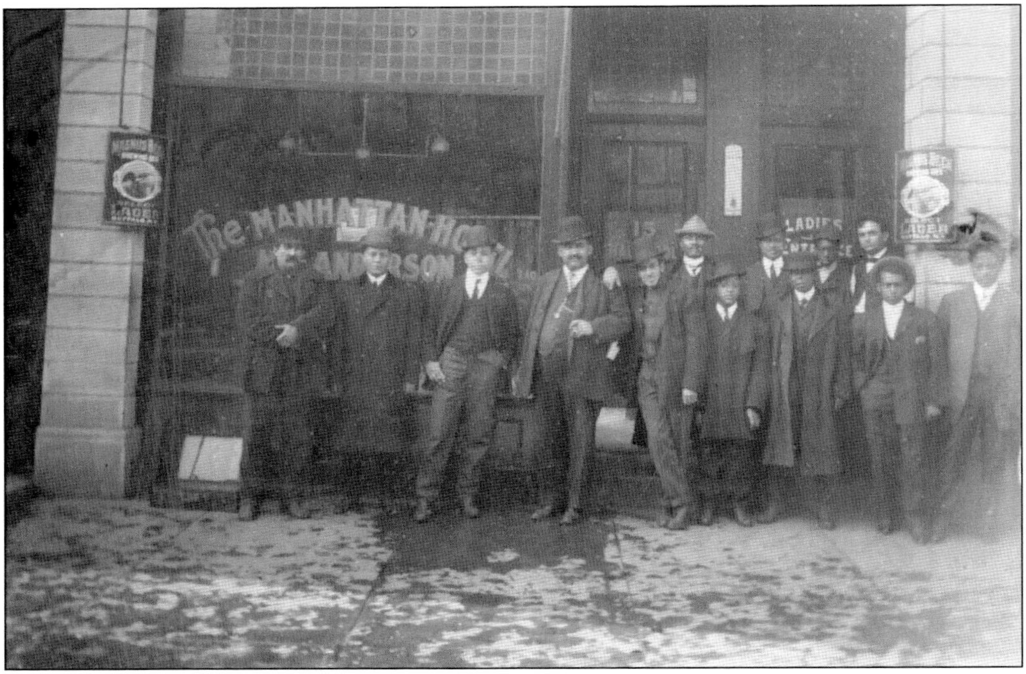

Mack Anderson is pictured fourth from left in front of his establishment, the Manhattan Hotel, located on the corner of William Street and Michigan Avenue. He is believed to have been the first African American to open a hotel in Buffalo. This c. 1910 photograph shows guests of the hotel—or perhaps patrons of the tavern located on the first floor.

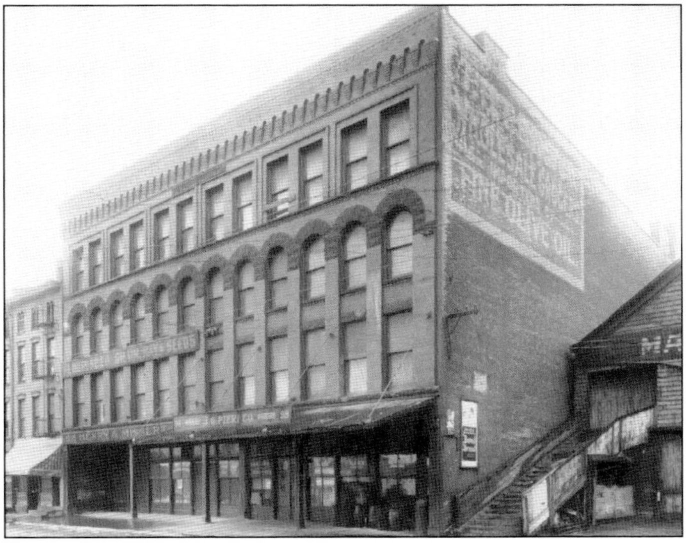

Wholesale grocer Pieri & Buscaglia opened in 1907 at 121 Michigan Avenue. By 1911, the name had changed to the J.G. Pieri Company, which was relocated to 96 Michigan Avenue, where it remained until 1932. That year, the Niagara Frontier Food Terminal opened on Clinton Street, and the J.G. Pieri Company moved into the terminal. In 1940, the company moved to 611 Bailey Avenue, then moved one last time to 240 Scott Street, where it operated until it closed in 1967.

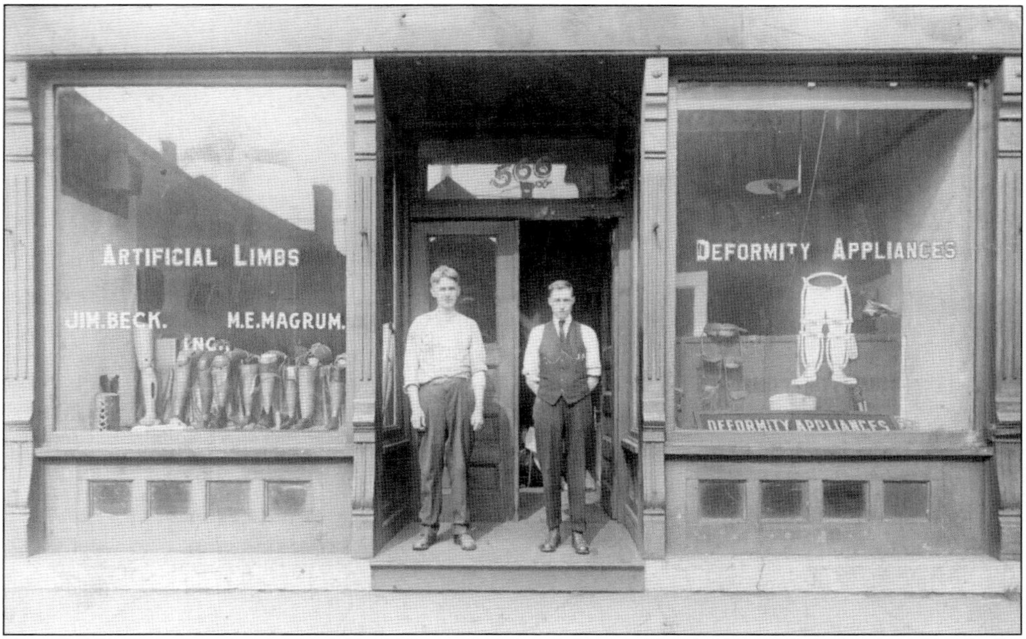

James Beck, who used an artificial leg, opened the James Beck Artificial Limb Company, located at 566 Michigan Avenue between Broadway and Sycamore Street, in 1910; it was a local leader in the industry for over 40 years. In 1923, the company moved to a larger space at 180 Broadway, where it remained in business until 1958. Above, Beck is pictured at left in the doorway, and below, he is in the background of a photograph of the factory. (Both, courtesy of Jill Frommer.)

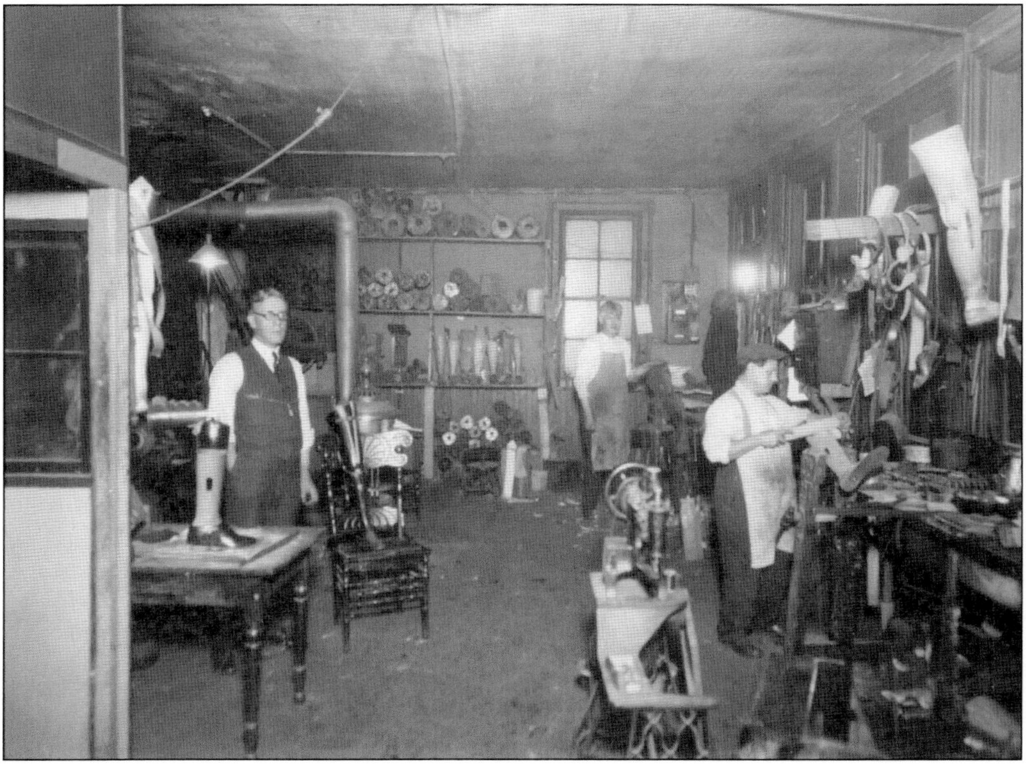

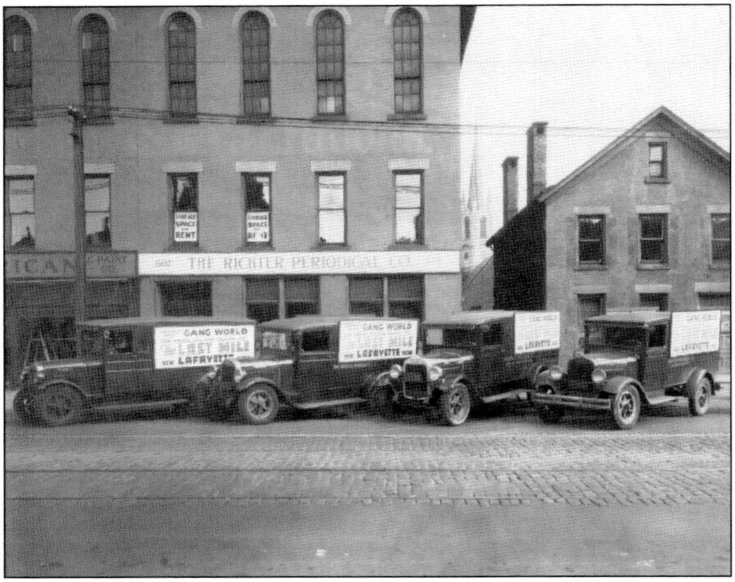

The Richter Periodical Company, located at 567 Michigan Avenue between Broadway and Sycamore Street, was owned by George and Anne Richter, who started the company in 1925 at 348 Ellicott Street, moving into this larger facility in the early 1930s. In addition to delivering newspapers around the city, it supplied bookstores and individual customers with various mass-produced books. The company closed in 1959.

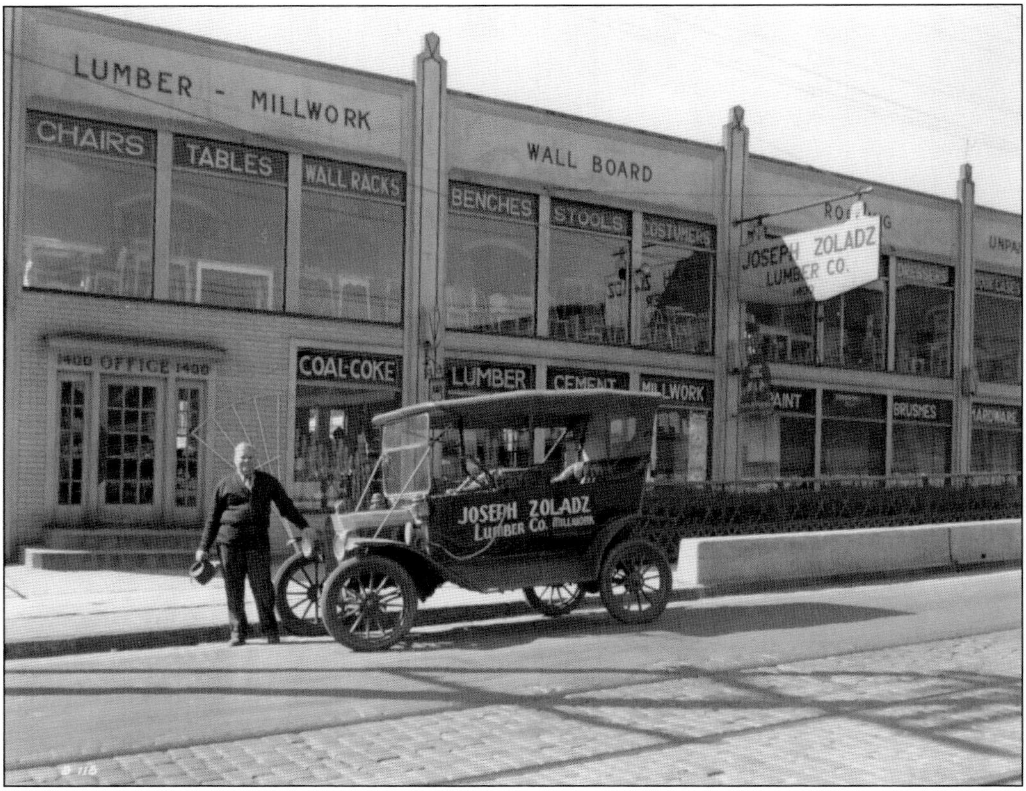

The Joseph Zoladz Lumber Company is pictured here around 1927 with Joseph Zoladz standing in front of the car. Located at 1400 Bailey Avenue near the intersection of Stanley Street, the company provided lumber and other supplies for all facets of construction, as the signage suggests. The 1920 city directory includes a Joseph Zoladz who worked as a chair-maker, and in 1924, the lumber company opened. In 1943, Zoladz was a member of the Professional and Businessmen's Association, which was composed of mostly Polish businessmen. The company closed in 1995.

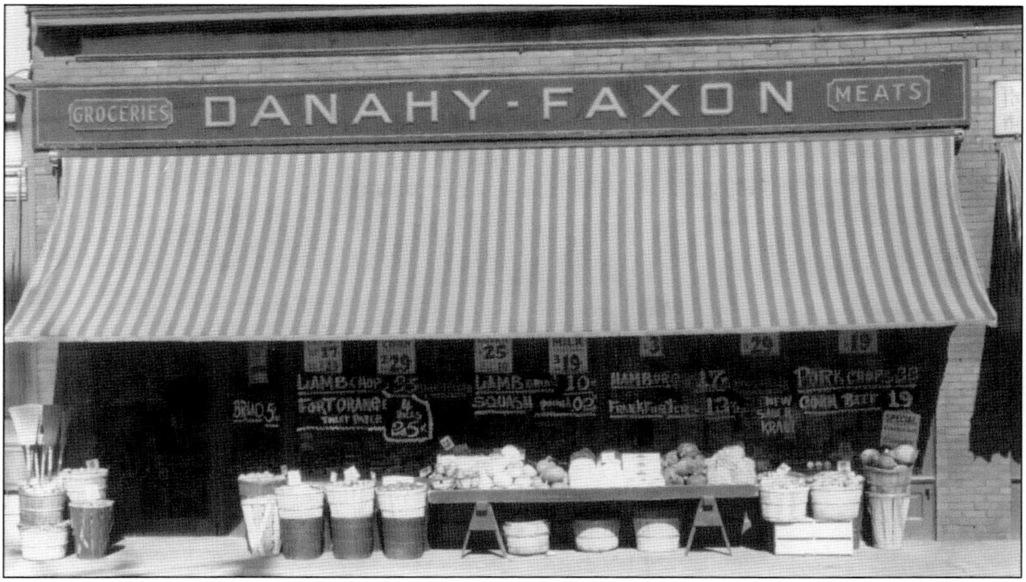

This Danahy-Faxon Grocery Store, located at 1585 Bailey Avenue, was part of a larger network of stores that resulted from a merger between grocery store chain Thrift-Faxon and the Danahy Packing Company. By 1937, the network grew to 147 stores after Danahy-Faxon purchased the Larkin Food Stores. Through various mergers and buyouts, the company eventually became Bells Supermarkets, which closed their doors in 1993.

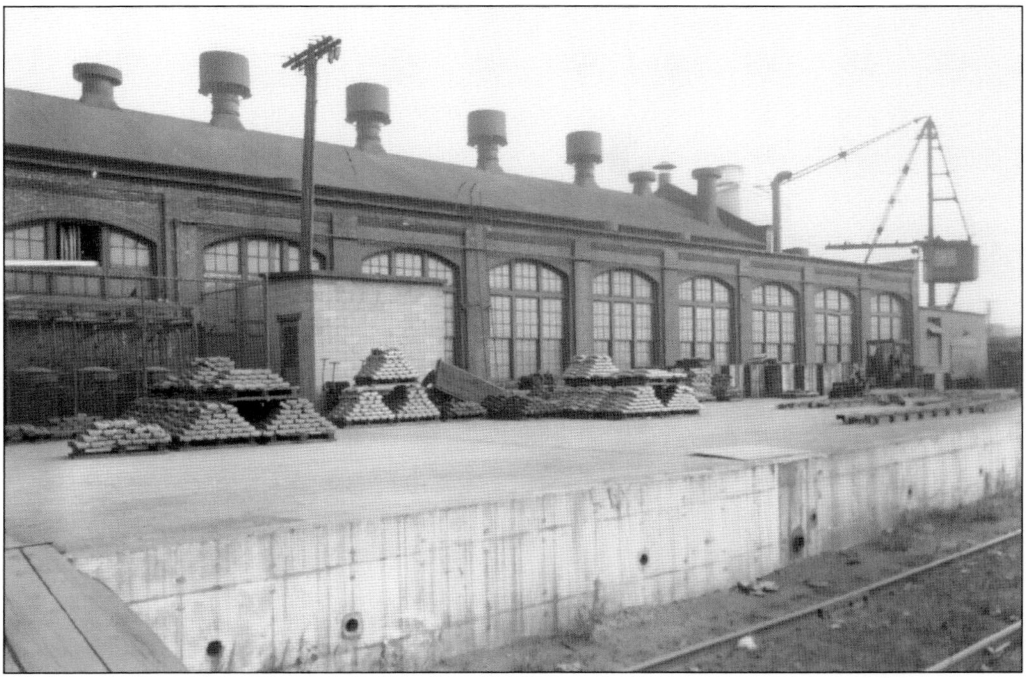

The American Brake Shoe Foundry Company, which produced castings and brake pads for locomotives, was located at 1673 Bailey Avenue (near the roundhouse shown on page 31). The company was founded in New Jersey in 1902 and also had factories in Maryland, Illinois, New Jersey, and Tennessee. It held stock interests in several other companies, including American Malleables Company, Dominion Brake Shoe Company, and the Southern Wheel Company.

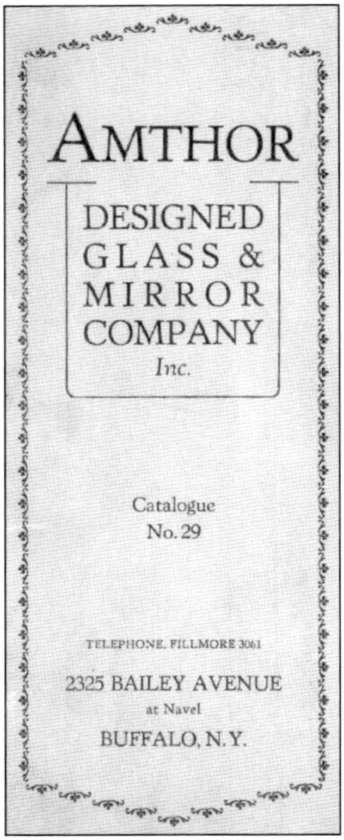

AMTHOR

DESIGNED GLASS & MIRROR COMPANY

Inc.

Catalogue No. 29

TELEPHONE, FILLMORE 3061

2325 BAILEY AVENUE

at Navel

BUFFALO, N.Y.

The Amthor Glass & Mirror Company is still in existence today. This catalog lists the company's address as 2325 Bailey Avenue; it is currently located at 1822 Bailey Avenue. The Amthor family owned and operated the company until 1947, when Jack Strauss purchased it. David M. Saunders purchased the company in 1958; he moved it to the new location in 1978, and the company is now run by his son, Charles.

Edna Noah ran a candy and chocolate shop at 3146 Bailey Avenue near East Amherst Street for a year in 1926. This 1926 photograph of the shop's interior shows Noah, who is listed as a clerk in the 1920 city directory. Sometime between 1921 and 1925, she became a widow, and this life change may have pushed her in a new direction. By 1927, she is listed in the directory as a saleswoman, and the store listing is gone.

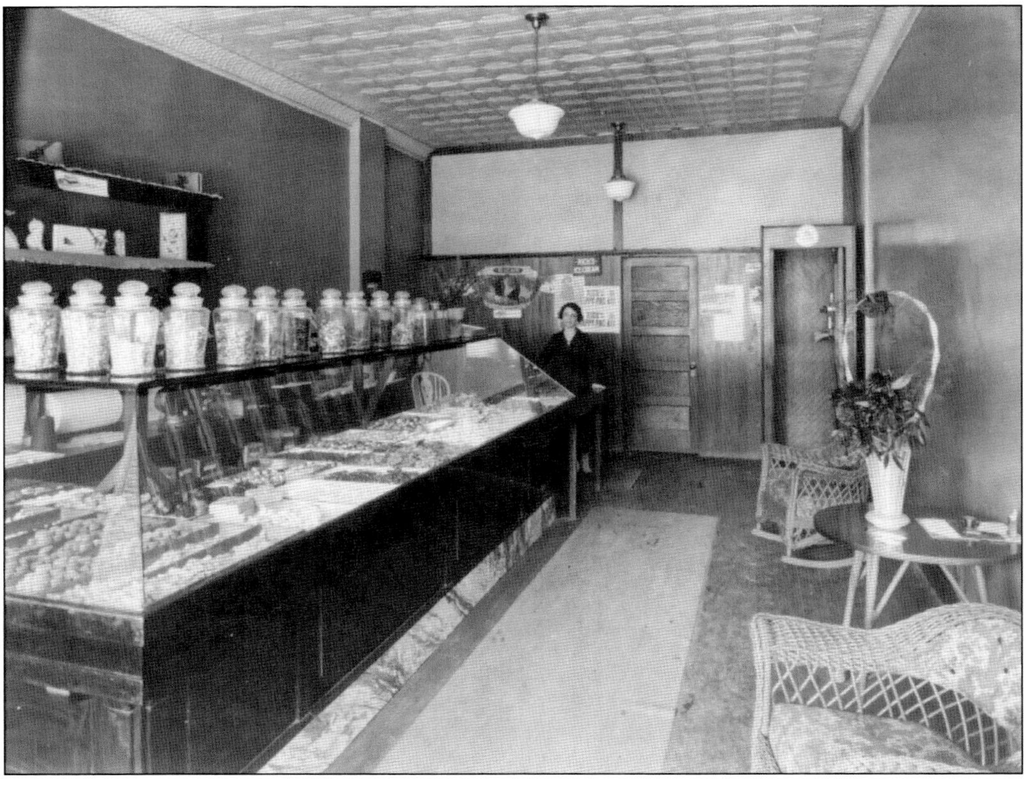

Six

Seneca and South
Down by the River

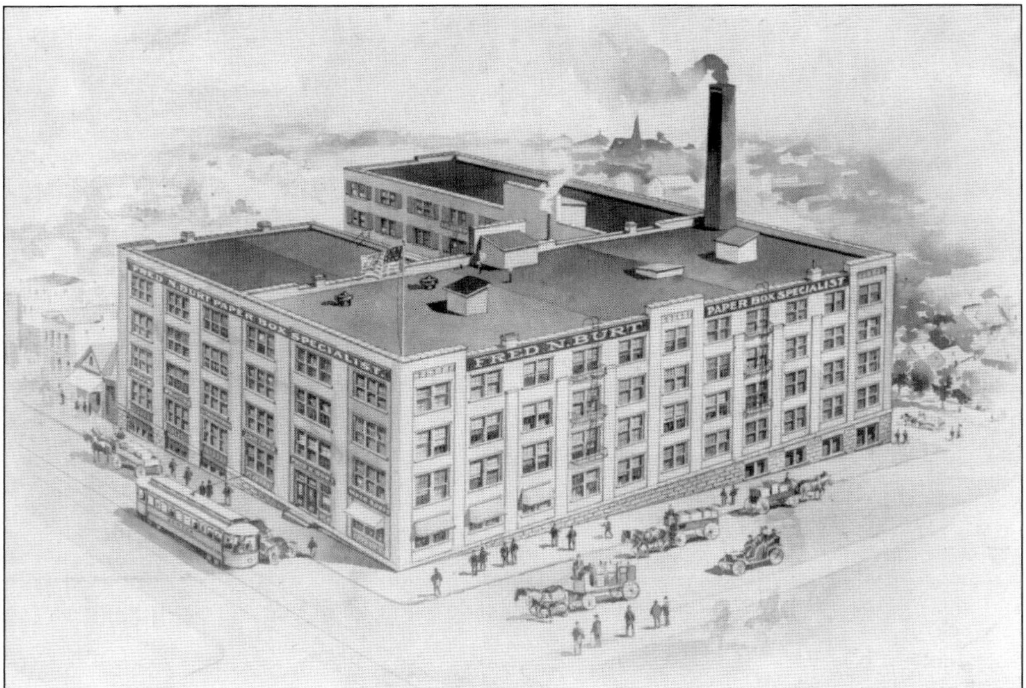

The F.N. Burt Company, located at 500 Seneca Street, has recently been reborn as a commercial and residential space. Frederick N. Burt opened the box company in 1884, and it was a leading producer of cigarette boxes. In 1909, the company became a subsidiary of the Moore Corporation Limited, a business form and sales book company. Soon after, it started producing 90 percent of all cigarette boxes made in America. The company closed in 1999.

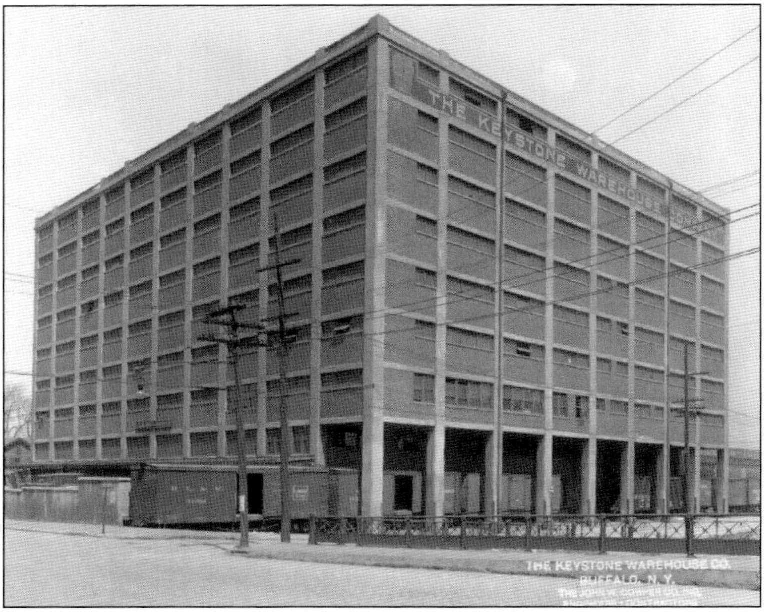

The Keystone Warehouse Company was located at 515 Seneca Street. With its proximity to various rail lines, as shown in this photograph, it became a storage and transportation facility for many companies. This photograph was taken before the building was expanded to the east. It was torn down in 2002.

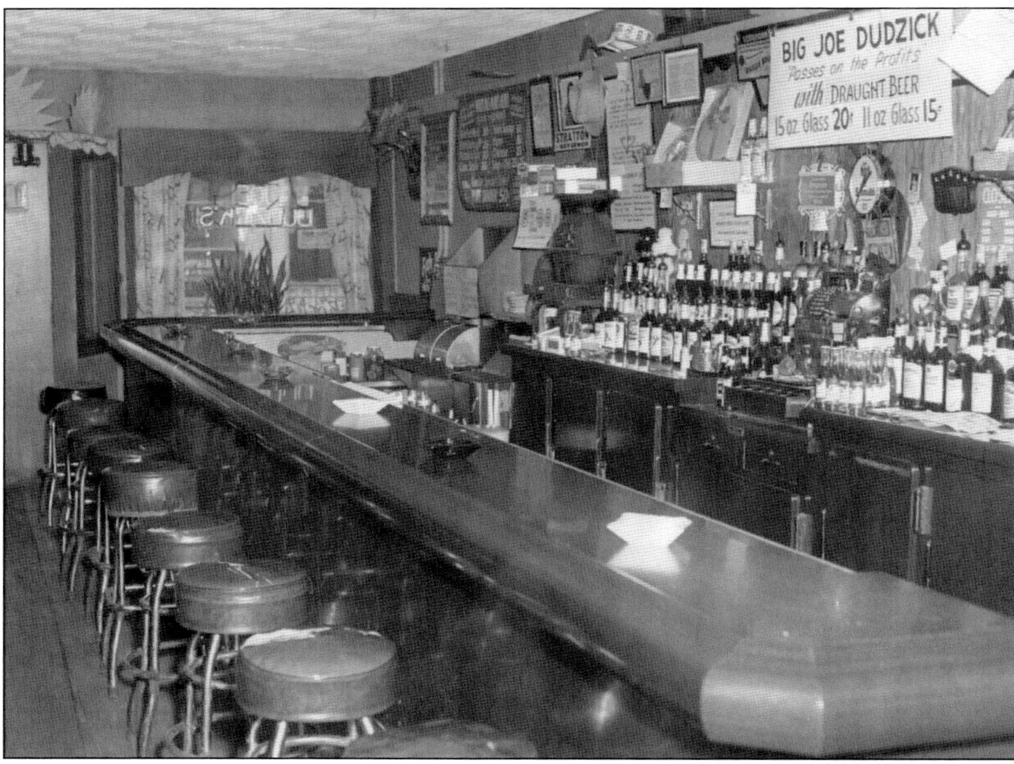

From 1946 to 1966, Big Joe Dudzick's Tavern, located at 770 Seneca Street near Hydraulic Street, was an important part of social life on the East Side. Joe, an accomplished basketball player and member of Buffalo's Common Council, and his wife, Alyce, greeted workers and patrons throughout the day. The building was torn down in the 1980s. One of Joe and Alyce's sons, playwright Tom Dudzick, portrayed the experience of living above this bar in his acclaimed play *Over the Tavern*.

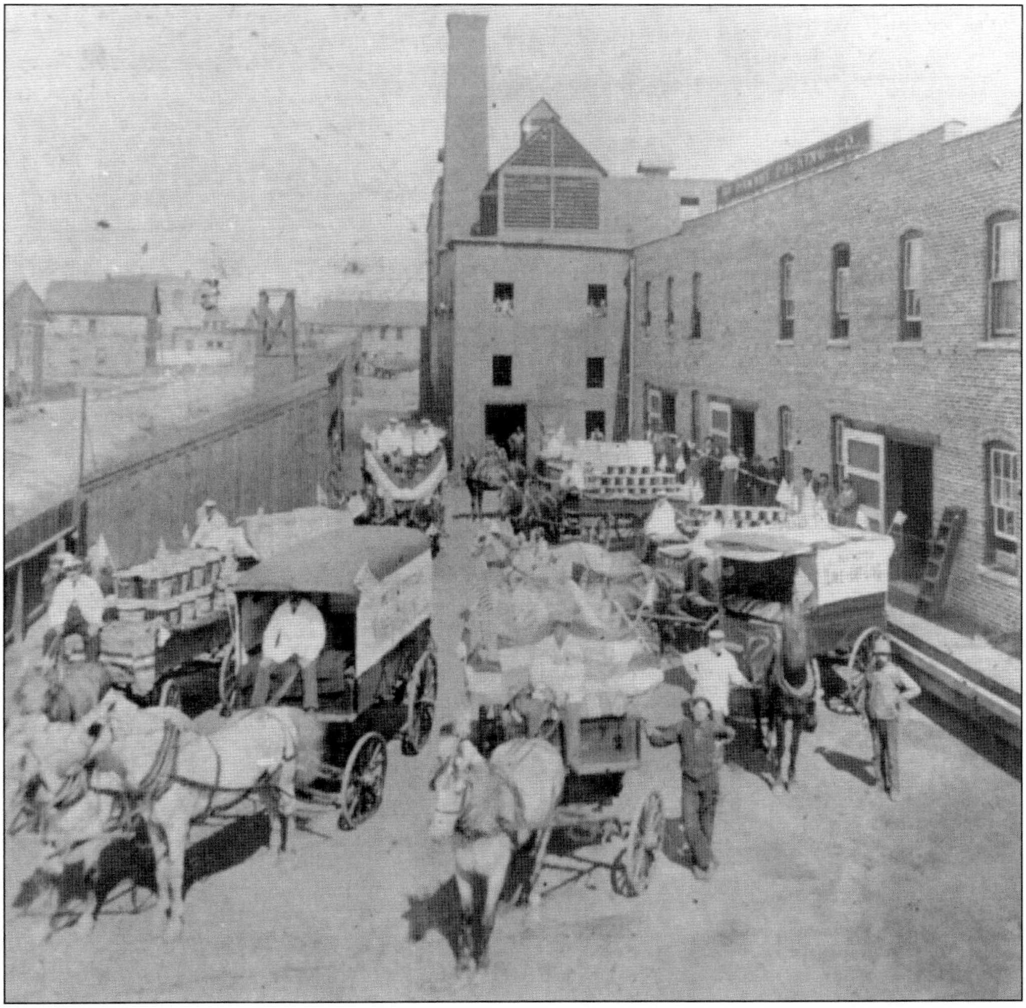

The Danahy Packing Company was established in 1887 near the corner of Seneca and Smith Streets. In 1916, changing technology in the meatpacking industry led Danahy Packing to construct a plant at Clinton and Metcalfe Streets, including a $20,000 cold storage facility. The photograph at right shows the original plant around 1890 with horse-drawn delivery carriages. The below photograph shows the cold storage facility at Clinton and Metcalfe Streets, which included a machine shop, slaughter rooms, washing rooms, seven cooling rooms, loading and unloading docks, packing rooms, and a sausage room. The plant had an enormous footprint, taking up a whole city block.

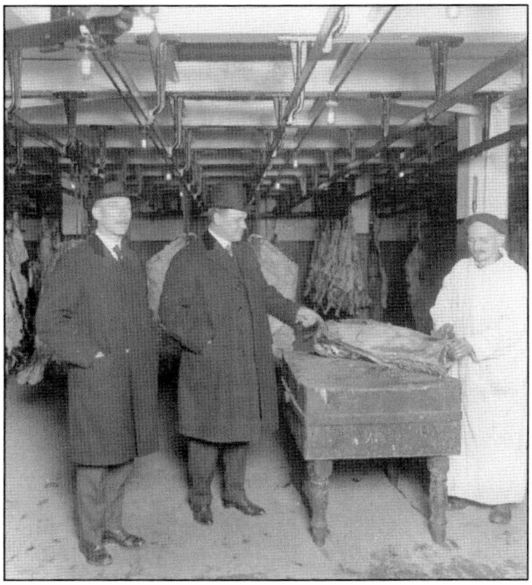

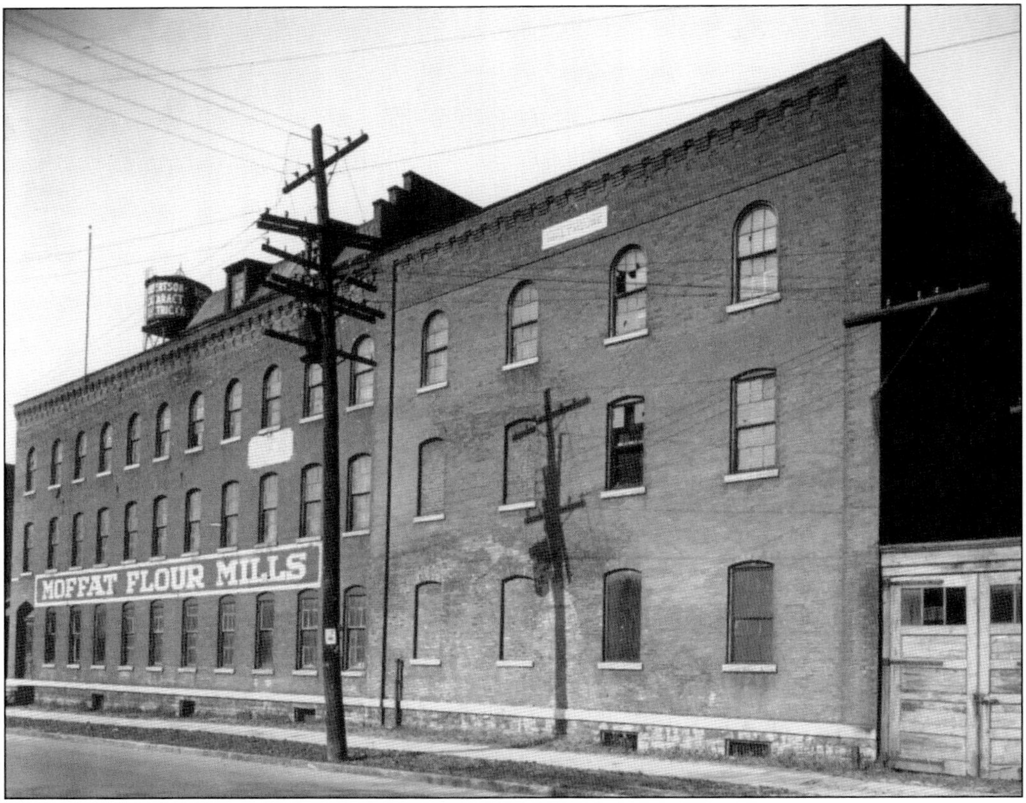

The Moffat Flour Mill Company, located at 1035 Seneca Street near Peabody Street and the Buffalo Belt Line, was first established in 1833 by John Moffat as an early brewery. The nascent company produced ales and porters and, at its height, sold roughly 20,000 barrels a year. With competition from many breweries, the brewery closed in 1918 and reopened as a flour mill, which operated until 1927. This image shows the new business next to the old malt house.

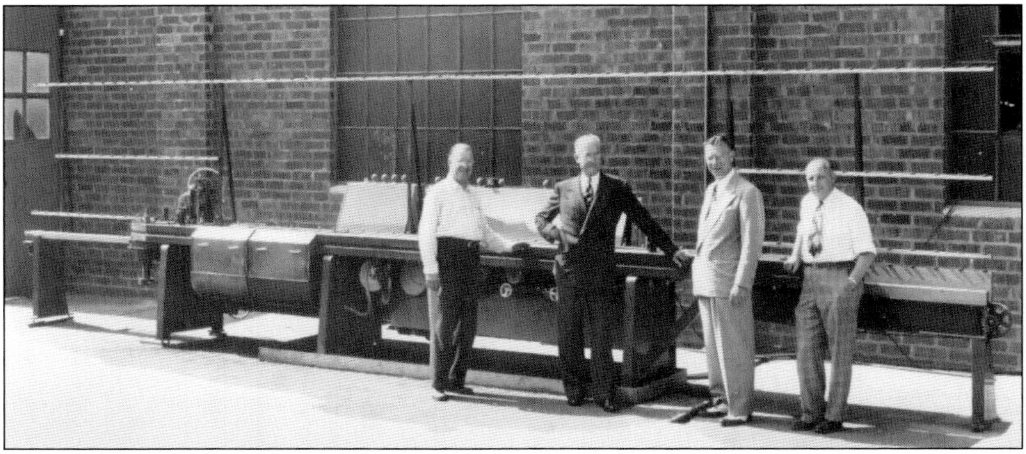
Wiesner-Rapp Corporation was located in the Clinton-Babcock section of the east side, which is shown in the aerial photograph on page 48. The company produced J-Box, Washer, Squeezer, and Saturator ranges for large industrial companies, which used many Wiesner-Rapp machines when they wanted to bleach their own products, such as cloth. In this 1949 photograph, employees stand in front of a Weber machine.

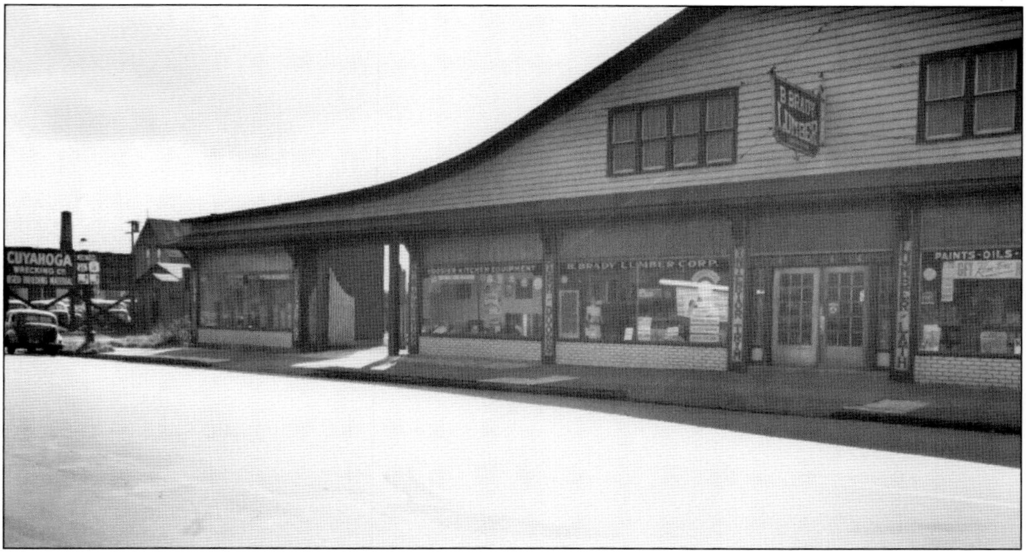

The B. Brady Lumber Corporation is one of the longest-running businesses included in this book. In 1890, Bernard Brady was listed in the city directory as a lumber inspector, and in 1895, he opened his lumber store at 711 Elk Street. One year later, he moved to 124 Fillmore Avenue, then moved to 1407 Seneca Street (the pictured location) in 1902. The company sold finishes, beaverboard, lathes, and shingles and was bought out in 1958 by the Len-Co Lumber Company, which has a lumberyard on this site and offices one block east at 1445 Seneca Street.

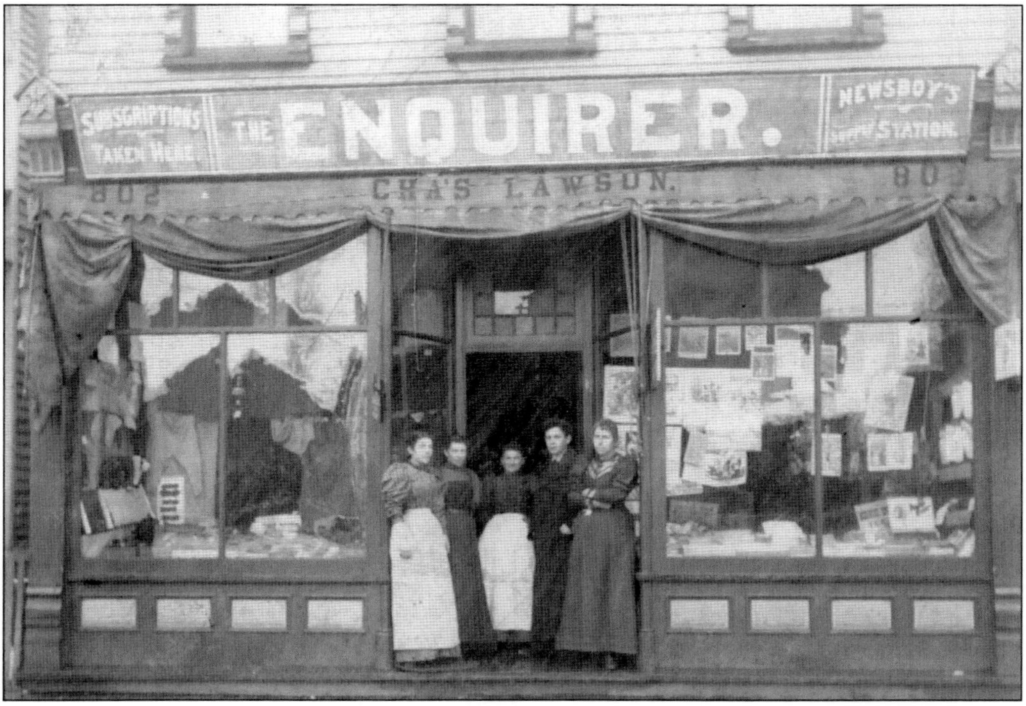

Charles Lawson's *Buffalo Enquirer* General Store is pictured with employees out front avoiding the rain. The *Buffalo Enquirer* newspaper ran from 1891 to 1925. The city had as many as 20 newspapers published during these decades—some dailies, some ethnocentric, and some very short-lived. Lawson's newsstand opened at 802 Elk Street in 1884 and remained in business until 1909.

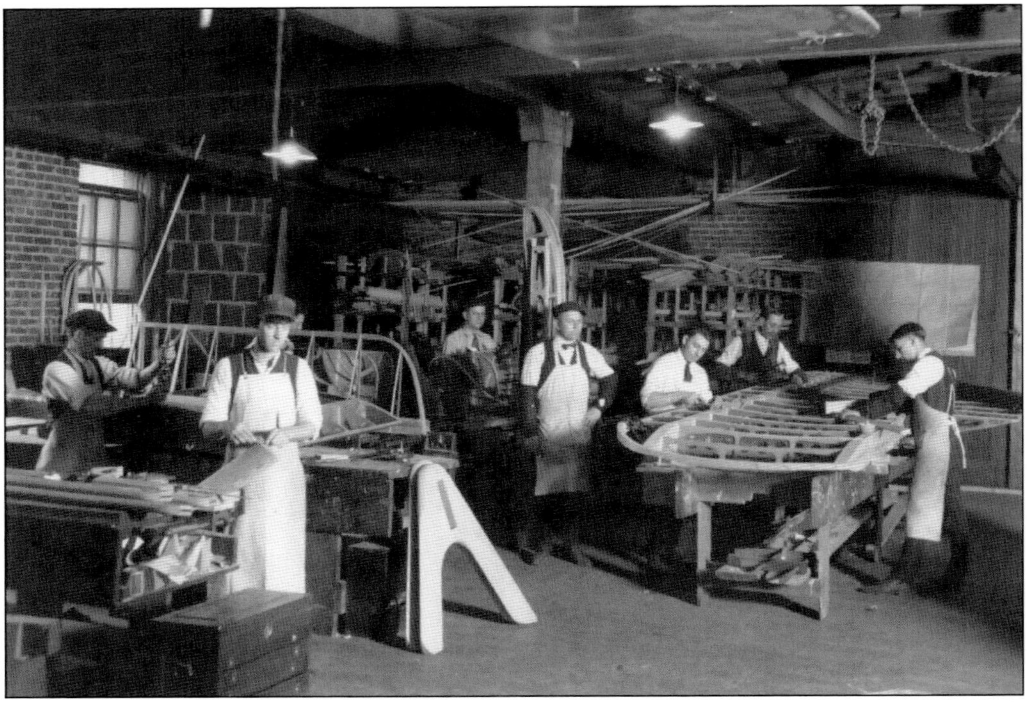

Brothers Gabriel and Abraham Elias founded the Elias & Bros. Company in 1881 on Churchill Street in the Black Rock neighborhood. For the company's first 37 years in business, the brothers ran a lumber and general millwork company; they switched to airplanes in 1919. By that time, they had moved to a larger facility at 965 Elk Street, where they primarily manufactured monoplanes for recreational and military use. These two photographs show the wing room of the factory (above) and an experimental plane (below). The plane was mostly made of wood, and its unidentified designer sits in the cockpit. The plane had one voyage, during which it crashed from 50 feet in the air, injuring its two pilots. The company, not able to carry on after the Depression, closed in 1934.

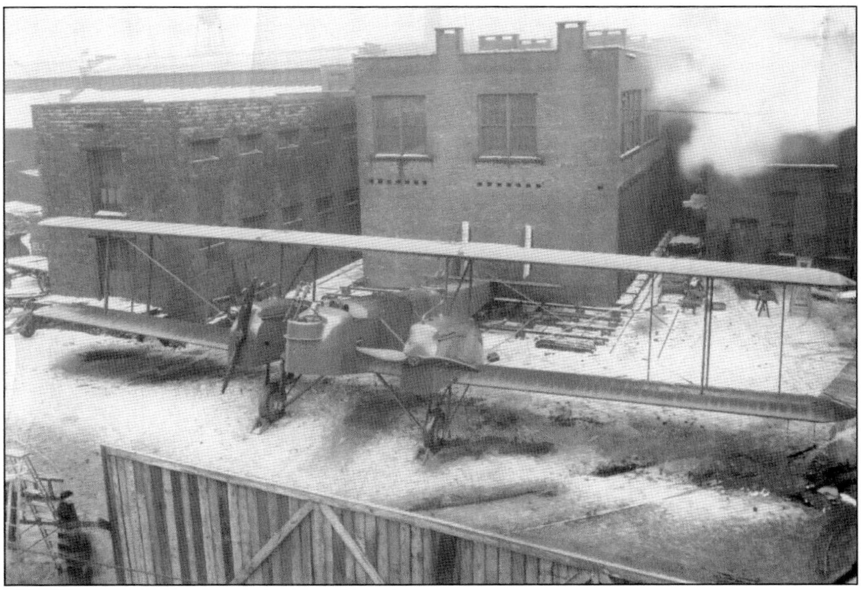

Seven

Into the Neighborhoods
Companies as Anchors

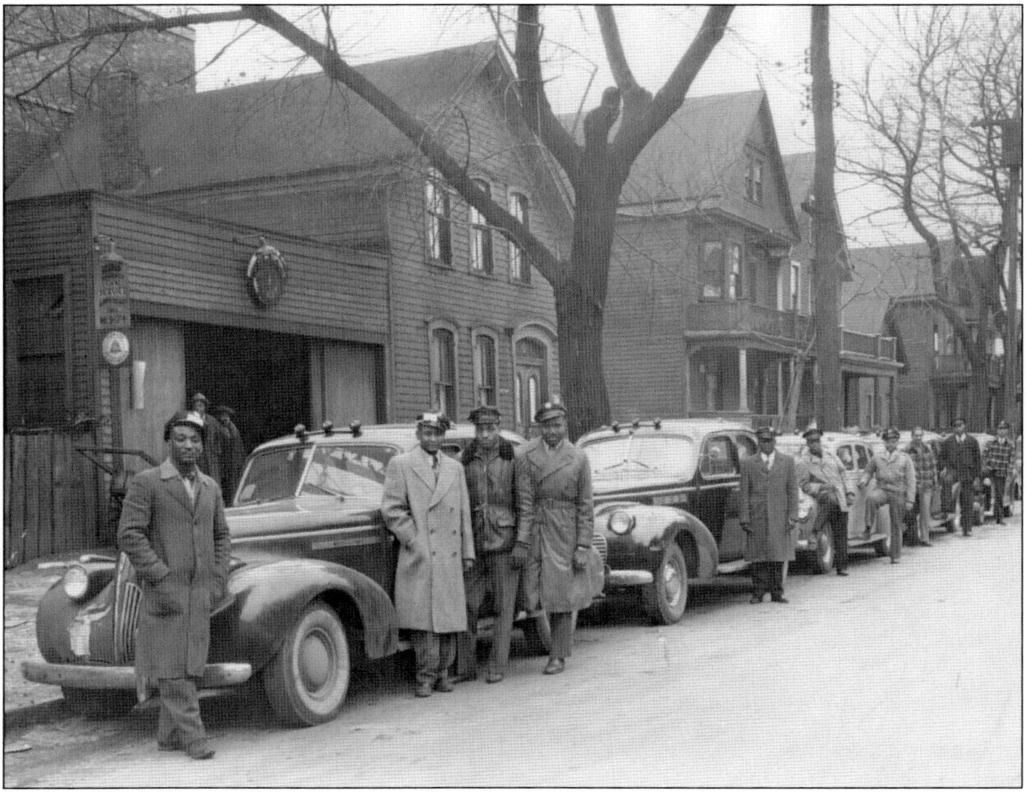

Brown Bomber Cab Service drivers are pictured outside company headquarters at 236 Hickory Street between William Street and Broadway. The service started in 1948 and remained in operation until 1970. The Brown Bomber Cab Service was a minority-owned business and showed the growing affluence of African Americans on the East Side.

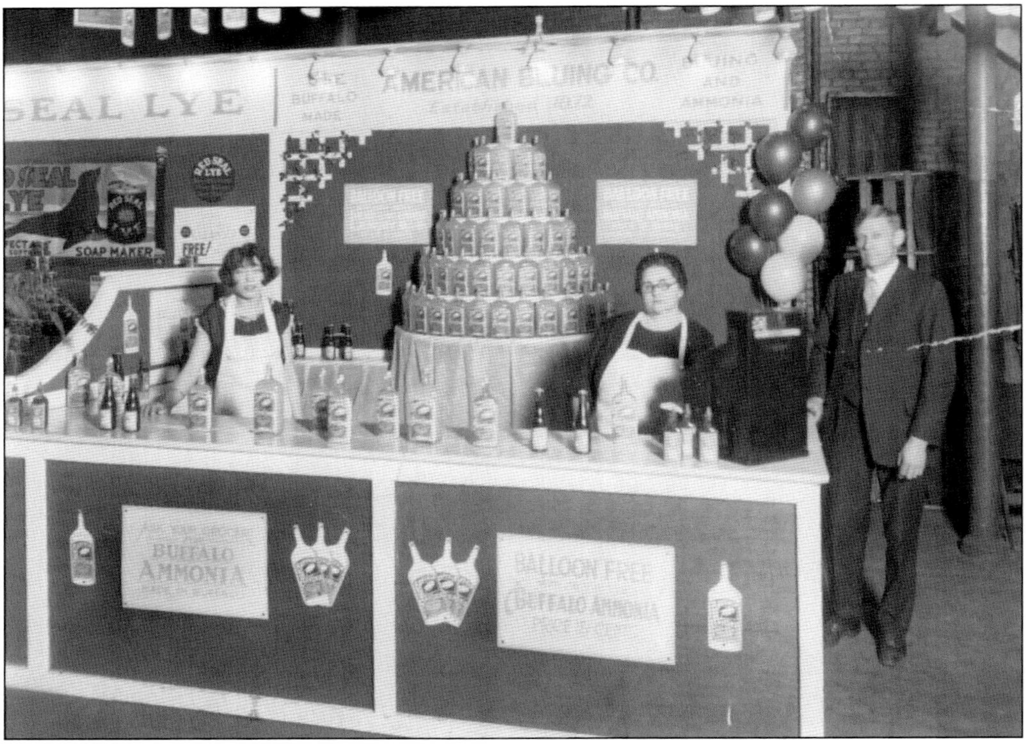

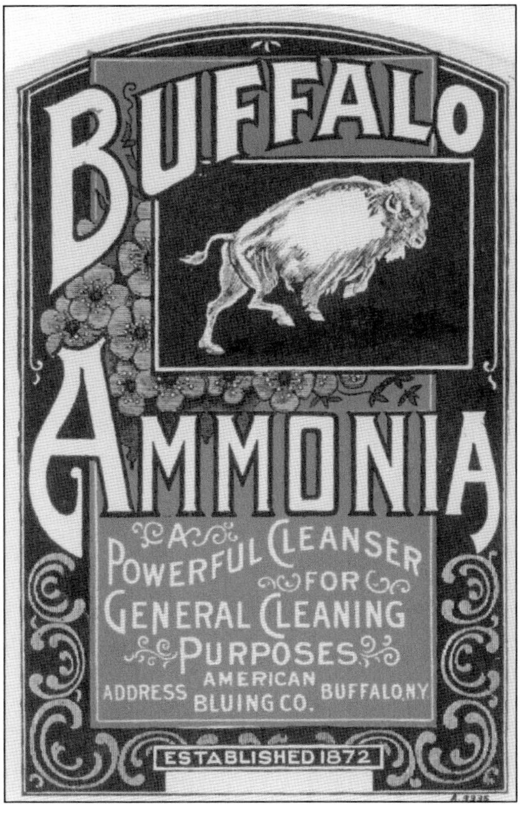

The American Bluing Company, established in 1872, was located at 56 Mulberry Street between Goodell and Virginia Streets. Joseph Hogg, who was asked to produce an herbal plaster as a cure-all for rheumatism, opened the company. The company primarily produced two products—Buffalo Bluing and Buffalo Ammonia—but also created cider vinegars and healing salves. Bluing, a light blue dye, was added to white laundry to give cloth an improved, clean appearance. Bluing products can be in liquid or solid form; the American Bluing Company produced the liquid form. The above image shows an American Bluing Company booth at a trade show, while the image at left advertises Buffalo Ammonia for "general cleaning purposes." The company lasted until 1977—for more than 100 years. However, the company's former site (56 Mulberry Street) currently shows no sign of the American Bluing Company's existence.

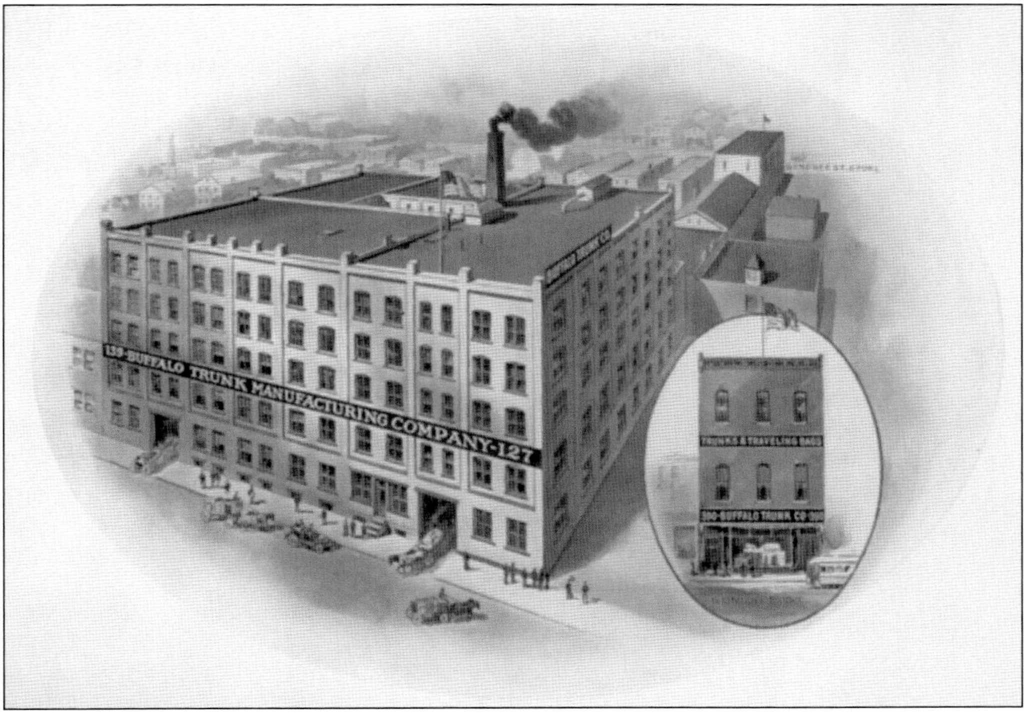

The Buffalo Trunk Manufacturing Company produced high-end luggage, suitcases, and bags. Owner William B. Knight opened the company in 1896 at 204–206 Terrace Street. In 1902, it moved from Terrace Street to 306 Genesee Street, opening a manufacturing plant directly behind it at 127–129 Cherry Street. This structure is still standing and was most recently occupied by Anthone Furniture Warehouse.

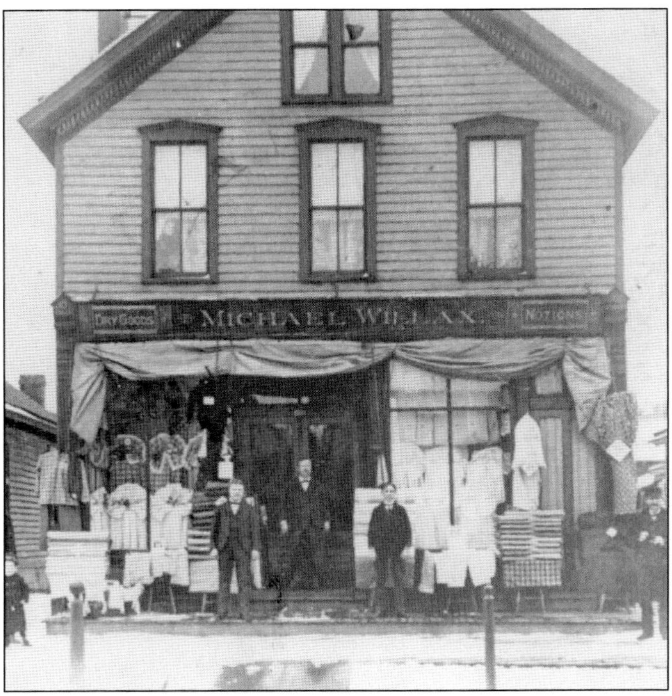

Michael Willax poses in the doorway of his store at 291 Cherry Street. Willax began his career as a shoemaker on Cherry Street, opening this store in 1893 and remaining there until 1899. That year, the business moved to 1268 Genesee Street, where Willax continued to sell dry goods and "notions," as indicated by the sign in the photograph. The last mention of the store in the city directory was in 1923.

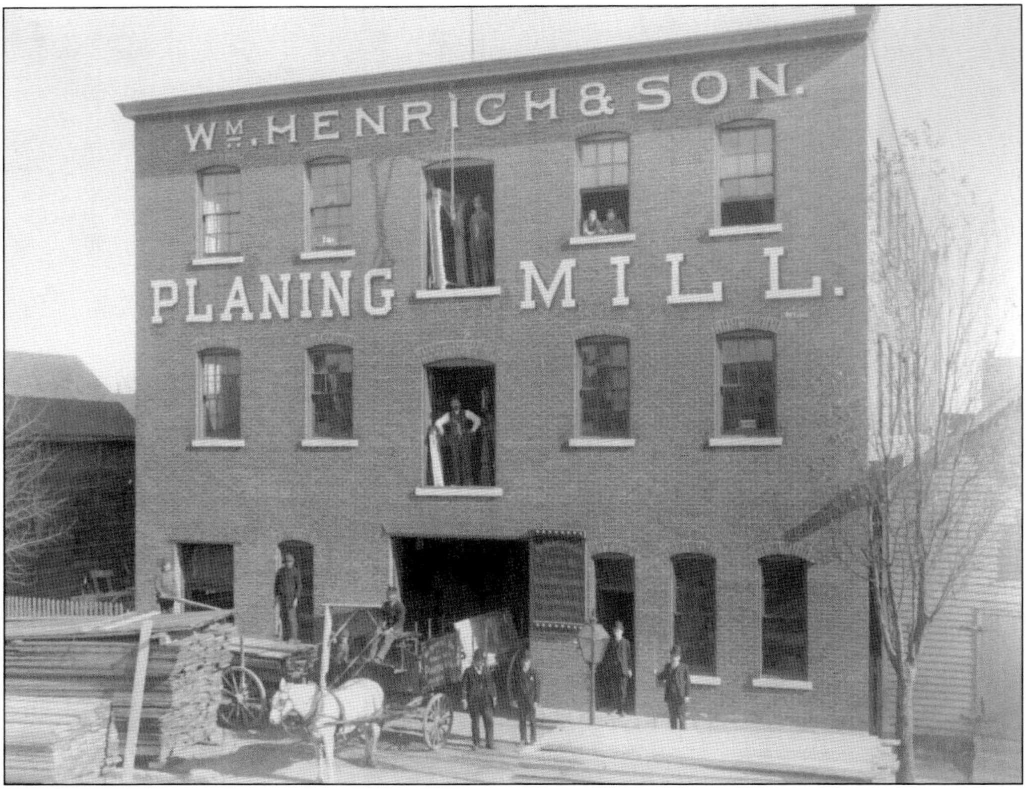

The lovely facade of Henrich Planing Mill, located at 193–195 Spring Street, is shown in the c. 1891 photograph above. William Henrich began as a carpenter in 1866, and his three sons joined him in the business before he died in 1888. The business operated a yard on Clinton Street. The below photograph shows a subsidiary business, Bison Lumber Co., in 1960. Henrich Lumber started in 1866 and lasted until 1964. The Henrich family also branched out into paneling and siding.

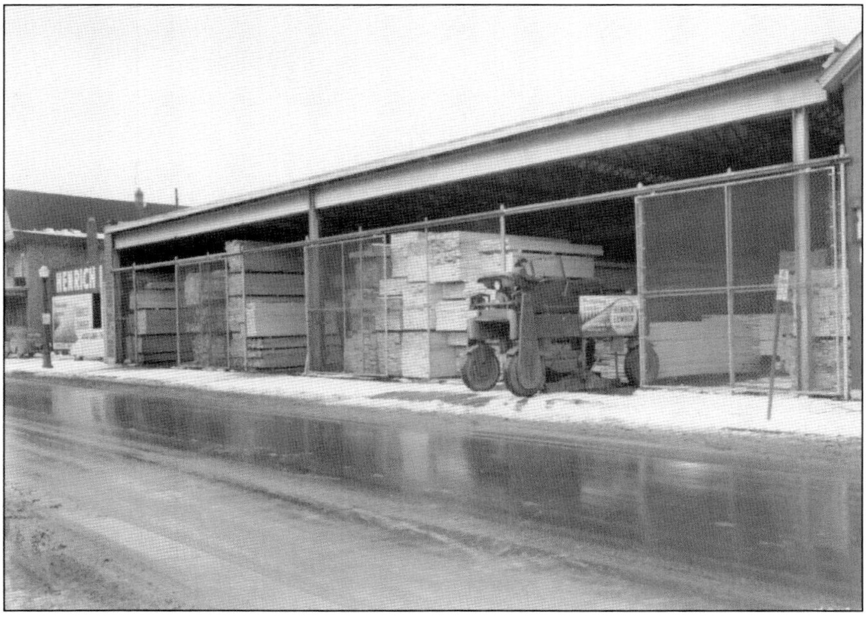

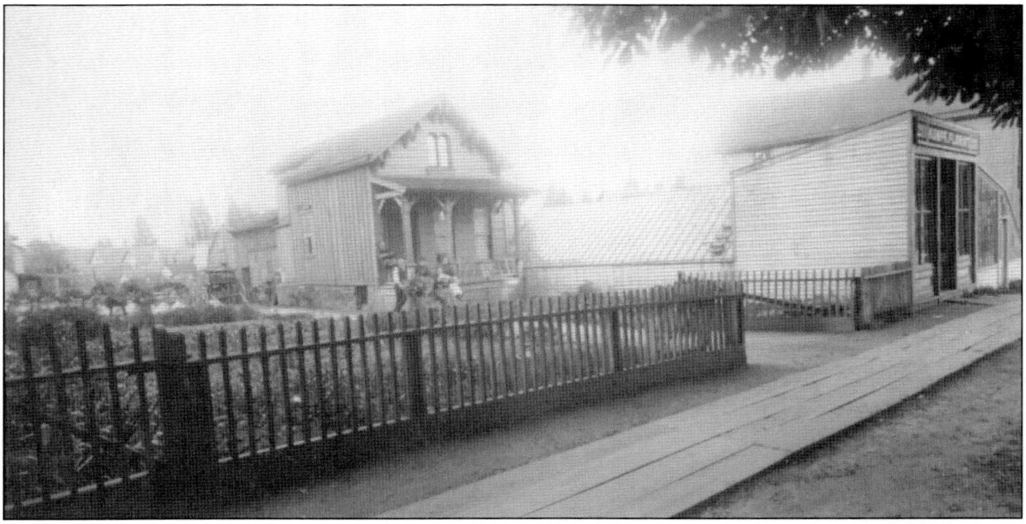

This undated photograph shows Kumpf Bros. Florists at 211 Peach Street and a plank sidewalk in front of it. Two brothers, August and Charles, founded the company in 1899, and it remained in business until 1943. In 1899, city directories indicate that the florist shop had two locations—one at the Washington Market and the other at this Peach Street storefront. The brothers vacated the Washington Market location in 1915 and then sold their goods exclusively at the Peach Street location. The company name was changed to Kumpf & Stall in its final years.

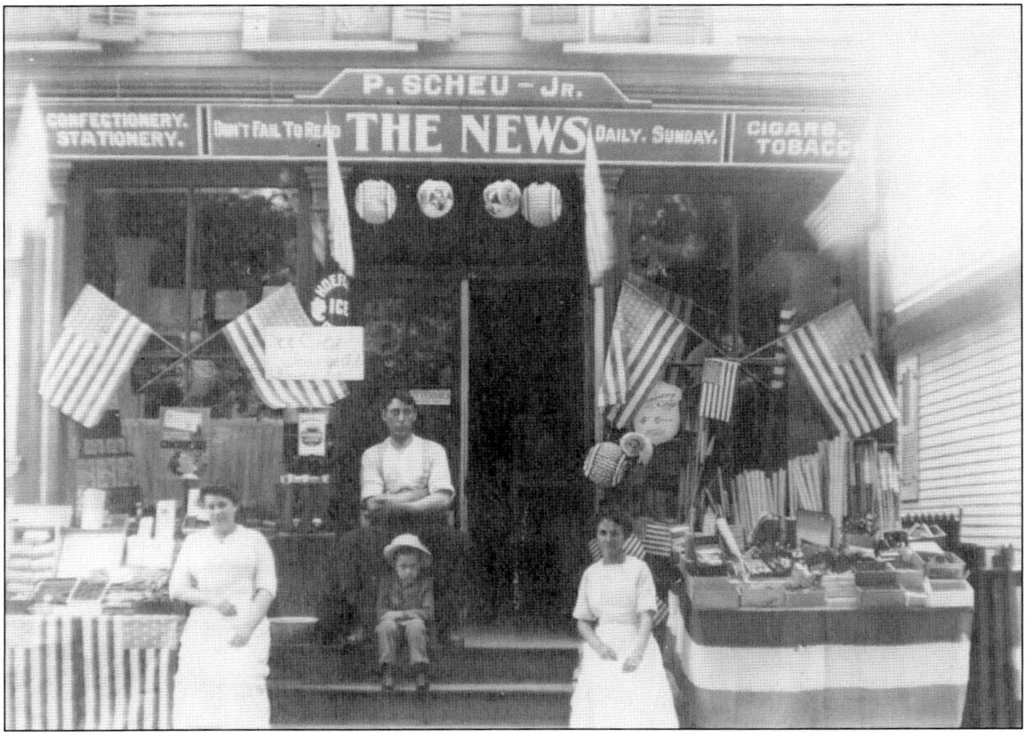

In this Fourth of July photograph from 1911, Paul Scheu Jr. poses with family members at his store. The confectionery and news store he ran did not last long, though. In 1910, his name shows up in the city directory as a houseman (constructor). In 1911, he opened his store at 16 Spruce Street between Broadway and Sycamore Street, and by 1914, this business was closed.

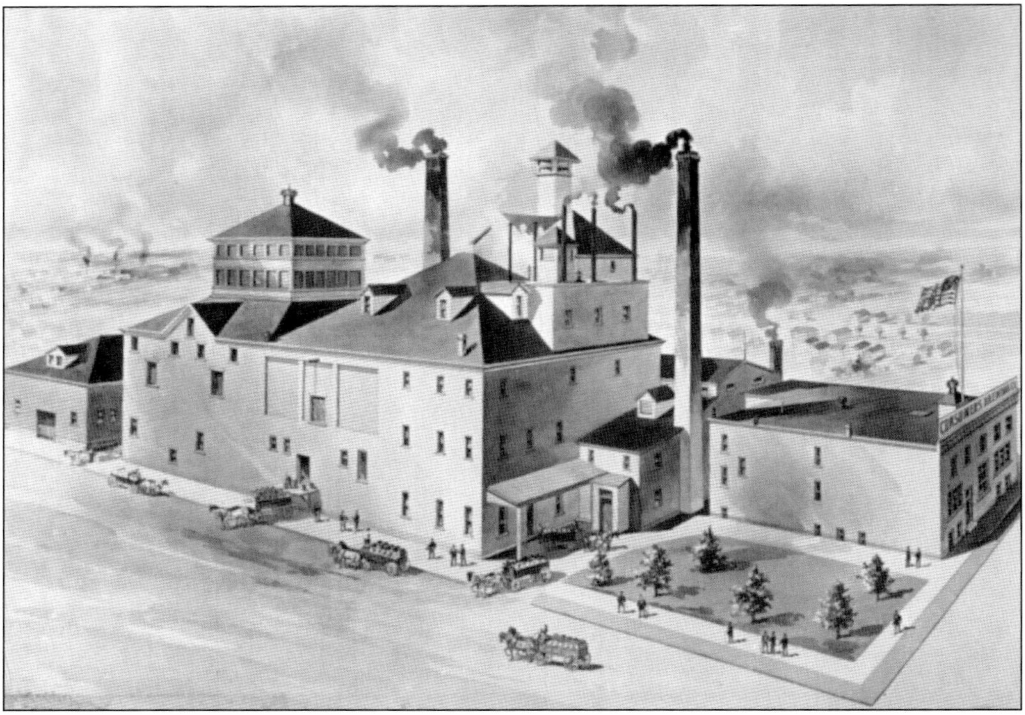

Consumer's Brewing, located at 1033 Jefferson Avenue on the corner of Best Street, was in operation from 1875 until the onset of Prohibition (1919 or 1920). George Rochevot opened the brewery in 1857 at Spring and Cherry Streets, where it remained until 1871, when the company constructed a larger brewery at Jefferson Avenue and Best Street. It changed names twice—in 1892, it became Lion Brewing Co., which lasted until 1904; it then operated as Consumer's Brewing until it closed.

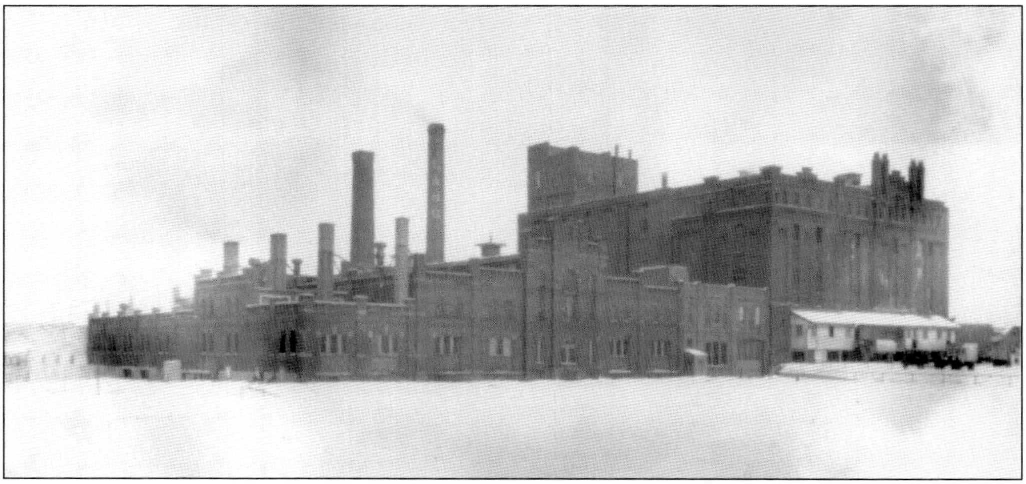

This 1935 photograph shows the Gerhard Lang Brewery at Jefferson Avenue and Best Street. Philip Born opened the company in 1840 as the Born Brewery located at 581 Genesee Street. In 1862, Gerhard Lang married Born's daughter and bought half of the company; the company's name then became Born & Lang, which existed from 1862 to 1876. In 1876, it became Gerhard Lang Brewery. At the end of the 19th century, it was the largest brewery in Buffalo; it closed in 1949 after 109 years in operation.

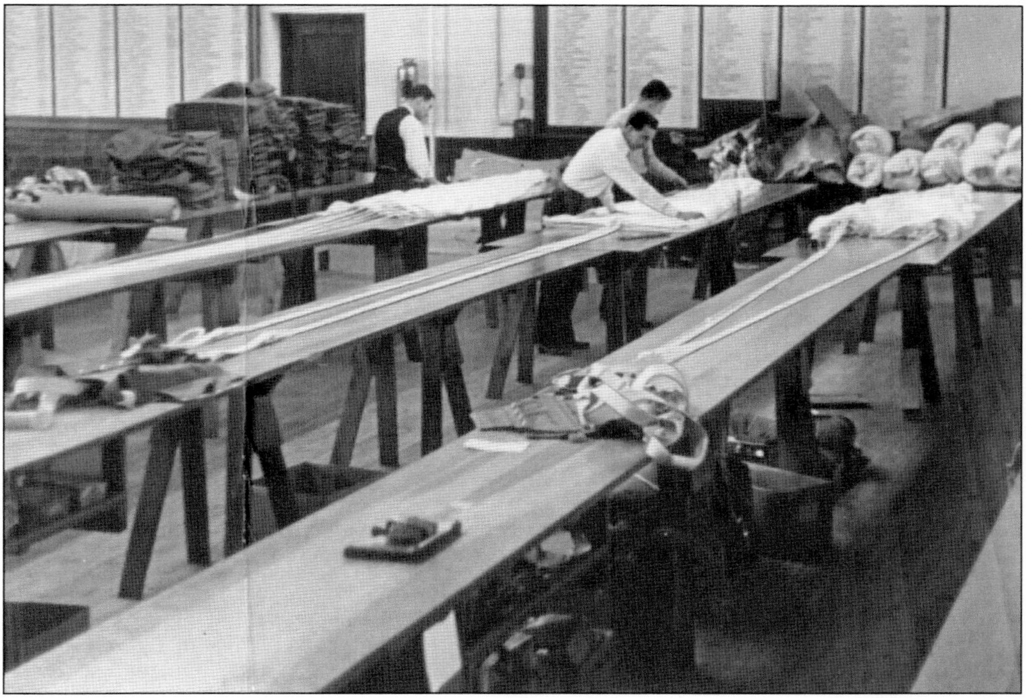

The Irvin Air Chute Company was the world's first producer of parachutes. Leslie L. Irvin started the business in 1919 at 760 Main Street and opened a second operation at 372 Pearl Street in 1925. By 1932, a need for more factory space led to the opening of the offices and plant at 1668 Jefferson Avenue between Florida Street and East Delavan Avenue. The company remained there until 1953, when it moved and also opened other plants around the country. The company is now known as Airborne Systems.

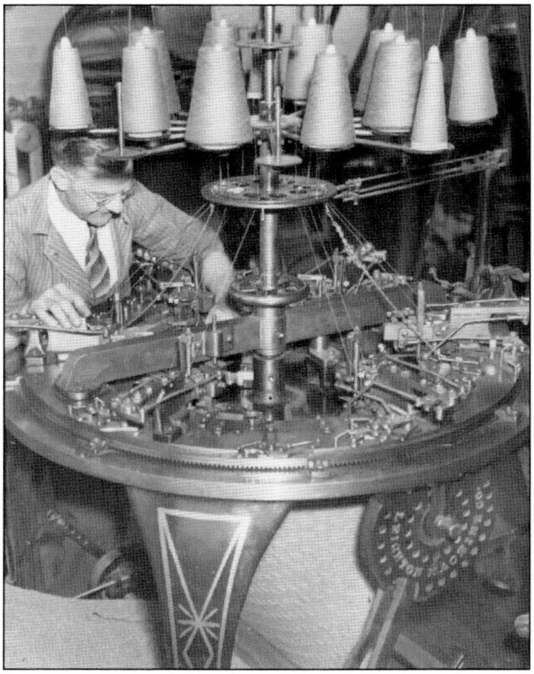

Rugby Knitting Mills began in 1905 as D.B. Levi & Bros., which produced men's knitwear at 89–91 Seneca Street. It became Rugby Knitting Mills in 1917 and moved to 1490 Jefferson Avenue in 1948. In 1965, it moved to Lord Street at the intersection of Seymour Street, where it became Rugby Sportswear Company in 1971 and closed in the mid-1970s.

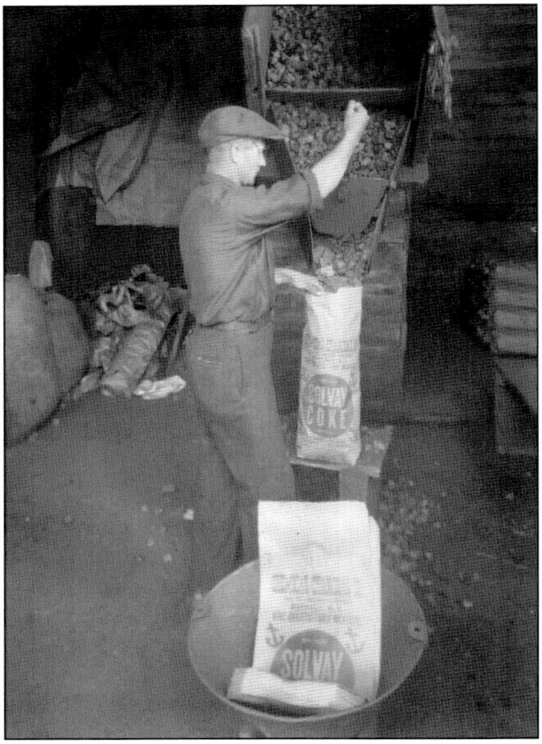

The Chemical Charcoal Company had a long history on Fillmore Avenue. In 1899, owner and manager Frank Hossenlopp opened the business at 211 Fillmore Avenue. In 1933, the company moved down the street to 188 Fillmore Avenue. It produced charcoal using the Solvay Coke process developed by the Solvay Coke Company in Milwaukee, Wisconsin, and the Solvay Process Company in Syracuse, New York. The Chemical Charcoal Company remained at 188 Fillmore Avenue until it closed in 1967.

Hall Baking Company, located at 2381 Fillmore Avenue on the corner of Main Street, later housed Kaufman's Bakery. Starting in 1912, Hall's Bakery was an East Side fixture for 50 years. The company opened its first location in 1912 at 2652 Main Street, near the corner of East Amherst Street, and built and moved into the Fillmore Avenue bakery in 1916, remaining there until 1963, when Home Pride Bakeries purchased the company.

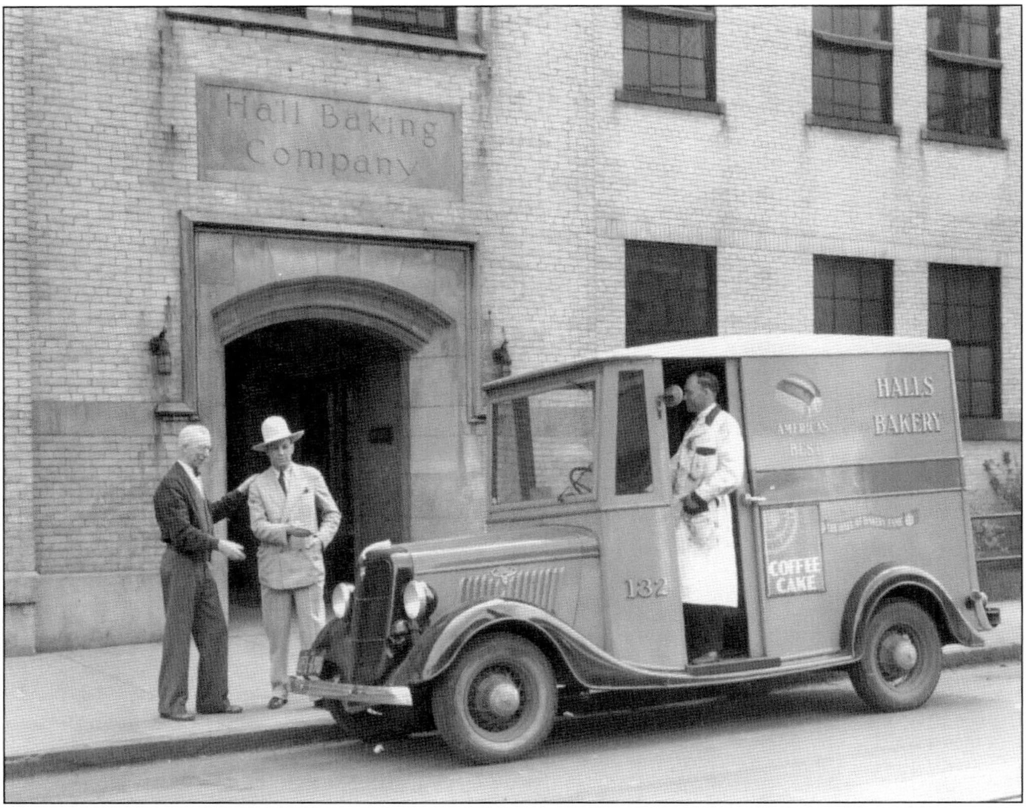

Sam Kaufman started Kaufman's Bakery in 1937 at 998 Broadway in the Sattler's Department Store, with an additional storefront in the Central Park Plaza. By the 1940s, a third storefront was added at 677 Hertel Avenue. In 1968, Kaufman's moved into the old Hall Baking Company/Home Pride Bakeries facility at 2381 Fillmore Avenue and consolidated its wholesale baking and manufacturing process. Kaufman's Bakery was in business until 2004. The memorable "Jolly Little Baker" emblem was once ubiquitous around Buffalo. These two photographs from the 1970s show a few steps in the process of making kimmelweck rolls.

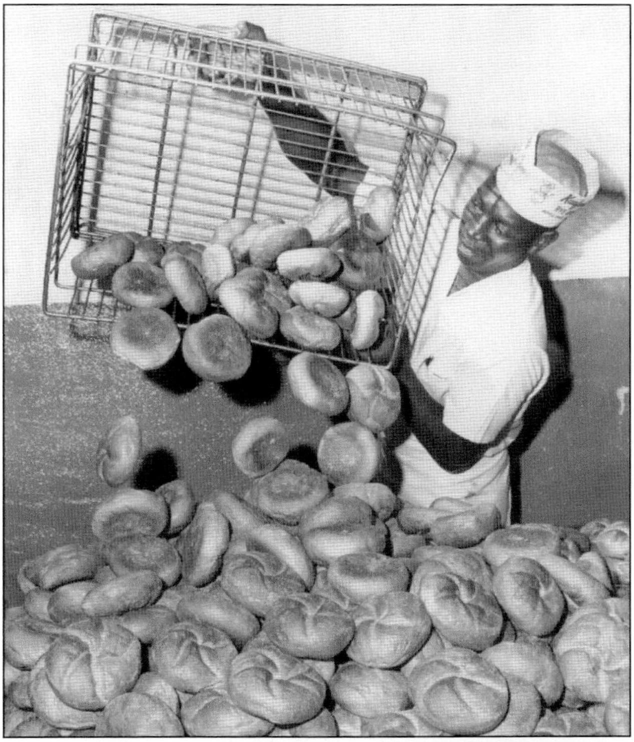

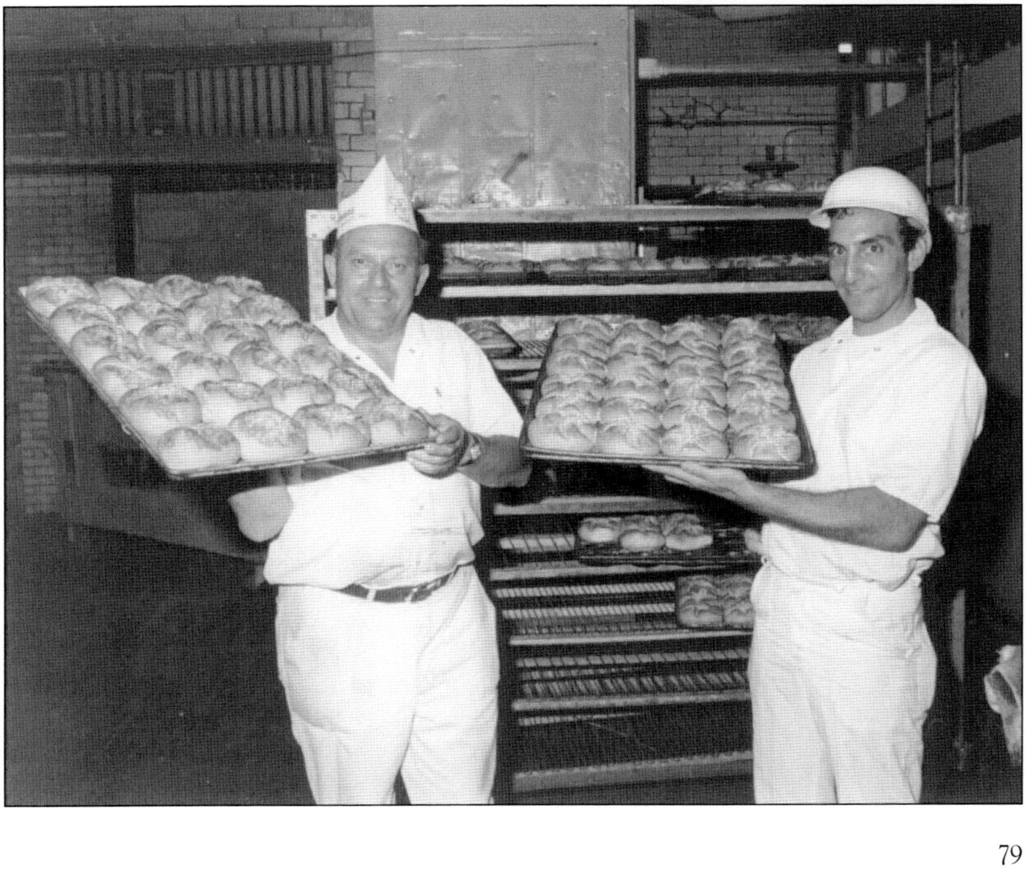

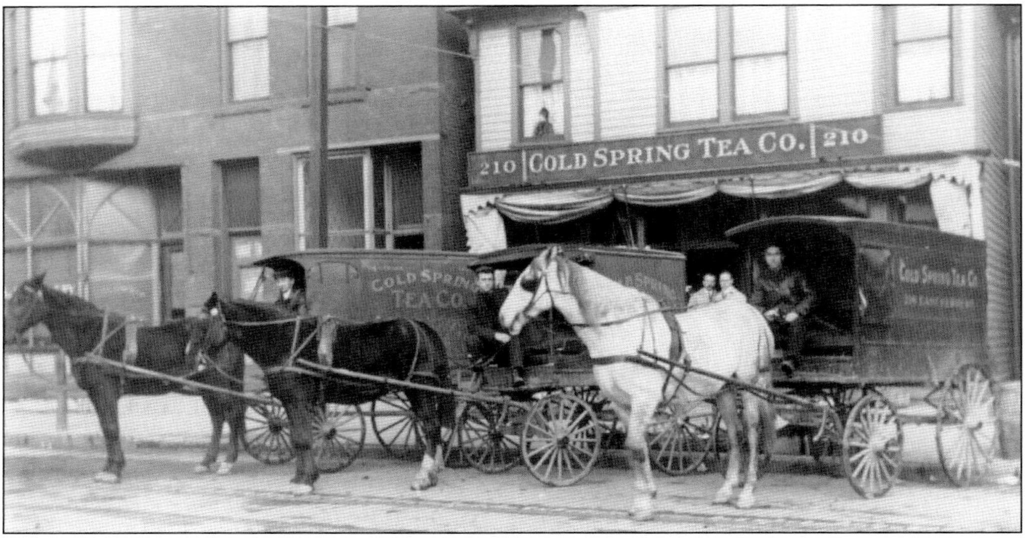

Emil Gerber and Joseph Weig stand in the doorway of their company, the Cold Spring Tea Company, around 1906. The two men founded the business, located at 210 East Ferry Street, in 1899 and remained in business until 1927. The company, which started out making and selling tea, turned into a coffee, soda water, and general grocery store.

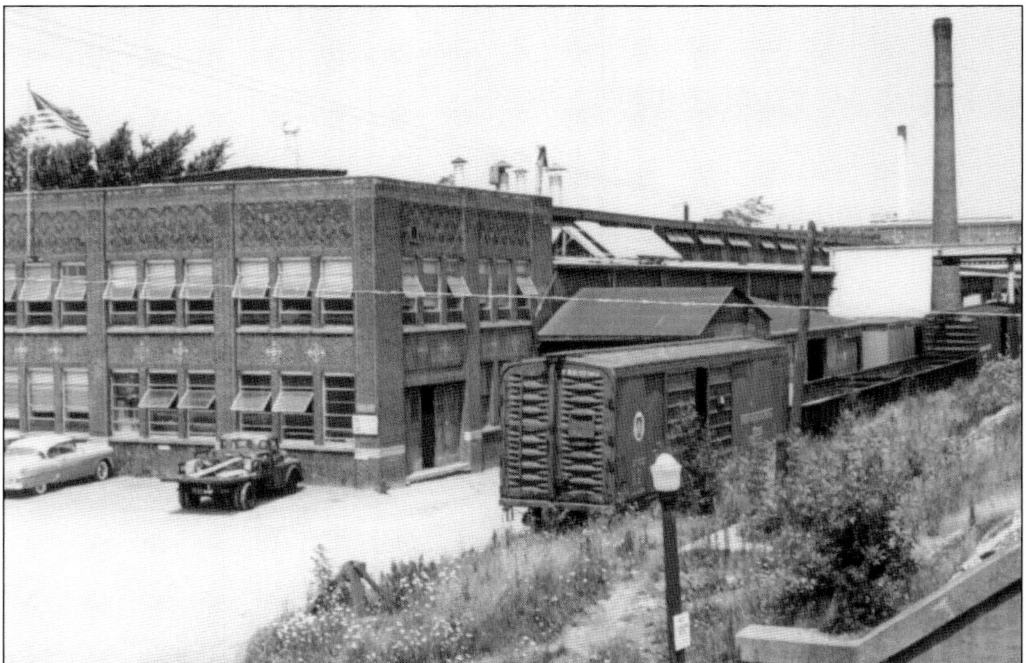

Taken at 1210 East Ferry Street, this photograph captures the Erie Railroad, Bettinger Coal and Coke Company (in the background), and Fenestra Steel Company (in the foreground). The Bettinger Coal and Coke Company, with the white smokestack, opened in 1933 and closed in 1971. The structure in the foreground housed multiple companies, including the Robert K. Glass Marble Manufactory, Detroit Steel Products Company, Fenestra Steel Company, and Demarkus Corporation. The last business to have this address was Speedway Conveyors, which remained open until 2013.

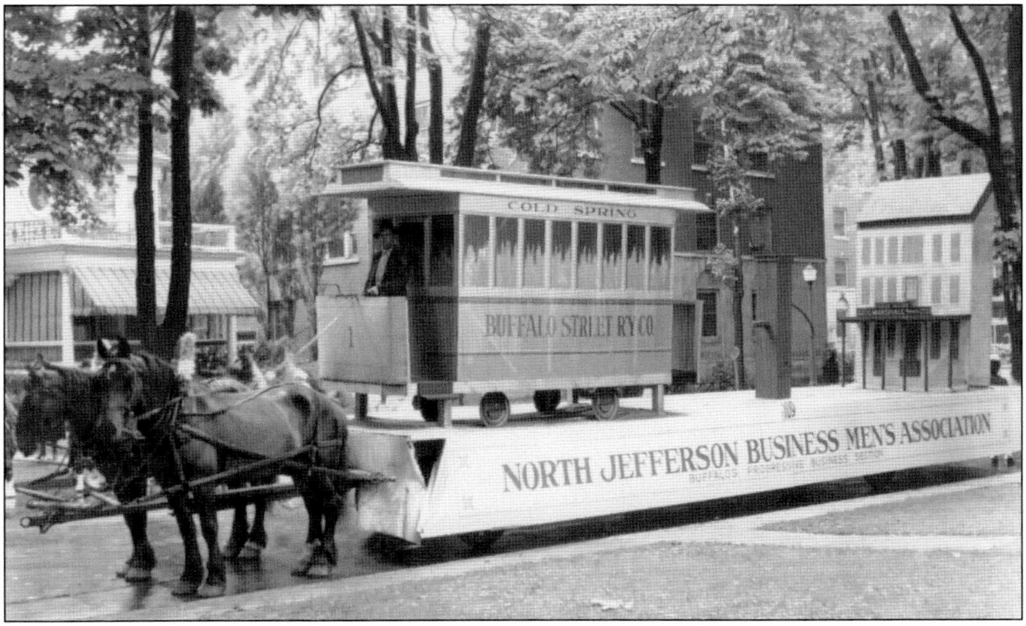

The North Jefferson Businessmen's Association served companies in and around the North Jefferson and Cold Springs neighborhood from 1927 to 1931. The association's offices were located at 1300 Jefferson Avenue; A.G. McDonald was president, and William E. Hyatt was secretary. Today, this group would be known as a chamber of commerce. Pictured is the association's float created for a parade in 1930.

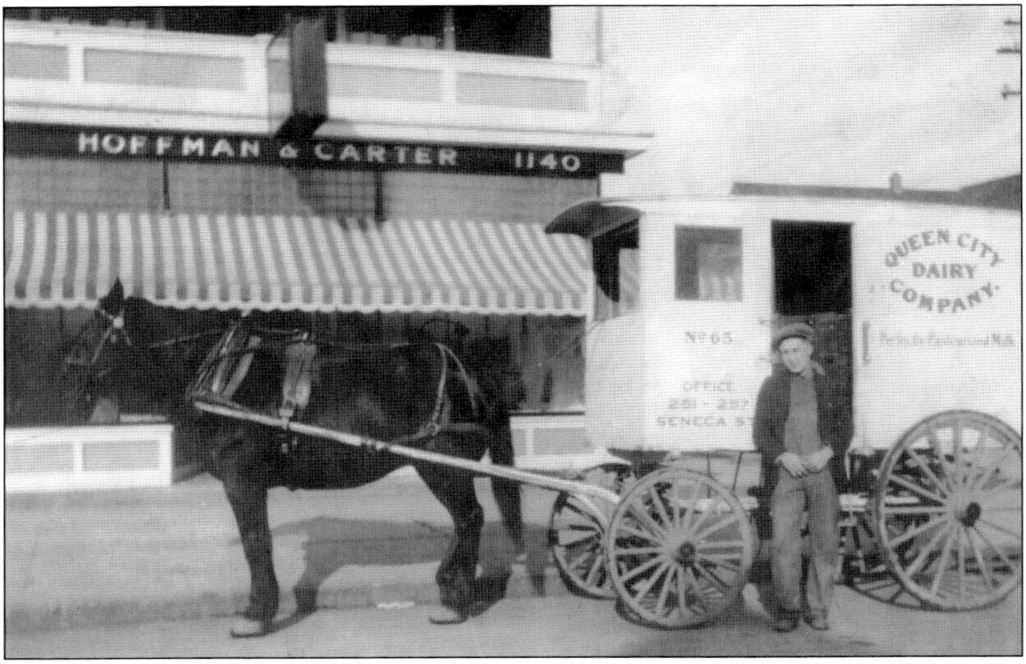

The Queen City Dairy Company sold dairy products from 1909 to 1927. The company started in 1909 at 885–895 Niagara Street. In 1913, they moved to 251–257 Seneca Street to aid with delivery to East and South Side businesses and residents. In this 1922 photograph, a delivery truck and driver pose outside of Hoffman & Carter, located at 1140 East Ferry Street.

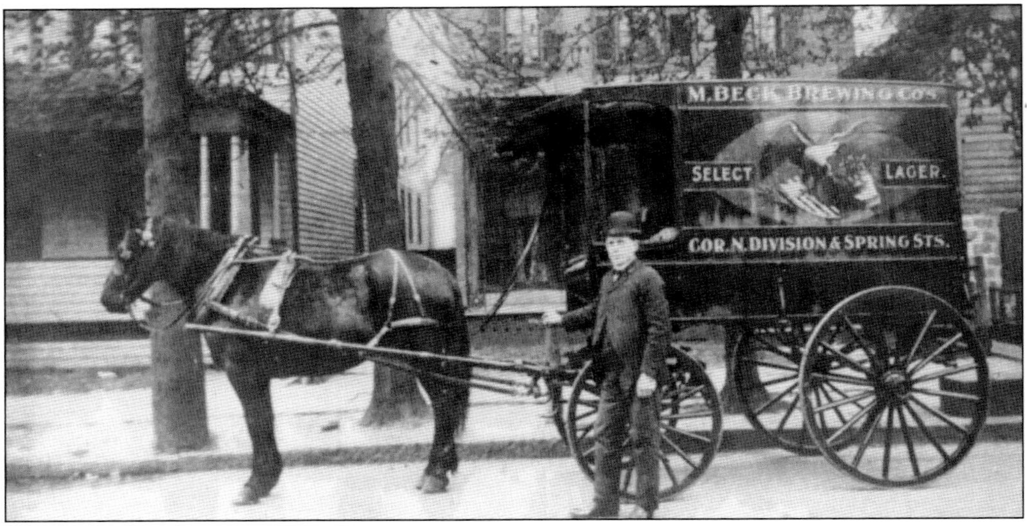

The Magnus Beck Brewing Company is another brewery with a long history in Buffalo. Joseph Freidman started the brewery in 1840 on Oak Street near Tupper Street. In 1855, Magnus Beck reorganized the company at 407 North Division Street. In 1883, Beck passed away, and for three years, his estate ran the brewery. In 1886, the brewery was moved to 466 North Division Street. Producing 11,000 barrels a year, it remained viable until 1920, when it closed during Prohibition. It reopened again in 1933 and produced beer until 1955.

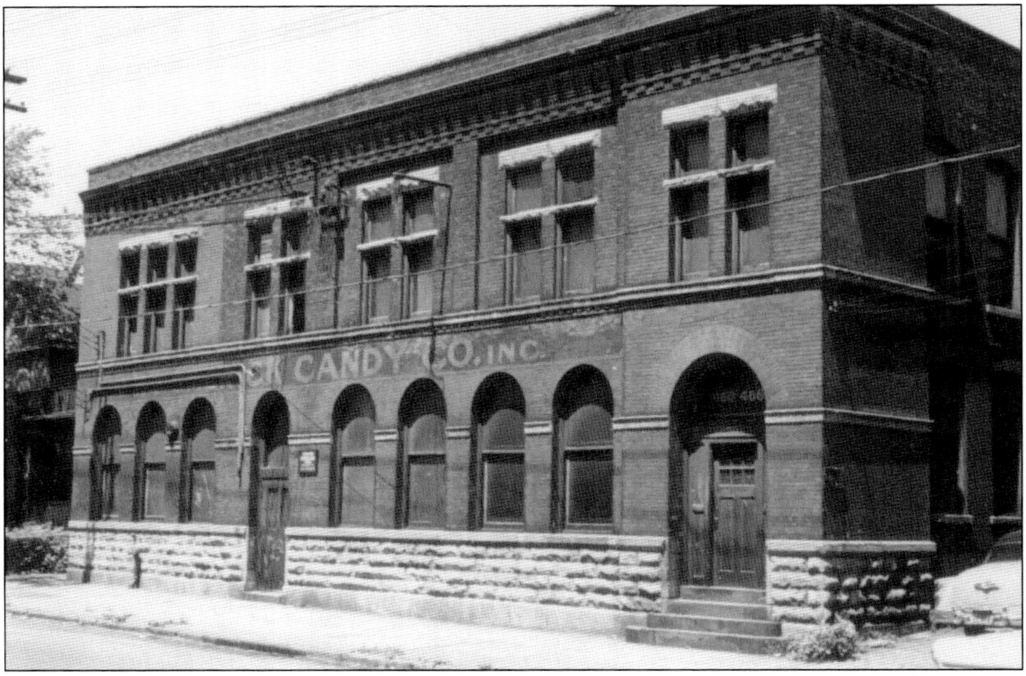

The Emerick Candy Company opened in 1917 at 1219 Main Street. In 1921, it moved to 461 North Division Street, where it remained until closing in 1959. The company started out as a wholesale producer of "chocolate specialties" and continued producing chocolates for its 42 years of existence. The last president and owner was William H. Emerick.

Although this undated pictorial evidence exists, there is not much historical evidence of the Samuel Anger Shoer Company. In 1889, Sam Anger was working a blacksmith, while his brother Lemuel Anger was a farrier listed at 571 Eagle Street. The sign in this photograph says "Sam Anger, Shoer," but there is no evidence that he was the farrier of the family. The company appears to have lasted from 1889 to 1893, when Sam disappears from the record.

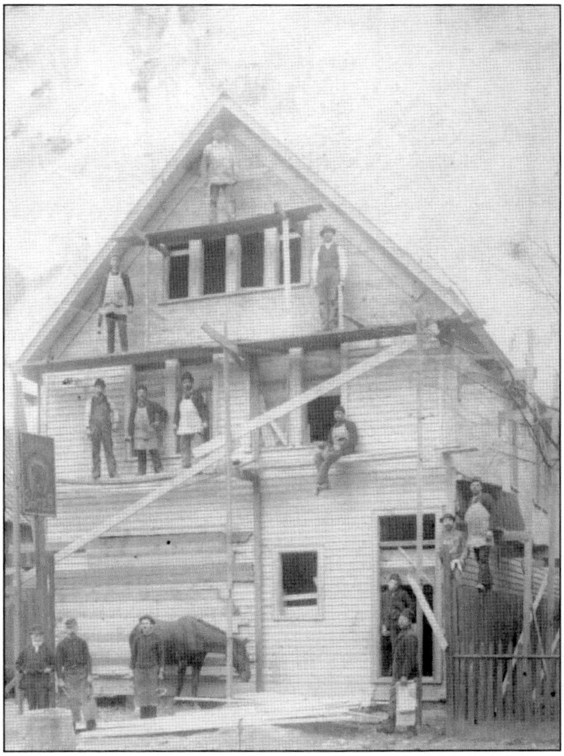

The Monroe Motor Car Company spent most of its existence on Main Street, near Lafayette Avenue, though it started at 24 Goodrich Street. The company produced automobiles from 1913 to 1930. After setting up a factory on Goodrich Street between Main and Ellicott Streets from 1913 to 1915, it moved to the Main Street location for the rest of its existence. Here, workers in the Goodrich Street plant pose with the chassis of an automobile.

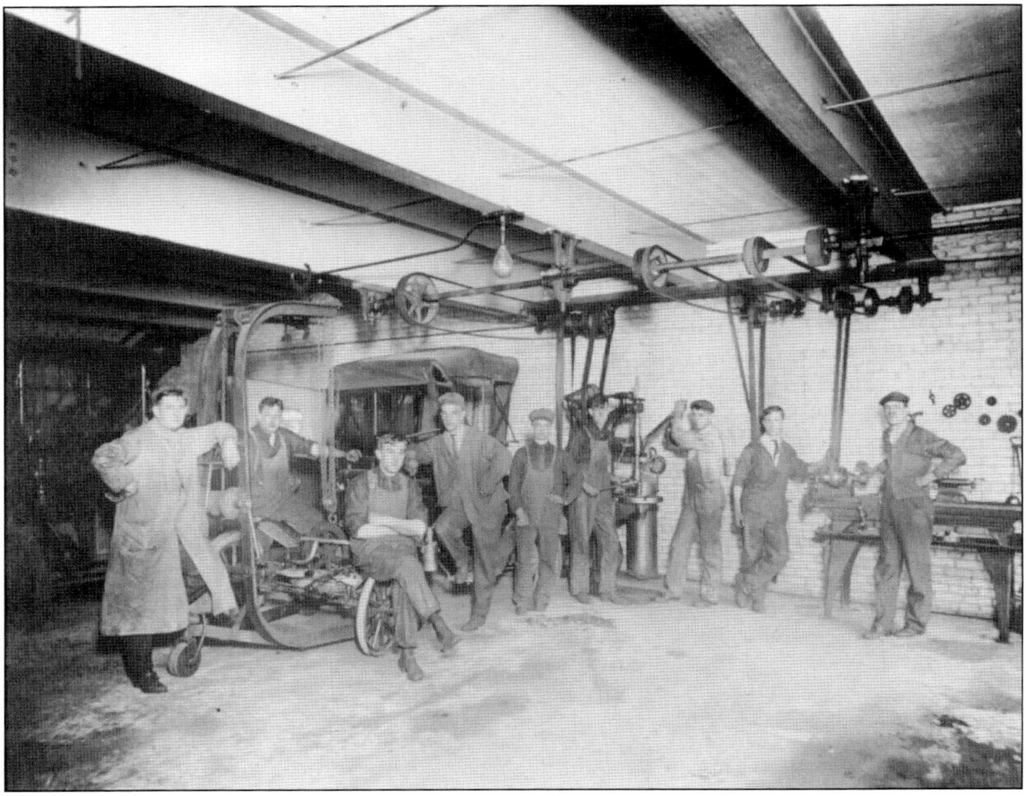

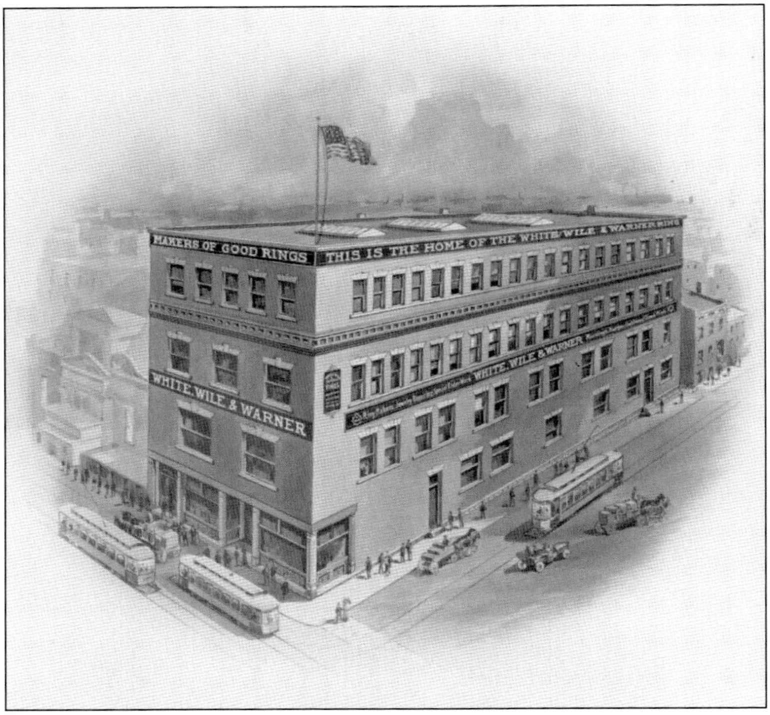

The White, Wile & Warner Ring Company was located at Goodrich Street at the corner of Main Street. The three jewelry makers and repairers merged in 1904 at 257–259 Washington Street. In 1912, the collective moved to 1021 Main Street, where it remained until 1932, when Philip Warner left the business to open a jewelry box store. The company closed after Warner left.

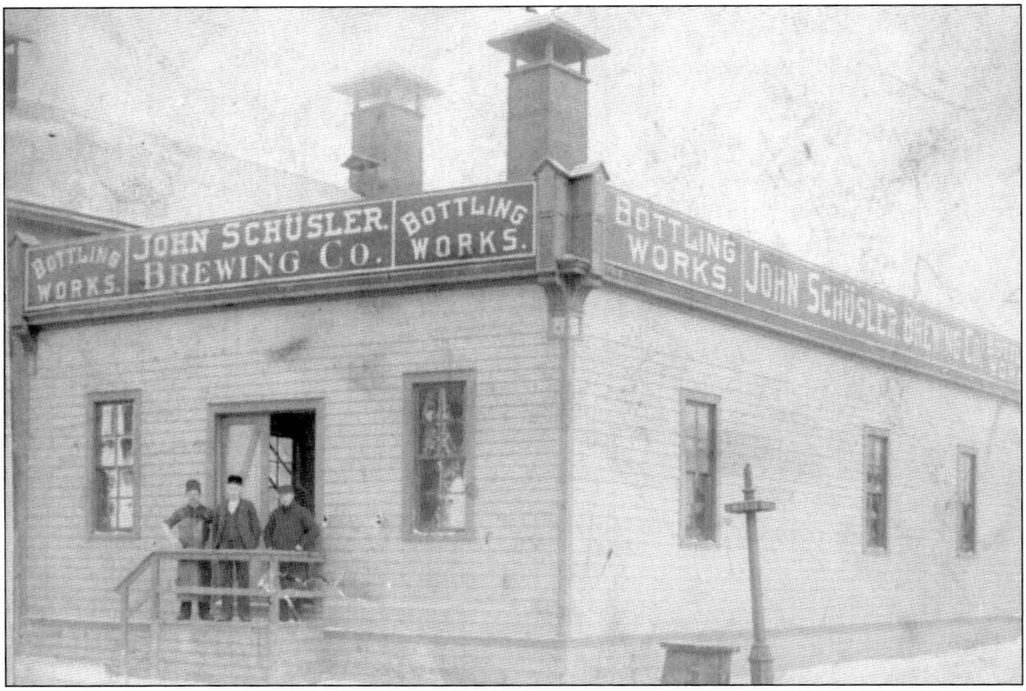

The John Schusler Brewing Company is another industry leader that remained open for 113 years. After Schusler opened the company in 1853 on Broadway, it expanded and moved to 143 Emslie Street in 1859. In 1894, William Simon, who worked at the brewery, became the owner of the business and expanded again at 127–161 Emslie Street, where the company became the Simon Brewery, which remained in existence until 1972.

At the end of its existence, the Phoenix Brewery was owned by International Breweries. Opened in 1869 at 298–300 Emslie Street by John M. Luippold, it operated as the East Buffalo Brewing Company from 1879 to 1920, when it closed during Prohibition. It reopened in 1934 under the name Phoenix Brewing Corporation and closed its doors for good in 1959. The brewery is pictured here in 1940. It is not to be confused with the Phoenix Brewery on Washington Street.

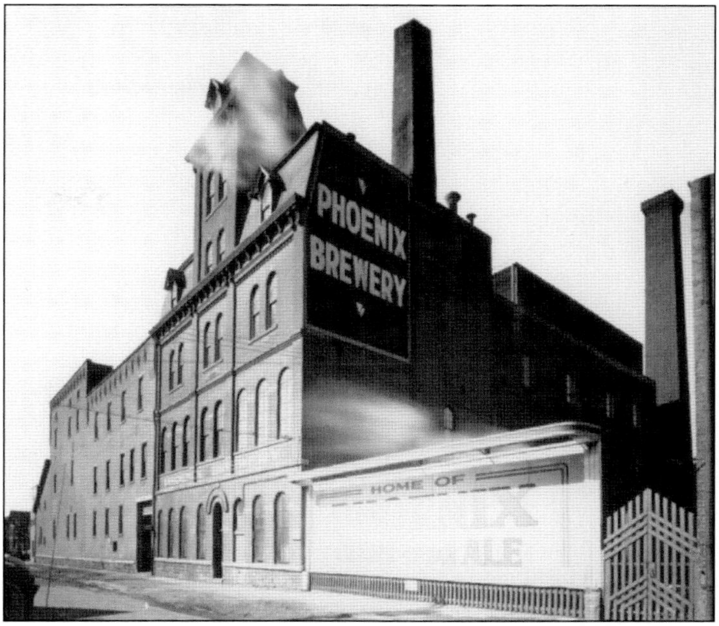

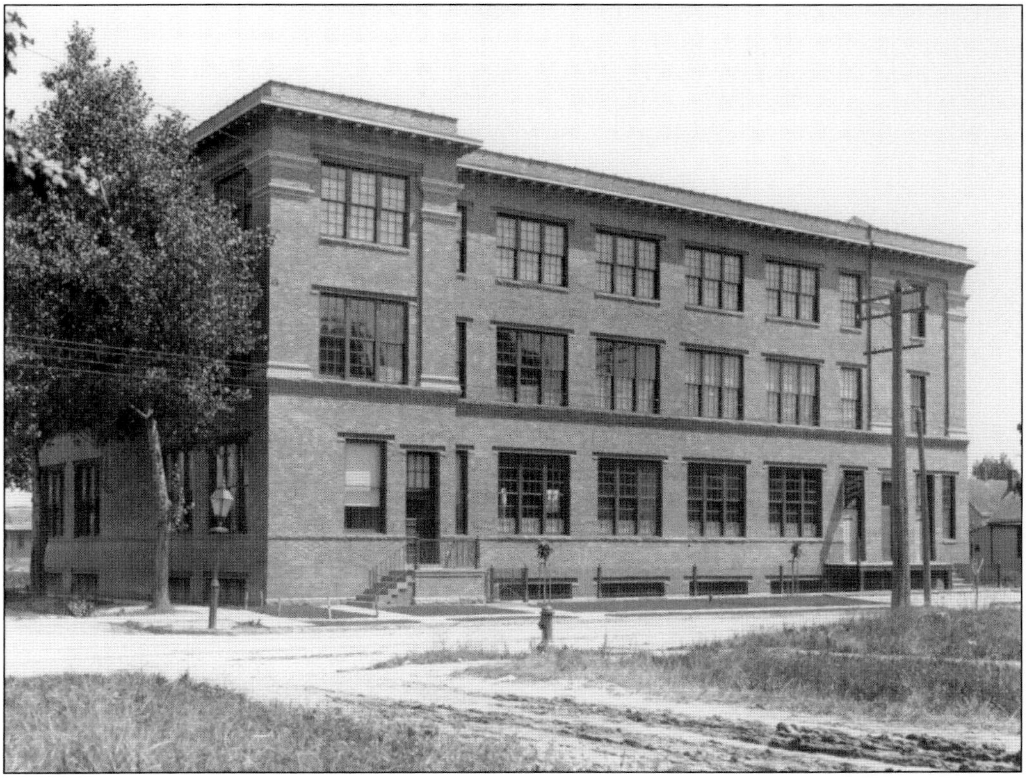

The Buffalo Dental Manufacturing Company lasted for 94 years. Opened in 1867 at 247–249 Main Street, it moved farther down Main Street in 1871. During the 1870s and 1880s, the factory was located on Commercial Street, and in 1905, the whole operation— office and factory—moved to 145 Kehr Street, where this photograph was taken. In the 1950s, it was reorganized as Buffalo Dental, Inc., selling equipment and supplies. The company closed in 1961.

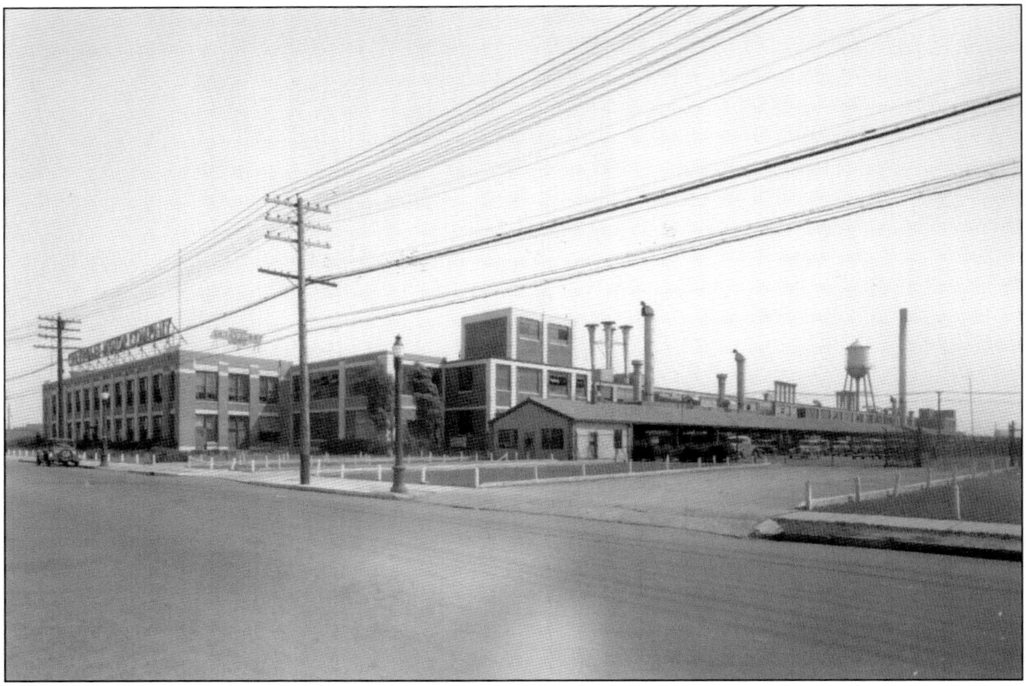

This plant on East Delavan Avenue opened its doors in 1923 as a General Motors–Chevy assembly plant; it is thought to be the first Chevy automotive plant built outside of Michigan. After the plant assisted with the wartime effort during World War II and the Korean War, it switched production lines and began making axles for passenger vehicles. It joined the Saginaw division of GM in the 1980s and was spun off to American Axle and Manufacturing Co., which managed it until its closure in 2009. The plant covered roughly 80 acres and featured a 400,000-gallon water tower. With a yearly payroll of $81 million, it was the bedrock of the community and spurned growth of the East Side's middle class. These two photographs show the facade around 1928 (above) and 1957 (below).

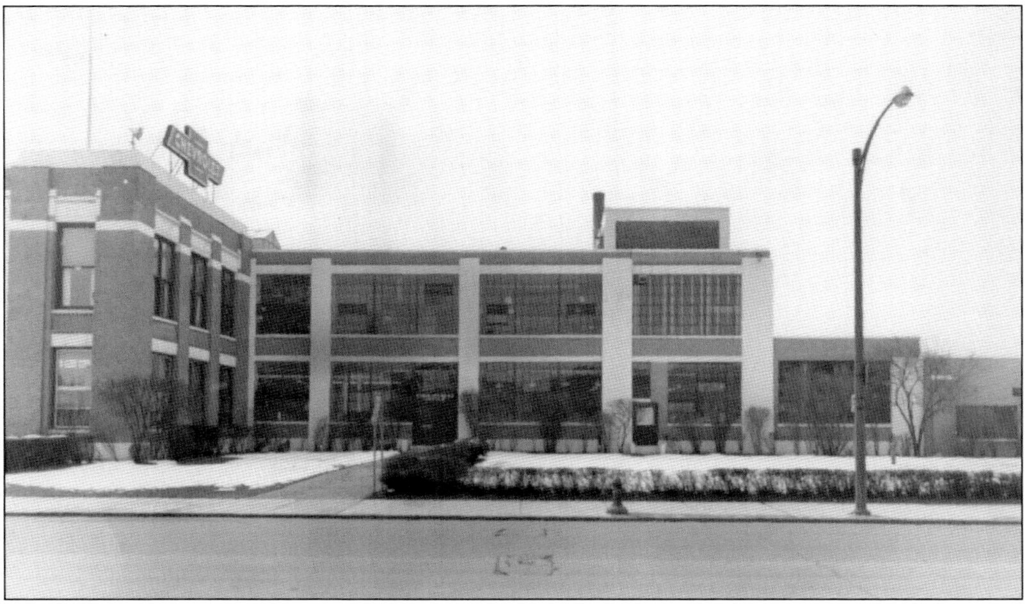

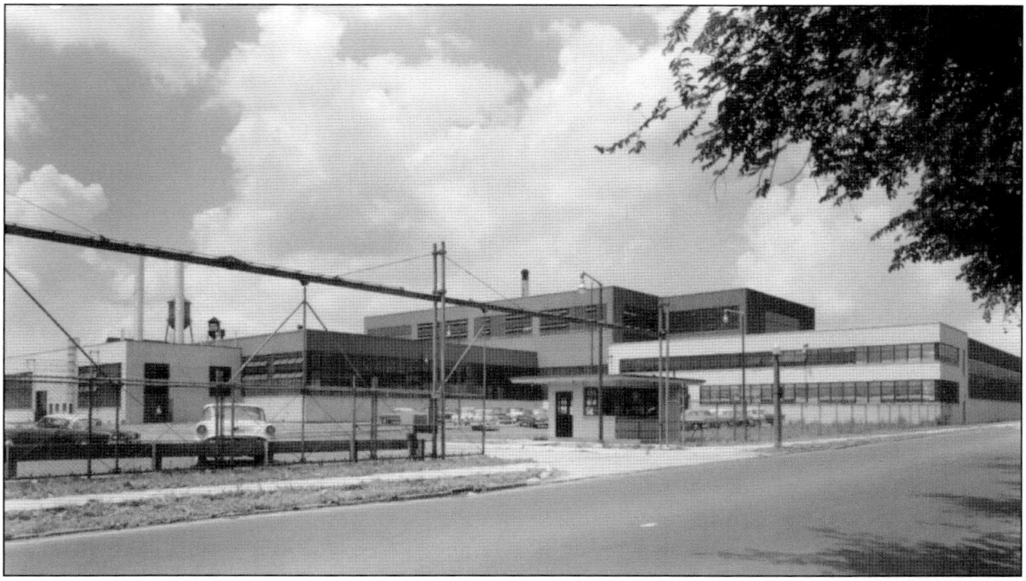

The Curtiss-Wright Aeroplane and Motor Corporation opened in 1916 and left an immense footprint on Buffalo's industry. Curtiss combined two companies, the Curtiss Aeroplane Company and Curtiss Motor Company, and moved his newly created company to Buffalo. After establishing the company on Churchill Street, it quickly outgrew its factory, and the company opened plants on Elmwood Avenue, Military Road, and Genesee Street in Cheektowaga. The company diversified and in 1951 purchased two buildings—the Otis Elevator Plant and an adjacent structure—in the Belt Line's Northland Grider corridor. These became the Curtiss-Wright Metal Processing Divisions. This photograph shows the exterior of the plant at Northland and Dutton Avenues in the Northland Grider area in 1953.

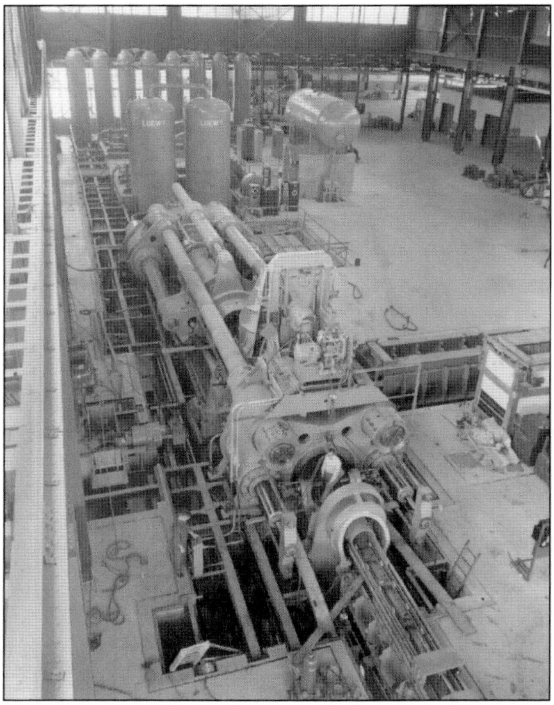

The photograph at right shows the interior of the Curtiss-Wright plant at Northland and Dutton Avenues in 1955. The image features the world's largest horizontal steel extrusion press. The press was able to squirt steel or titanium into any desired shape.

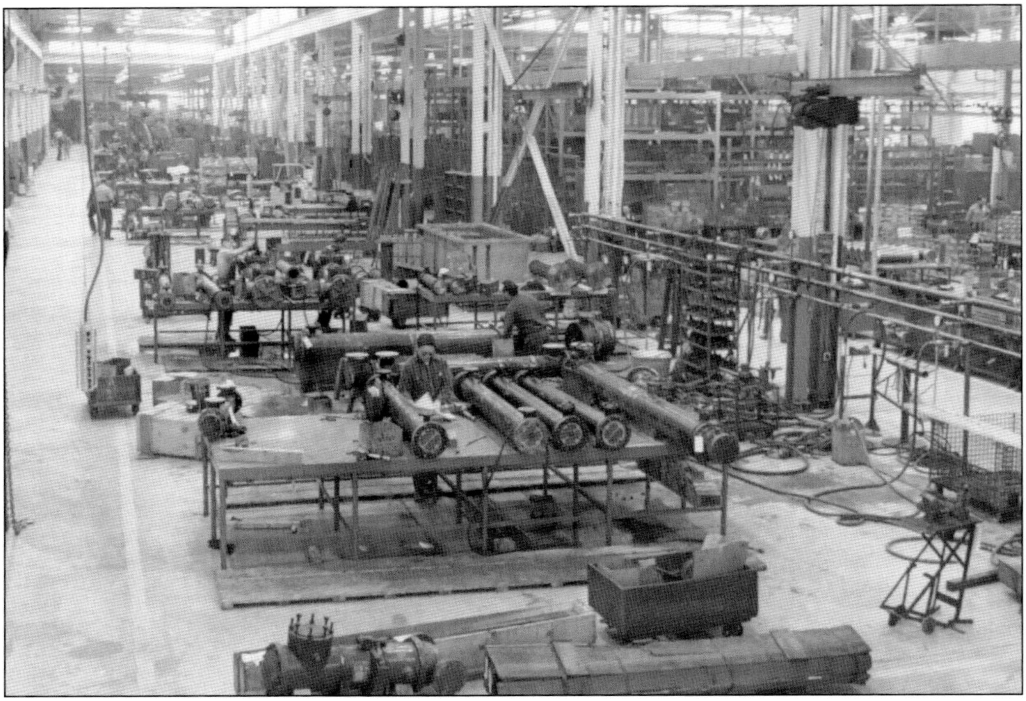

Glenn Curtiss was an early pioneer in naval aviation, and in 1929, his company merged with the Wright Aeronautical Corporation to form the largest aircraft company in America. This photograph offers a view of the interior of the Curtiss-Wright Metal Processing Division plant at Northland and Dutton Avenues. During World War II, the Curtiss-Wright factories employed between 9,000 and 12,000 Buffalonians, and million-dollar contracts for military vehicles were flowing from the federal government to the company.

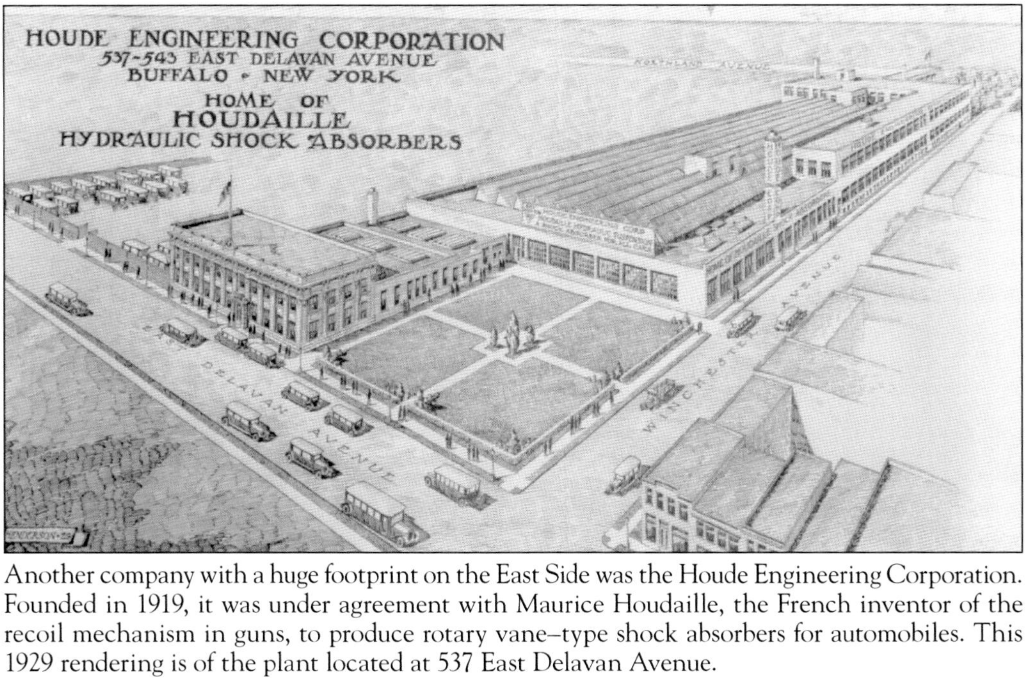

Another company with a huge footprint on the East Side was the Houde Engineering Corporation. Founded in 1919, it was under agreement with Maurice Houdaille, the French inventor of the recoil mechanism in guns, to produce rotary vane–type shock absorbers for automobiles. This 1929 rendering is of the plant located at 537 East Delavan Avenue.

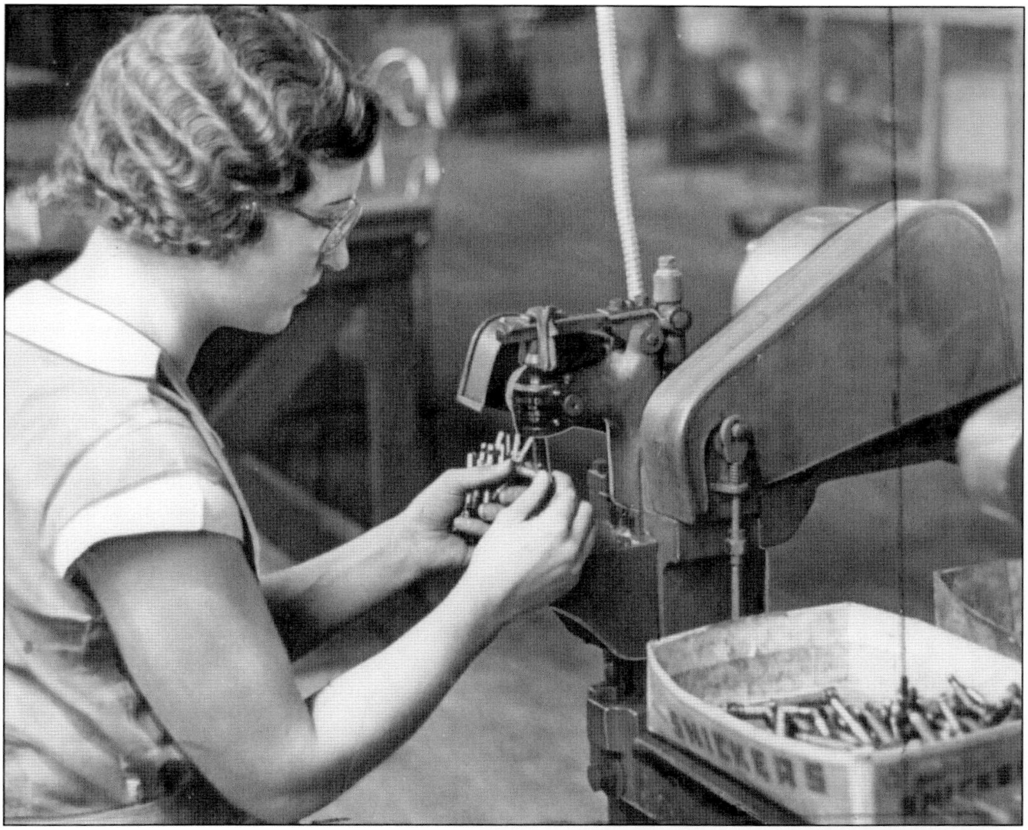

Houde Engineering Corporation's first plant was located on West Avenue near Forest Avenue on the West Side but moved into the Northland-Grider neighborhood—at 537 East Delavan Avenue—in 1925. As automotive technology grew, so did Houde, by expanding from hydraulic shock absorbers in cars to those in planes and trains, as well. Pictured above is Mildred A. Schell riveting valve parts in 1936; these parts provided thermostatic control for the absorbers. The other image shows "Rosie the Riveters" working on hydraulic retracting cylinders during World War II. As at Curtiss-Wright, wartime production increased at Houde, and at its height, the company employed 2,800 men and women. The company remained in business until 1988, when a collection of smaller companies moved into the 537 East Delavan Avenue structure.

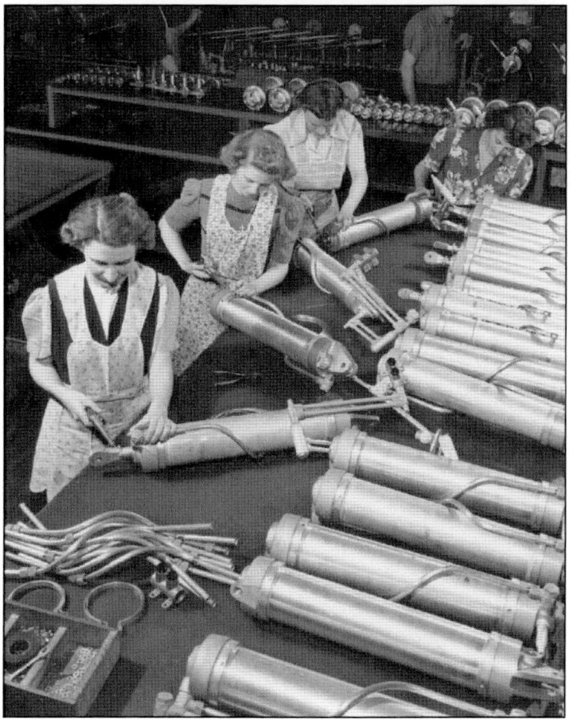

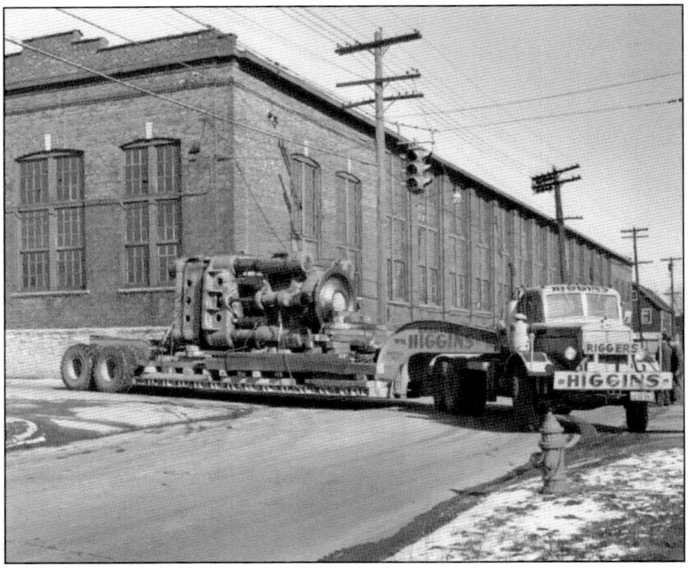

The Otis Elevator Company factory was designed by famed Buffalo architects E.B. Green and William Sydney Wicks in 1913. From 1913 to 1951, the company manufactured rails, overhead beams, frames, and buffers for elevators. Located at the corner of Northland and Grider Avenues, Otis employed 450 Buffalonians and shipped one million feet of rails—used in elevators throughout the country—every year. After the Curtiss-Wright Corporation bought Otis Elevator Company in 1951, it repurposed the plant.

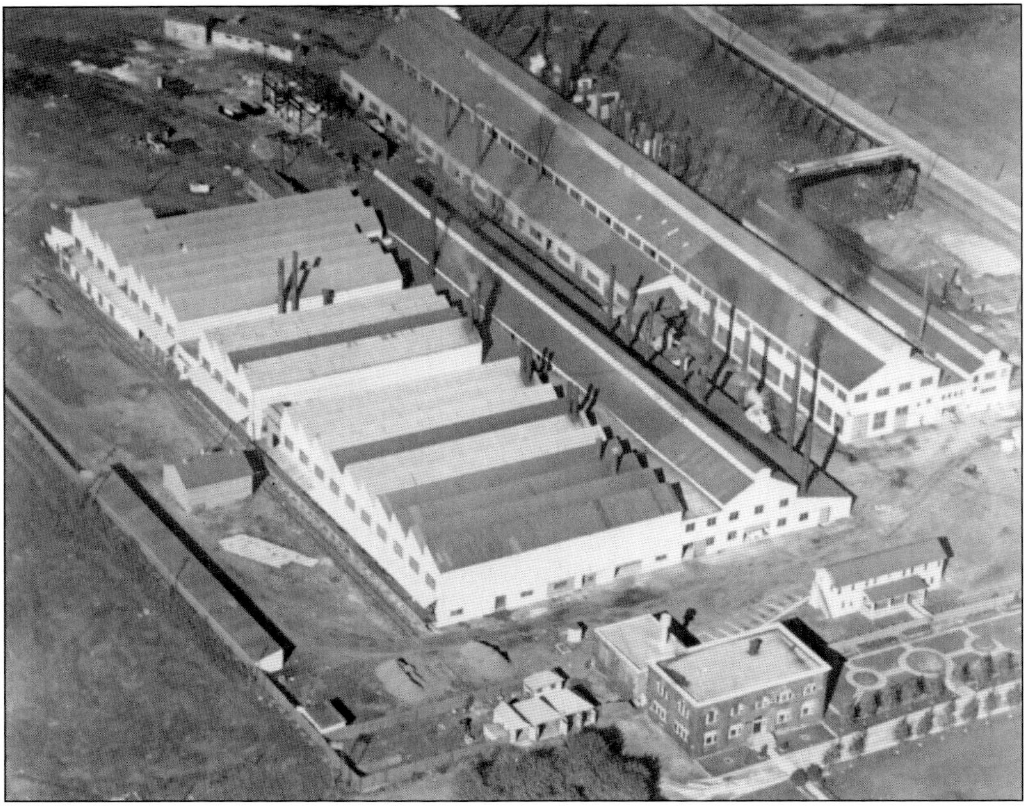

This 1956 aerial image is of the Harrison Radiator Corporation Plant, located at 56 Clyde Avenue southeast of Bennett High School. Opened in 1905 by Herbert Harrison, this plant was originally the factory for General Cable. When Harrison was purchased by and merged with General Motors in 1946, this plant—together with the General Motors plant in Lockport, New York—became the world's largest producer of automobile temperature control systems. This plant remained open until 1993.

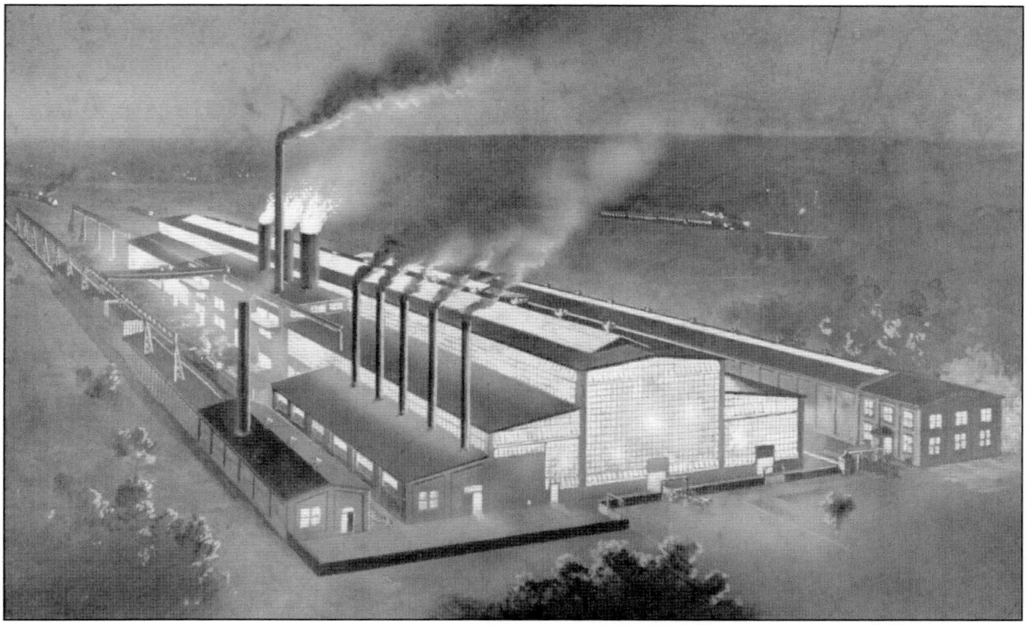

The Buffalo Foundry Company, opened by Charles F. Dunbar in 1899 at the corner of Mississippi and Perry Streets, moved to its current location at 750 East Ferry Street in 1904. After merging with David Bell Engineering Works in 1907, it became the Buffalo Foundry and Machine Company, which still manufactures processing equipment for the food and chemical industries; it recently expanded into the waste treatment and bioenergetic industries as well. In 1945, it changed names to Buflovak, a division of Blaw-Knox Food and Chemical Equipment. The plant had the ability to manufacture heavy and large machine parts weighing up to 120 tons. The above image shows the Buffalo Foundry Company prior to 1907, and the below photograph shows the interior of the pattern shop in 1929. The company is still located at 750 East Ferry Street and has been in business for 116 years.

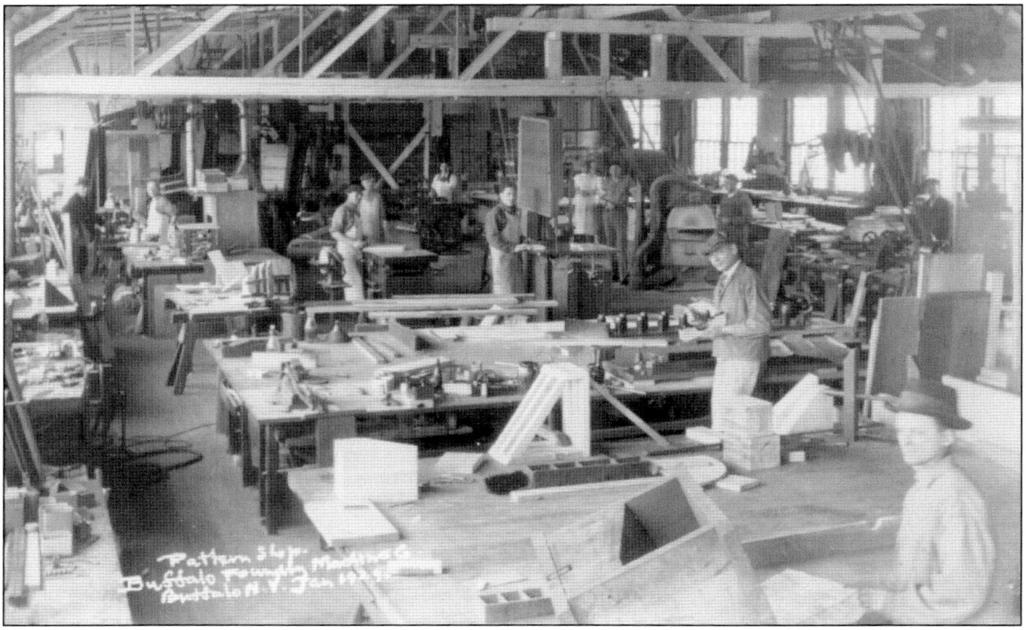

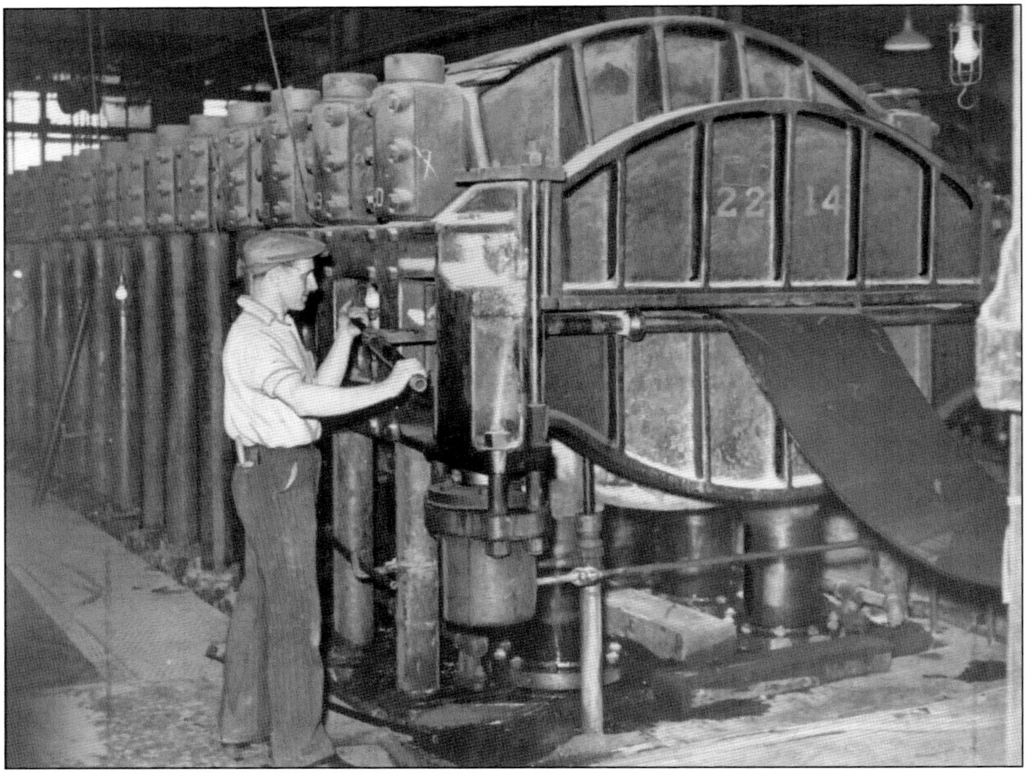

H.H. Hewitt founded the Hewitt Rubber Company in 1909 to manufacture rubber material for railroad companies. In 1918, Hewitt started producing rubber tires and tubes for automobiles and trucks. Since the company was located at 240 Kensington Avenue, within feet of the Buffalo Belt Line, train cars had the ability to stop at the loading dock to take on product. Pictured here is an employee helping to manufacture a conveyor belt. The company remained open until 1974.

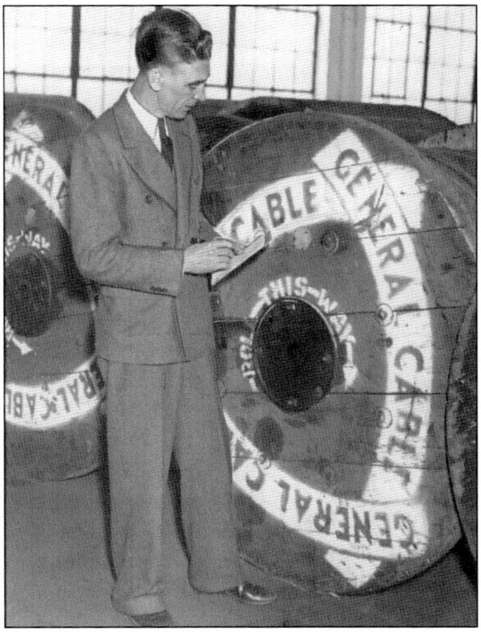

General Cable Corporation originally owned the 56 Clyde Avenue plant that became Harrison Radiator in 1946. The wiring company's Buffalo plant, which had 400 employees at its peak, fabricated single- and double-wound wiring for various industries. During World War II, General Cable, which officially incorporated in New Jersey in 1927, was awarded the largest federal contract since World War I. The company opened the Buffalo plant in 1930 and vacated the factory in 1946, and in the ensuing years, only a sales office was listed in Buffalo city directories.

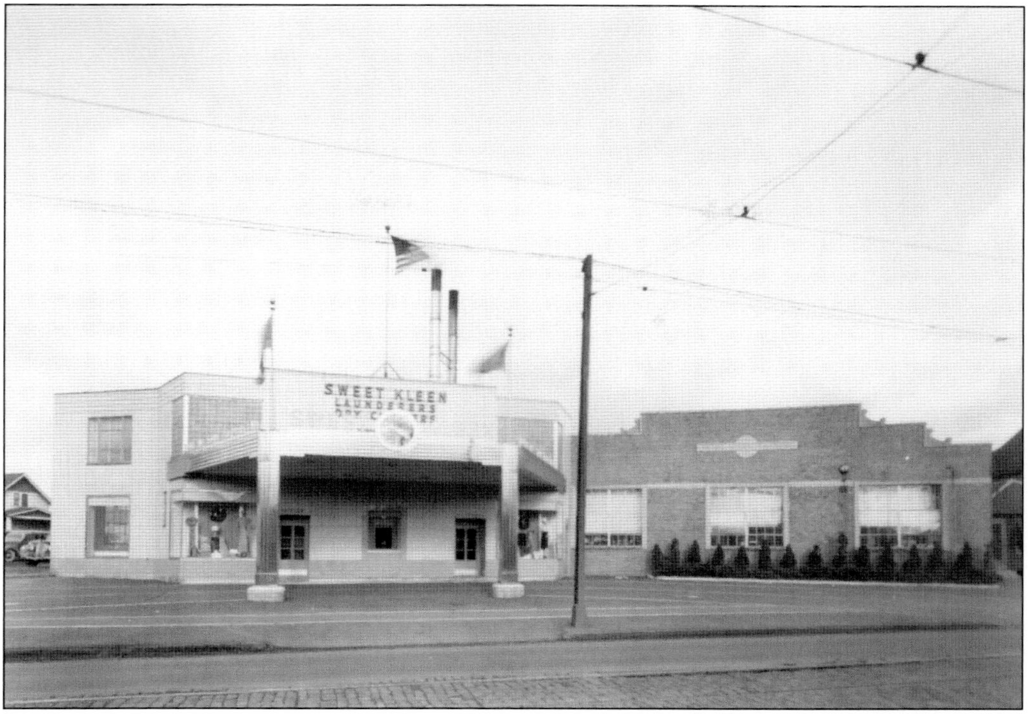

Sweet Kleen Laundry and Dry Cleaners opened in 1926 and catered to commercial businesses on the East Side. Located at 760–764 Kensington Avenue, the company expanded in the 1950s to include personal dry cleaning and opened four other locations in Buffalo and one in Snyder for this purpose. In the 1939 photograph below, employees pose outside Sweet Kleen headquarters. The company remained in business until 1993. In 2005, the Environmental Protection Agency demanded that the owners clean hazardous waste materials—including exposed asbestos and rusty industrial waste drums that sat out in public—from the Kensington Avenue site.

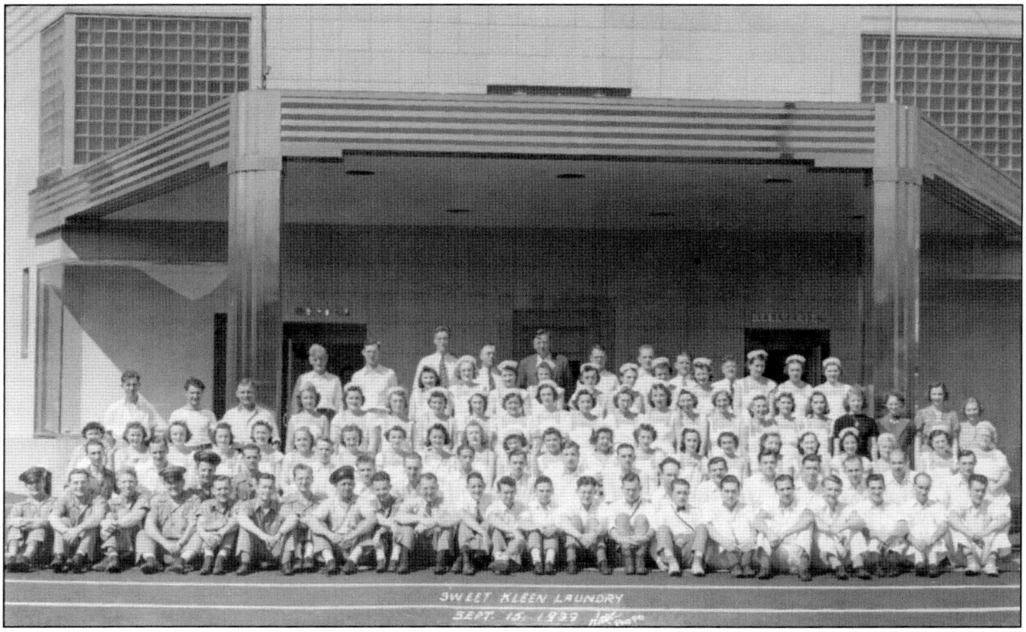

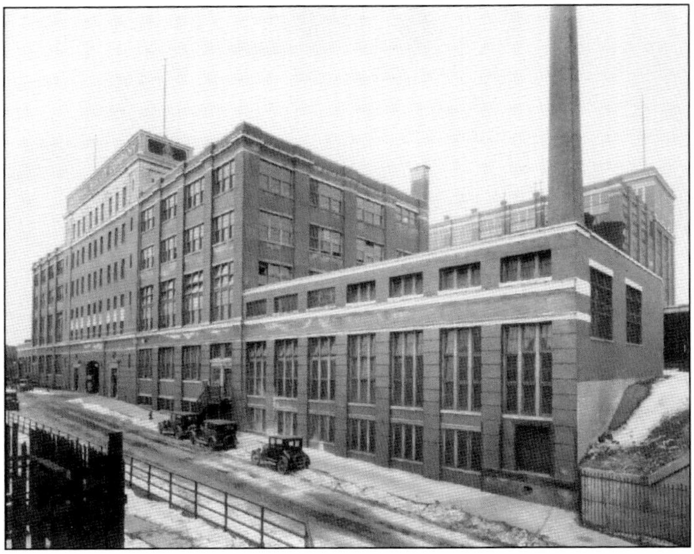

There are few names that carry the weight of National Biscuit Company—aka Nabisco—and this mammoth factory at 243 Urban Street was the first plant built by the company during its nationwide expansion. After it was constructed in 1927, the plant produced Nabisco crackers for its first 30 years. Since 1957, it has been the sole worldwide producer of Milk-Bone Dog Treats, producing 140 million pounds of treats a year.

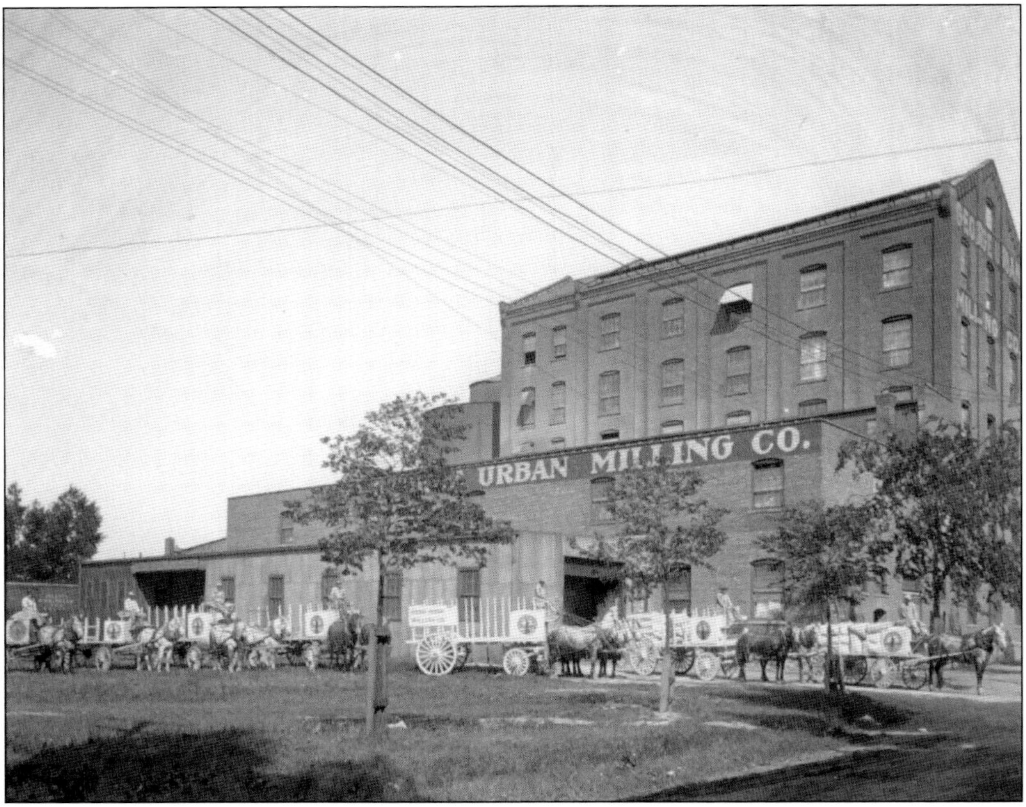

The Urban family name is ubiquitous in Buffalo. The George Urban Milling Company was in business for 147 years and became a national leader in the industry. George Urban Jr. entered the business in 1868 and instituted the "Hungarian system" of crushing grain with rollers, becoming one of the first American plants to do so. It was also the first mill in America to use alternating current. The plant, built in 1903 near the corner of Urban and Kehr Streets, is pictured here in 1910 with delivery wagons.

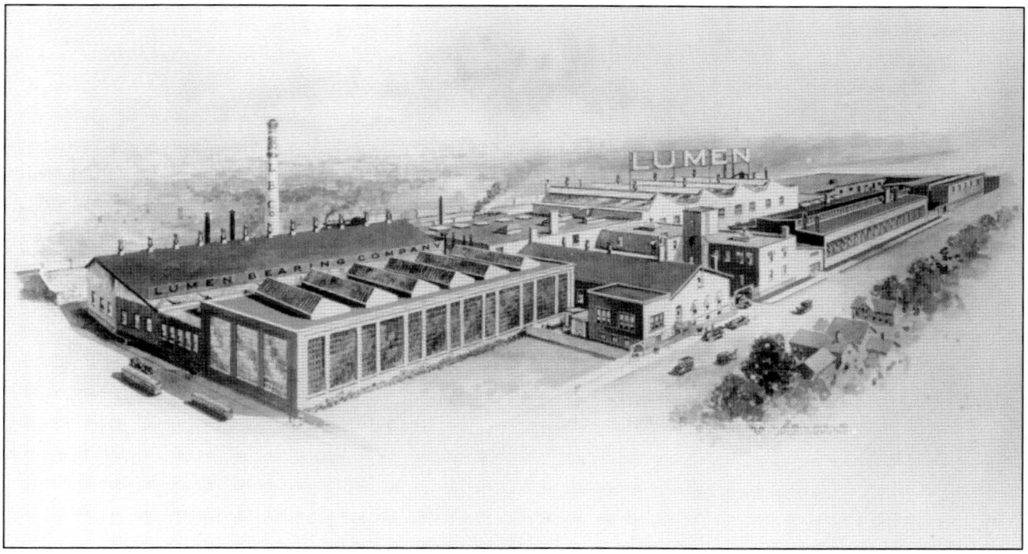

For 60 years, the Lumen Bearing Company was an East Side fixture. Founded in 1902 at 1155 Sycamore Street, it began by making bearings for automobiles and machinery. In 1904, it expanded its product line and started producing trolley wheels; in 1920, they began making brass works. The company moved in 1927 to 197 Lathrop Street, where it continued making bearings and machinery until closing in 1962.

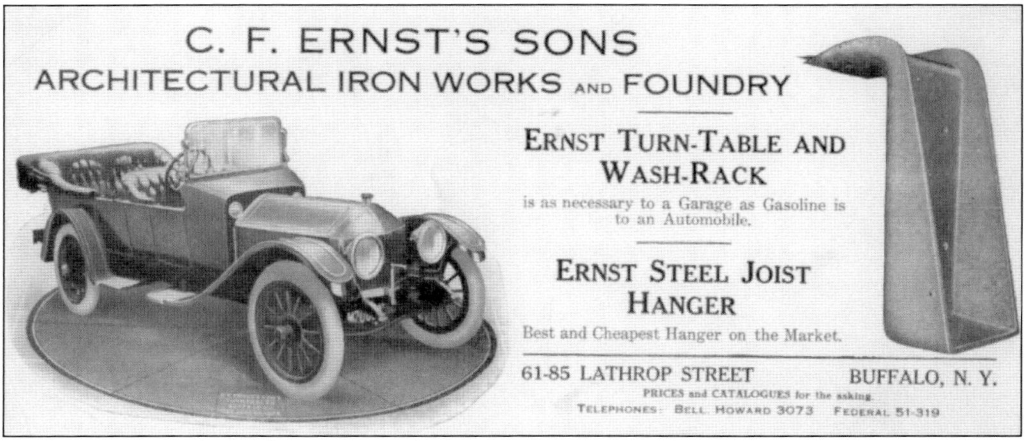

C.F. Ernst's Sons, located at 61–85 Lathrop Street, was a neighbor of Lumen Bearing Company. The company, founded in 1882 by Charles F. Ernst, began making iron fences at its location at 311 Walnut Street; in 1891, it expanded into producing iron railings. In the early 20th century, it started producing parts for the automobile and truck industry. In 1925, it moved to Lathrop Street, but in 1939, the business, which was then called Ernst Iron Works Company, closed. Pictured is an advertisement from 1906.

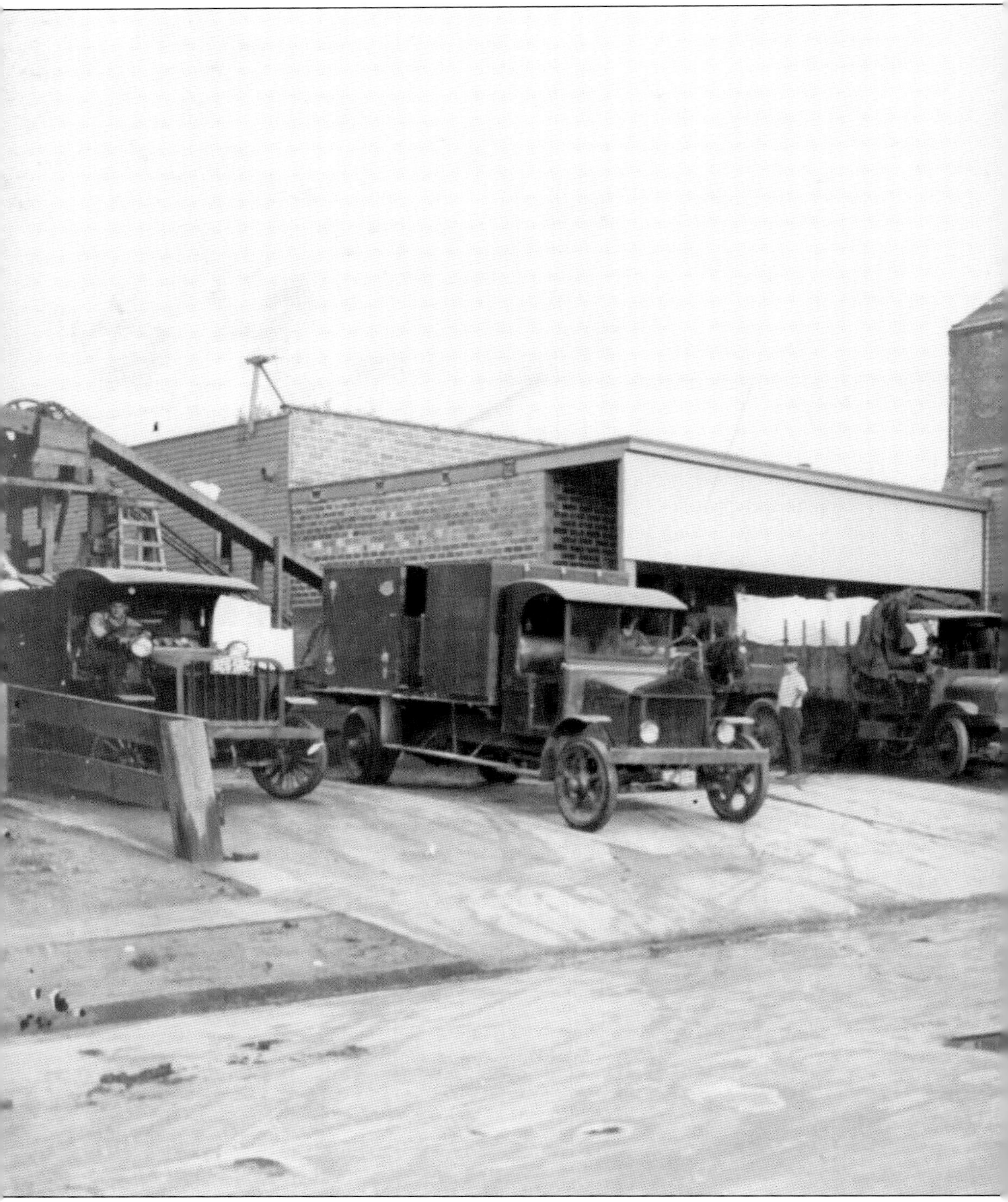

The Culliton Ice Cream Company, pictured here in 1920, was located at 172 Guilford Street between Genesee and Sycamore Streets. Two brothers, Louis R. and Edward H. Culliton, established the business in 1915. At the time, there were 11 other wholesale and retail ice cream producers in the city, including Rich's Ice Cream, which is still in operation today. This photograph, taken from the east side of Guilford Street, shows the factory, offices, and a large fleet of delivery trucks. By 1924,

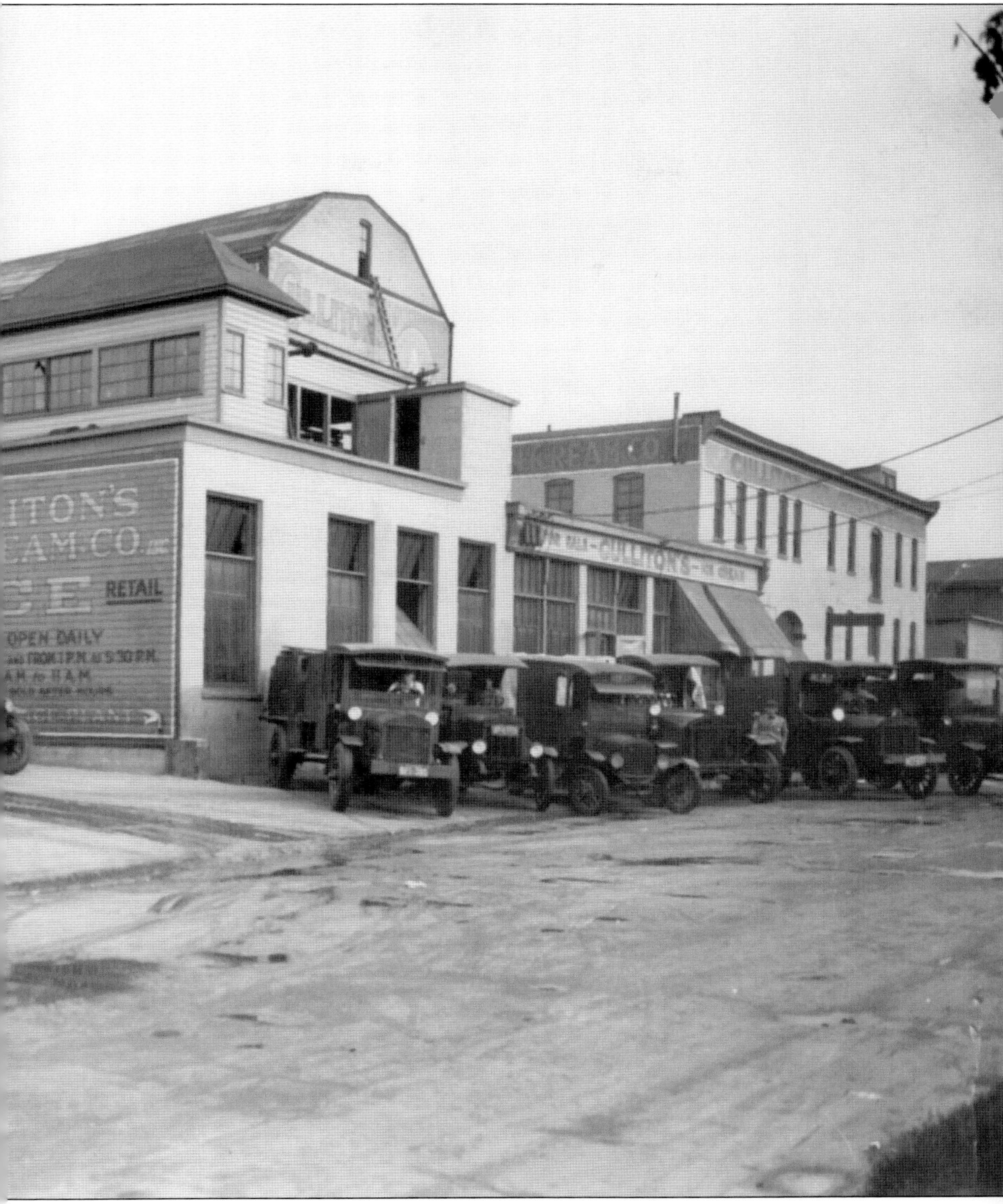

Culliton had begun to put a manufacturing focus on ice, addressing the growth in the local and national residential-freezer business. The ice cream factory moved west—closer to the city—on Pratt Street, also between Genesee and Sycamore Streets, while the ice manufactory remained in this building on Guilford Street. There are no remains of this structure, and the site is now an open field, although the sidewalk and driveway aprons are still vaguely evident.

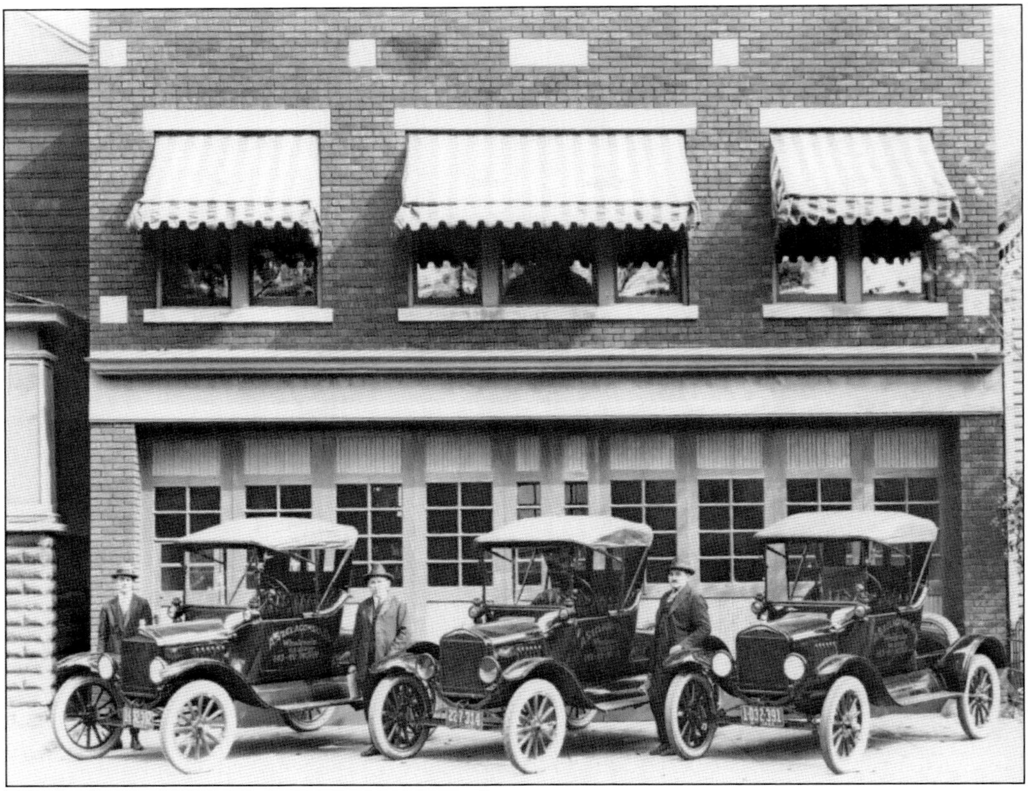

The 1900 city directory lists an Anton Szelagowski Meat Market as being located at 1428 Broadway. In the 1902 city directory, Szelagowski's first name, Anthony, is spelled correctly, with the business in the same location. In 1914, the company opened the pictured plant at 143–147 Mohr Street near Broadway. In this photograph, Szelagowski stands to the right of the center vehicle. The Szelagowski family sold the company in 1957, but former rival Wardynski & Sons reintroduced the Szelagowski "Shelly" brand of hot dogs and bologna in 2005.

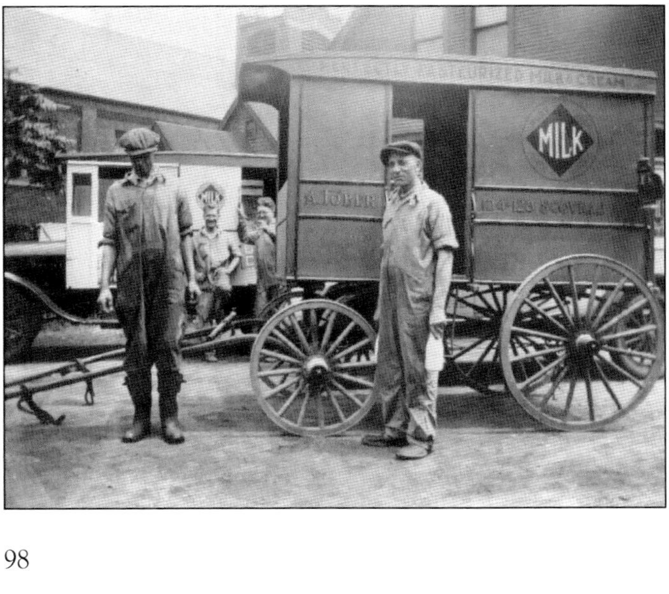

Pictured is the Adolf Tober Dairy, located at 124–128 Scoville Avenue. Tober is on the right, while the employees in the back appear to be having a laugh at the expense of the man on the left. The dairy opened in 1908 at 191 Scoville Avenue and expanded in 1915. This image shows that the company used the lot directly behind them fronting Gilbert Street. The church in the background, St. Paul's Evangelical Lutheran, still stands, though the company closed in 1928.

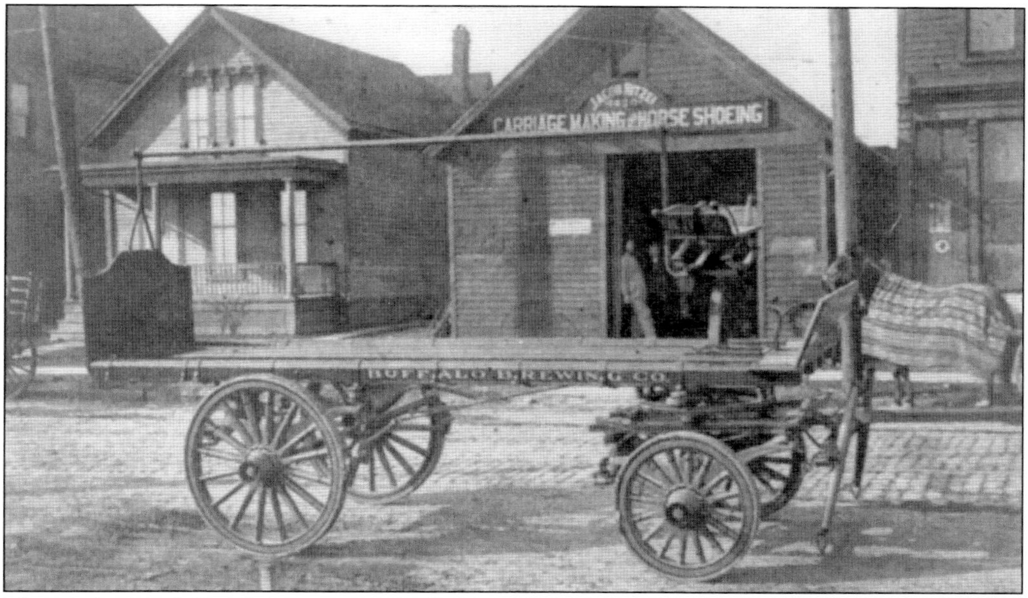

This is the Jacob Ritzel Carriage and Shoeing Shop. Ritzel entered the record as a blacksmith in 1889 at 13 Wilson Street. He briefly moved his shop to 741 Bailey Avenue, but by 1897, the business was located at 1420 William Street (pictured). Ritzel switched from blacksmithing to horseshoeing in 1901 and remained in the profession until 1909. In this photograph is a cart from the Buffalo Brewing Company, which was located at 1540 Clinton Street from 1910 to 1920.

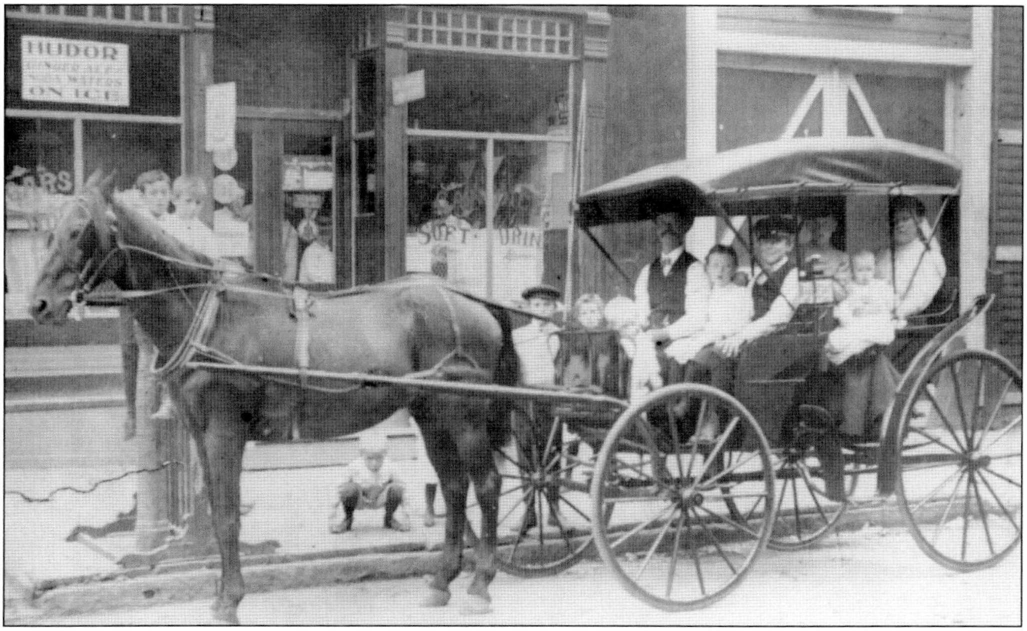

A Hudor Water Company sign—and a large unidentified family—appear in this image of Schlossin's candy shop, which was located at 113 Lovejoy Street (now Paderewski Avenue) in 1905. Owner Emil Schlossin appears in the city directory in 1899 as a laborer; in 1905, he opened a confectionery and soft-drink business at 403 Emslie Street. In 1906, he moved the business to 113 Lovejoy Street, where it remained open for another four years. By 1910, Schlossin was back to working as a laborer.

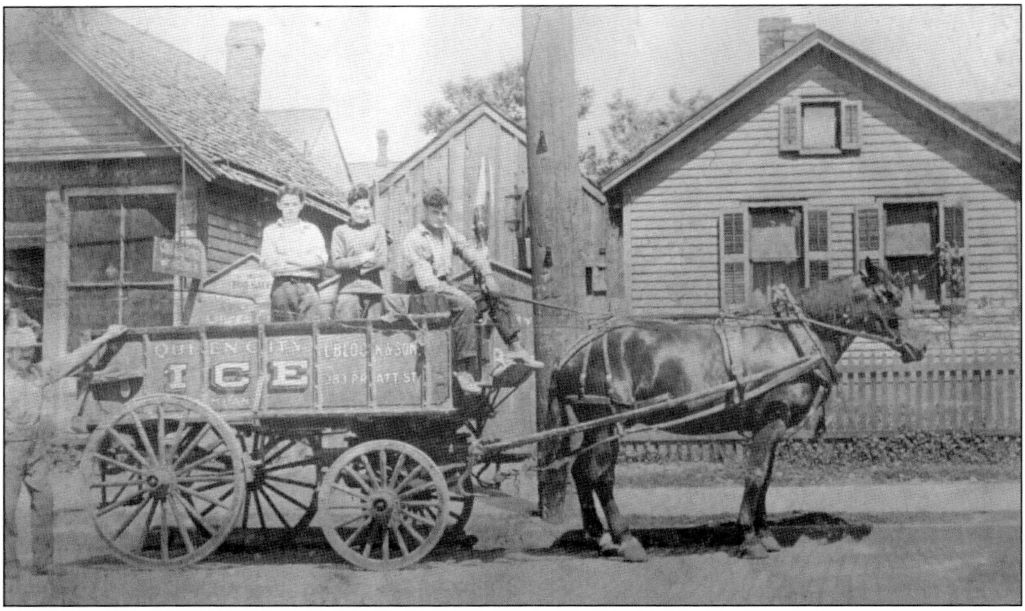

This photograph shows a Queen City Ice Company delivery cart, with employees sitting atop it, at the company's offices in 1896. The company was founded in 1860 at Main and Seneca Streets, where it remained until 1881. That year, it moved to 383 Pratt Street, one block away from the Roos Cooperative Brewing Company. In 1896, the company merged with the American Ice, Union Ice, and Buffalo Ice Companies to create the Citizens' Ice Company at 49 Niagara Street.

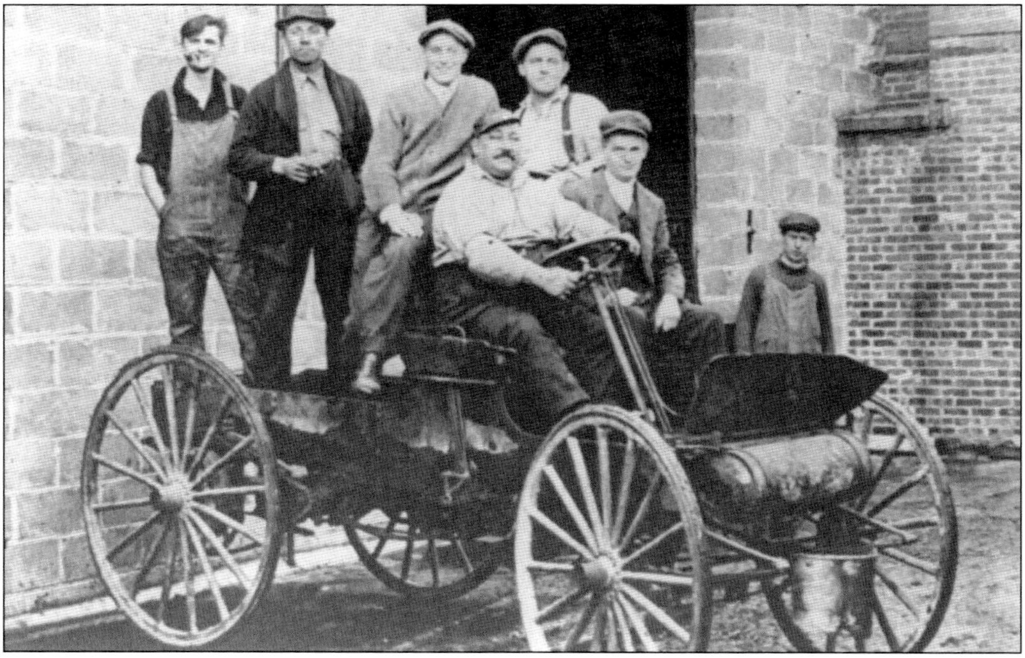

Iroquois Brewery, located on Pratt Street, was one of the largest and longest-lasting breweries in Buffalo. It opened in 1830 as the Jacob Roos Brewery and operated until in 1971. It survived Prohibition by converting its operations to brew "near beer" and sodas. At its peak, the brewery produced 600,000 barrels per year. These workers are pictured on a delivery vehicle in 1914.

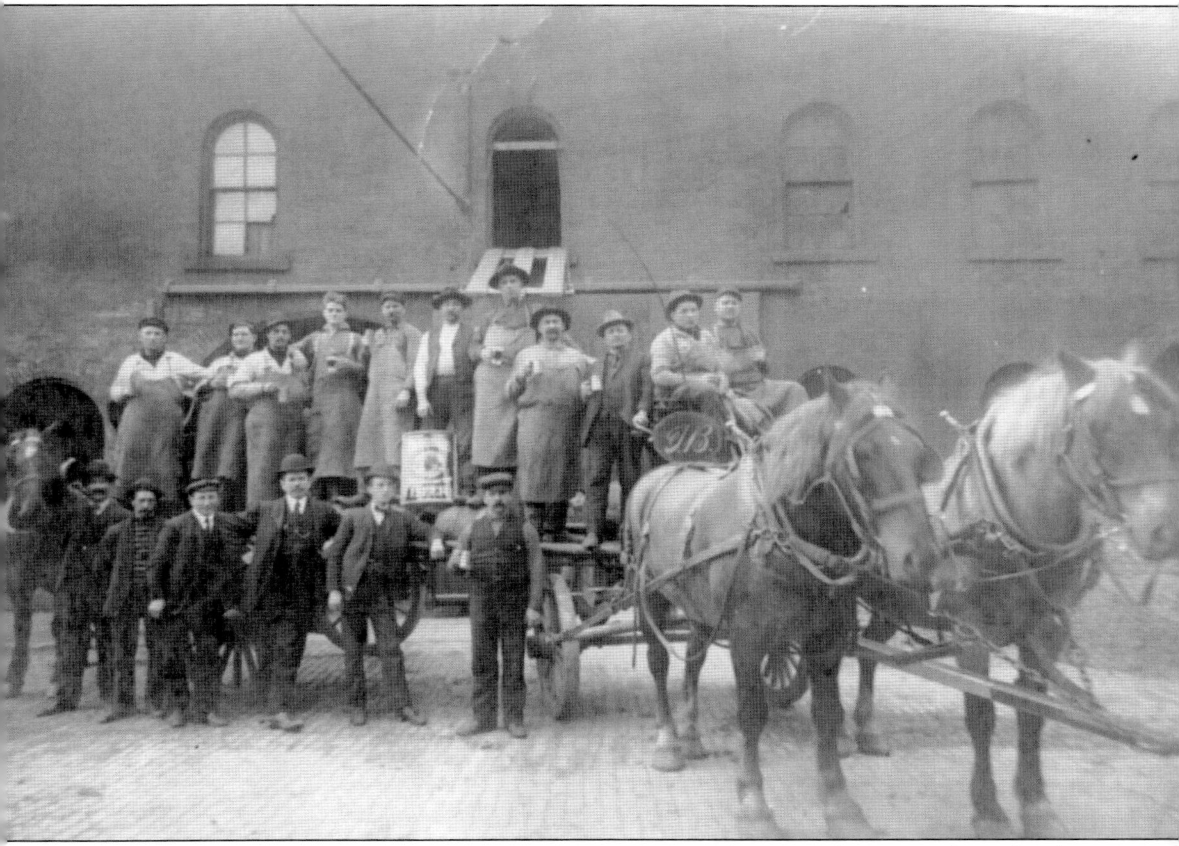

This 1900 photograph of the Iroquois Brewery on Pratt Street shows employees out front. Jacob Roos founded this brewery in 1830 between Church and York Streets, the border streets of the lost neighborhood of "Sandy Town." The brewery remained there until 1874, when it was taken over by Jacob's son George, who moved it to 95 Roos Street near Pratt Street. The company's name changed in 1887, and it was known as the Roos Cooperative Brewing Company until 1892, when the company moved to 210–256 Pratt Street and became the Iroquois Brewing Company, a name it kept (in various forms) until the company closed in 1971. The iconic "Indian Head" emblem was well known in Buffalo. At its peak, Iroquois Brewing Company employed over 500 people and had distribution offices in New York City, Baltimore, and New Orleans. There has been recent reinvestment in the former Iroquois plant on Pratt Street, and the East Side site may see some new development in the future.

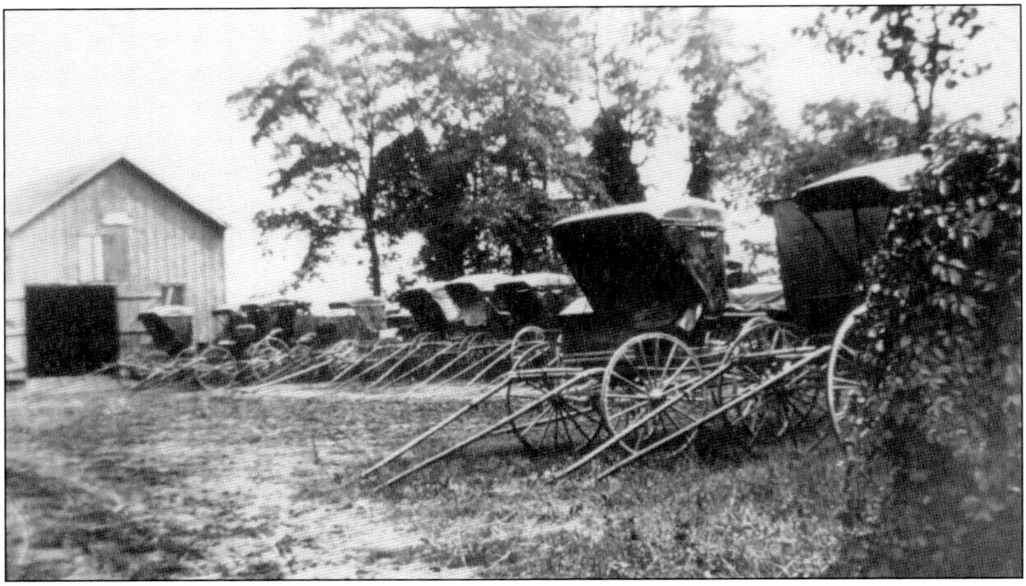

This photograph shows the carriages of the Crandall Horse Company, owned by Daniel Taylor, at 500 East Utica Street. For four years, starting in 1902, Taylor was vice president of the Hickok-Aldrich Company, a horse dealership on Cassy Street, which was a rural road near present-day Newell Street (off William Street). In 1906, Taylor opened the Crandall Horse Company at his residence, and it remained open until 1926.

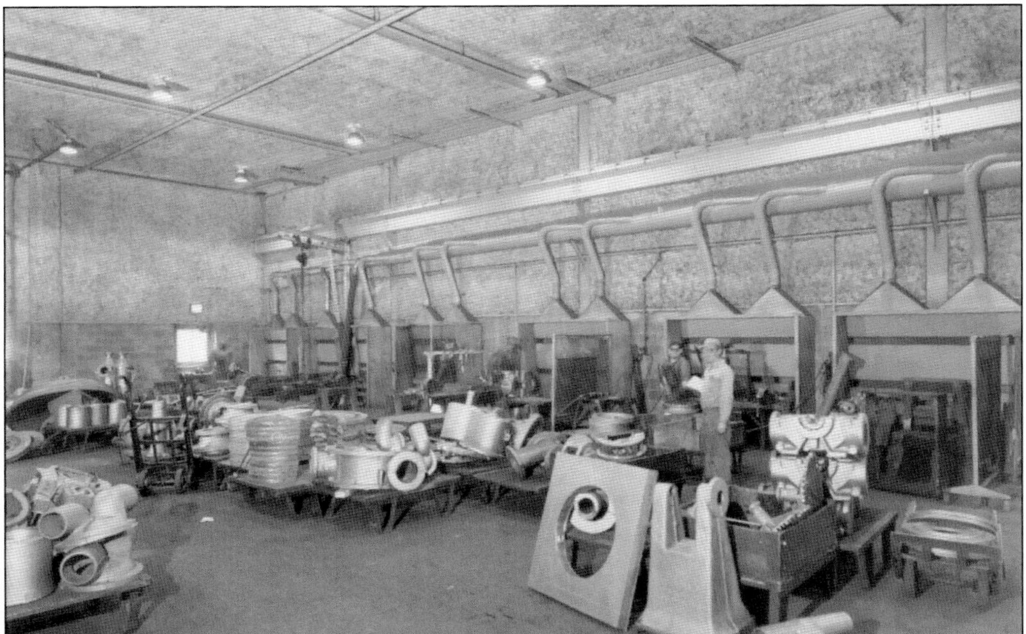

The Pohlman Foundry was in operation for 113 years, finally closing its doors in October 2002. The company, located at 205 Baitz Avenue, made iron castings for various pump and compressor manufactures, including Cooper Turbocompressors in Cheektowaga, New York. The company was independently operated until Lionheart Industries purchased the plant in 1998. Pictured are workers with Gold Bond Thermostatic iron castings.

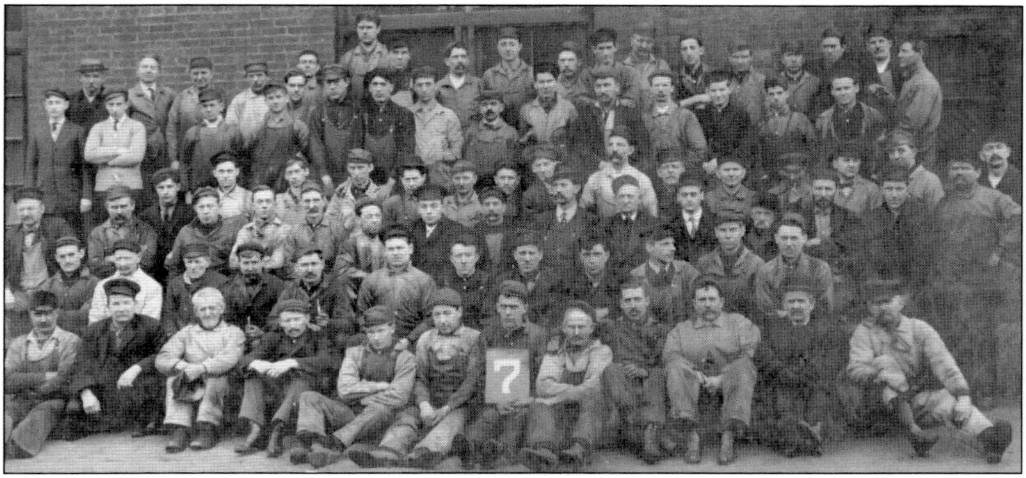

The mass of buildings on Roberts Avenue off Clinton Street are the remnants of the Worthington Pump Company–Buffalo Works Company division. Opened as the Snow Steam Pump Company in 1889, the business specialized in small single and duplex steam-driven and power pumps. In 1899, the company merged with four other pump companies—The Worthington Company, Blake and Knowles Steam Pump Works, Holly Manufacturing Company, and Laidlaw-Dunn-Gordon Company—to form the International Steam Pump Company. After the merger, the Buffalo plant was known as the Snow Holly Steam Pump Works and, eventually, the Buffalo Works Company. The 1906 photograph above shows "Gang 7," presumably a shift of employees who worked on a particular mechanism of a pump. Below are the mammoth pump ends for six vertical triple expansion-pumping engines bound for Cincinnati, Ohio. The pump ends are so large that the two employees shown are almost hidden in the 1906 photograph.

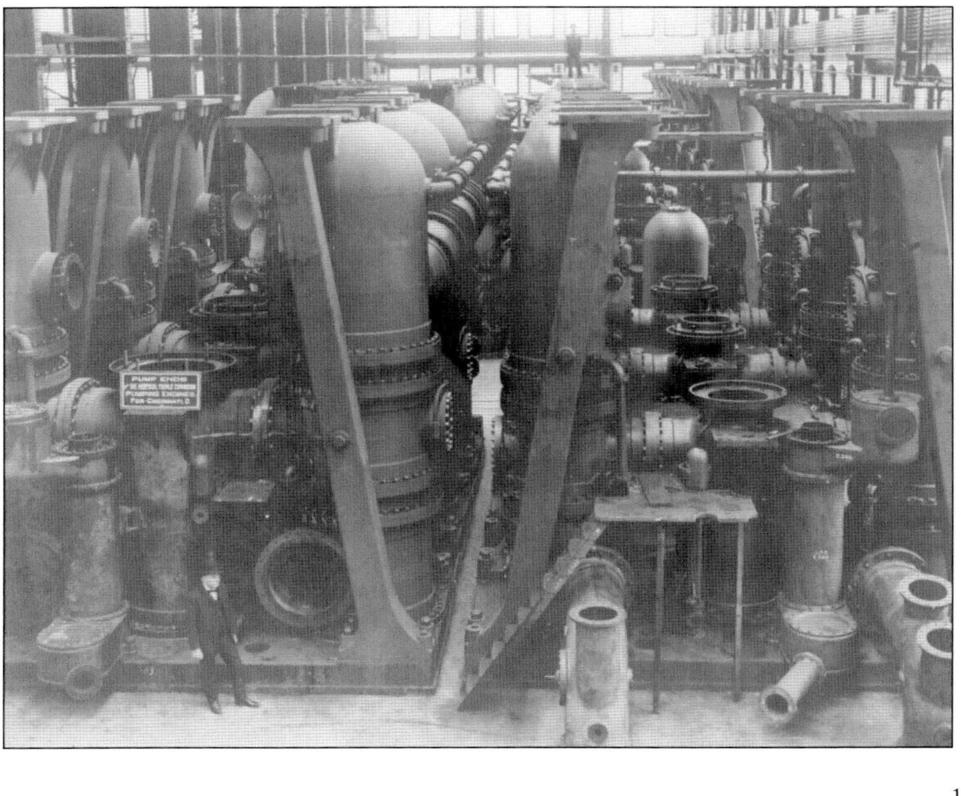

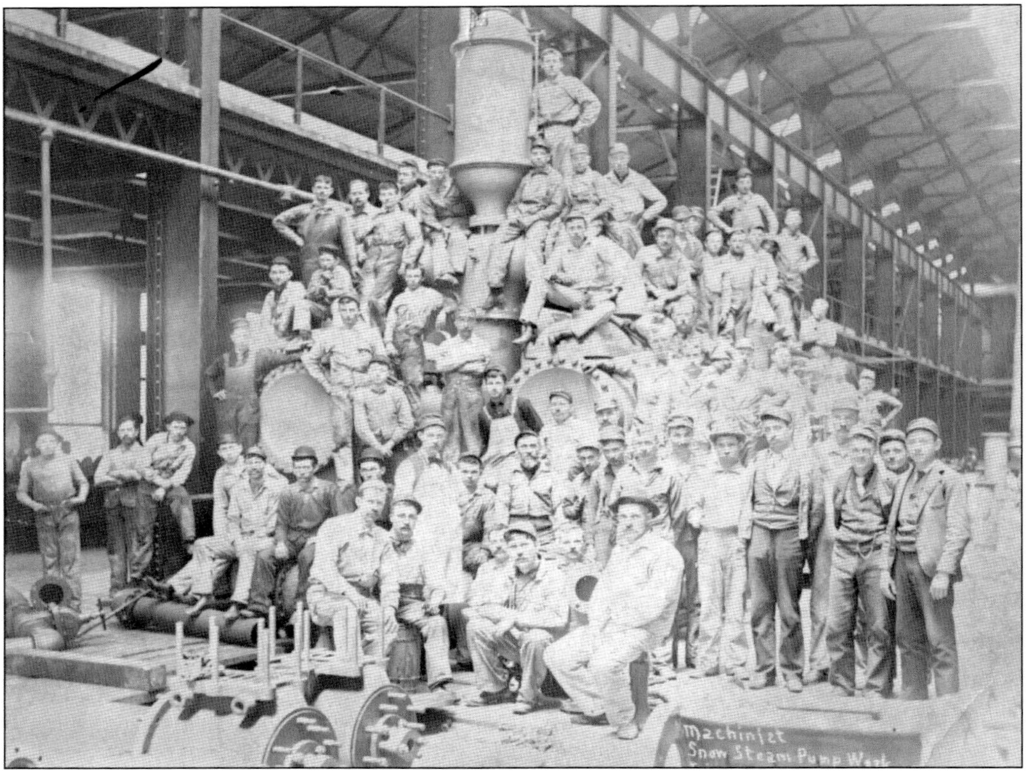

The Worthington Pump Company's Buffalo Works Company division continued to expand when work from other divisions was transferred to Buffalo. Throughout the 1950s and 1960s, the plant consisted of 72 buildings, covering 32 acres, with 1,800 employees. The Buffalo Works Company division was an integral asset for 88 years, and the first completely American-designed diesel engine was produced at the plant in 1912. Many engines for naval vessels were also constructed there. In the 1980s, the corporation was losing so much capital that parts of the company were sold off to Dresser Industries, and work was shifted to that company's plant in Olean, New York. Above, a team of machinists surround a pump in 1912, and below is an example of a colossal Worthington pump.

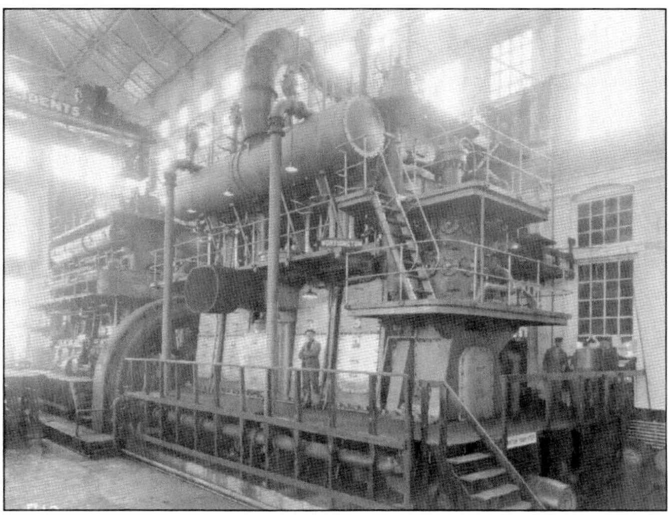

The storage yard and plant of the Rood & Brown Car Wheel Works Company is pictured around 1895. The company was founded in 1880 at the corner of Howard and Thomas Streets near William Street. Rood & Brown produced wheels for trains and locomotives. At its height, it manufactured 150 wheels per day and was located along the Buffalo Belt Line for easy transportation of products.

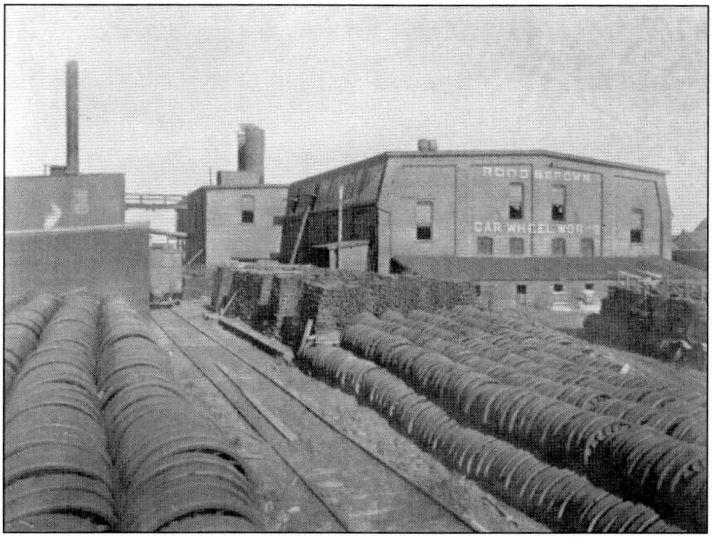

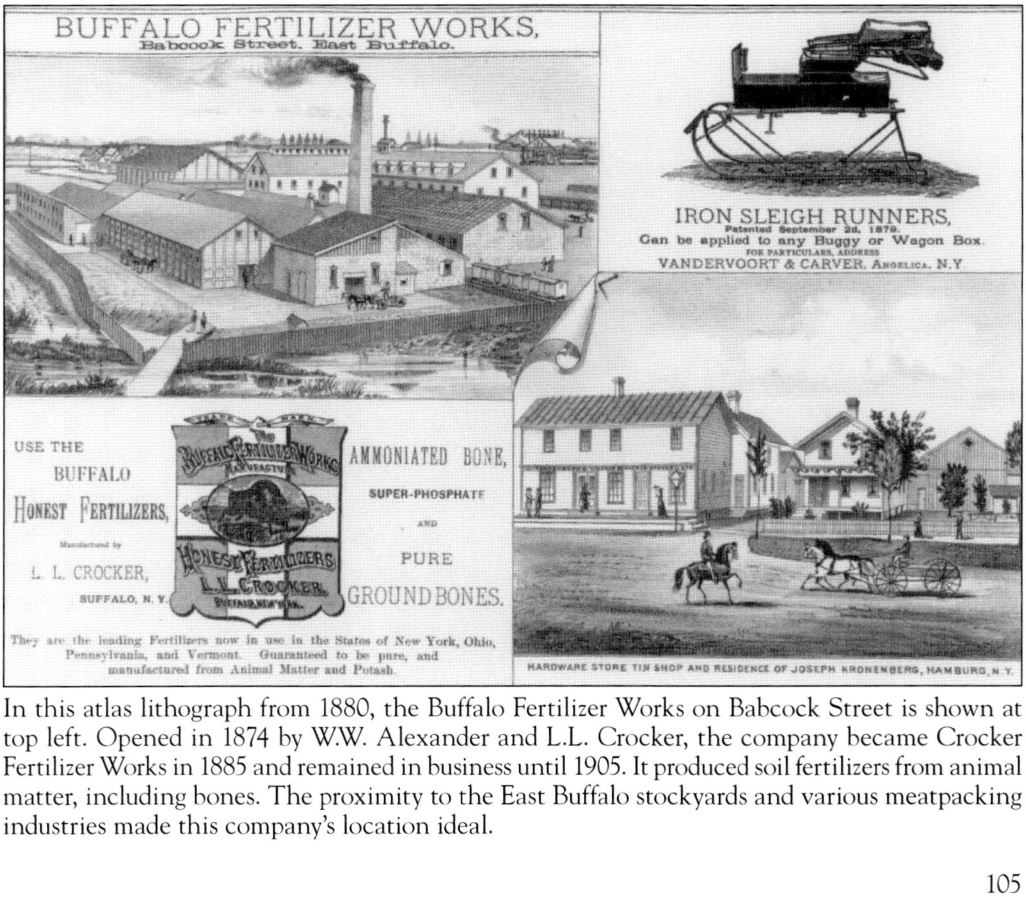

In this atlas lithograph from 1880, the Buffalo Fertilizer Works on Babcock Street is shown at top left. Opened in 1874 by W.W. Alexander and L.L. Crocker, the company became Crocker Fertilizer Works in 1885 and remained in business until 1905. It produced soil fertilizers from animal matter, including bones. The proximity to the East Buffalo stockyards and various meatpacking industries made this company's location ideal.

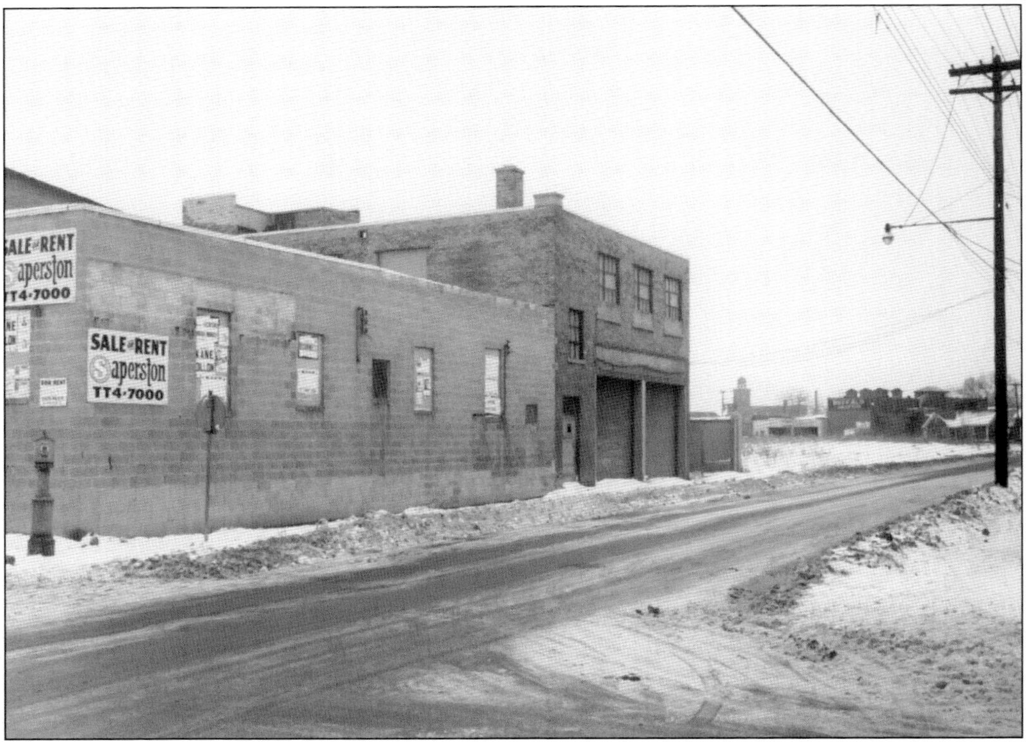

The old Malecki Company meatpacking plant at 524 Howard Street near Metcalf Street is pictured here in 1963. Based on Buffalo city directories, this plant closed in 1948, and the operations were consolidated at the other Malecki plant at 191 Person Street. In 1967, the Malecki Company opened its new headquarters and packing plant at 2320 Clinton Street, visible from the Interstate 190 and Interstate 90 West Thruway exchange. The company closed in 1977.

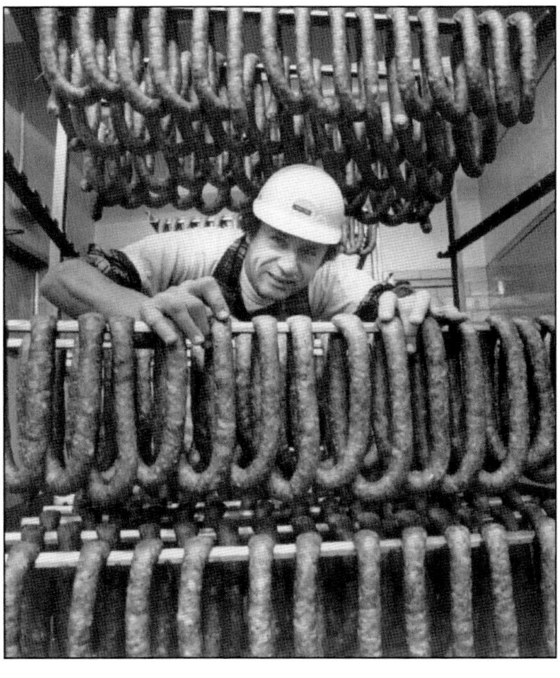

Paul Redlinski opened his meat market in 1947 at the Broadway Market after running a family farm in Elma, New York. After 20 years and strong sales, the company built a meatpacking and sausage-making plant on the block next to the Broadway Market on Sienkiewicz Street. In 2002, to much dismay, Redlinski Meats left the Broadway Market, and the company is currently headquartered at 1585 Walden Avenue.

Christian Klink founded Klink Bros. Meat Packing Company on Seneca Street in 1856. Klink is considered to be the first meat-packer in Buffalo. The company soon outgrew the Seneca Street plant and moved to Depot Street and a larger production plant. Klink Bros. was eventually sold to Allied Packers, based in Chicago, and then to Hygrade Food Products in the late 1920s. After the sale to Allied Packers, the Klink Bros. opened Klink & Schaller, with a plant at 620 Babcock Street.

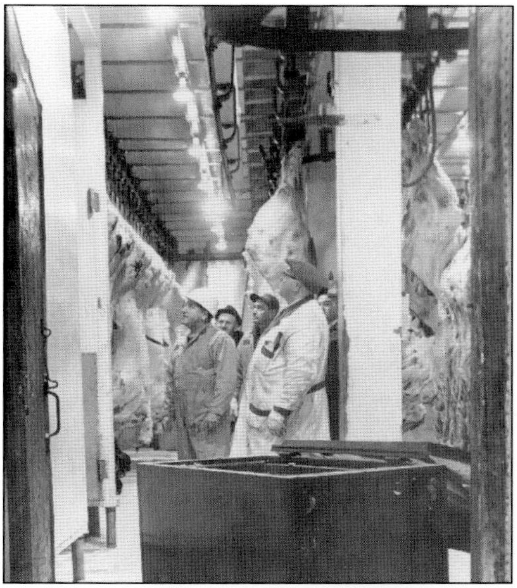

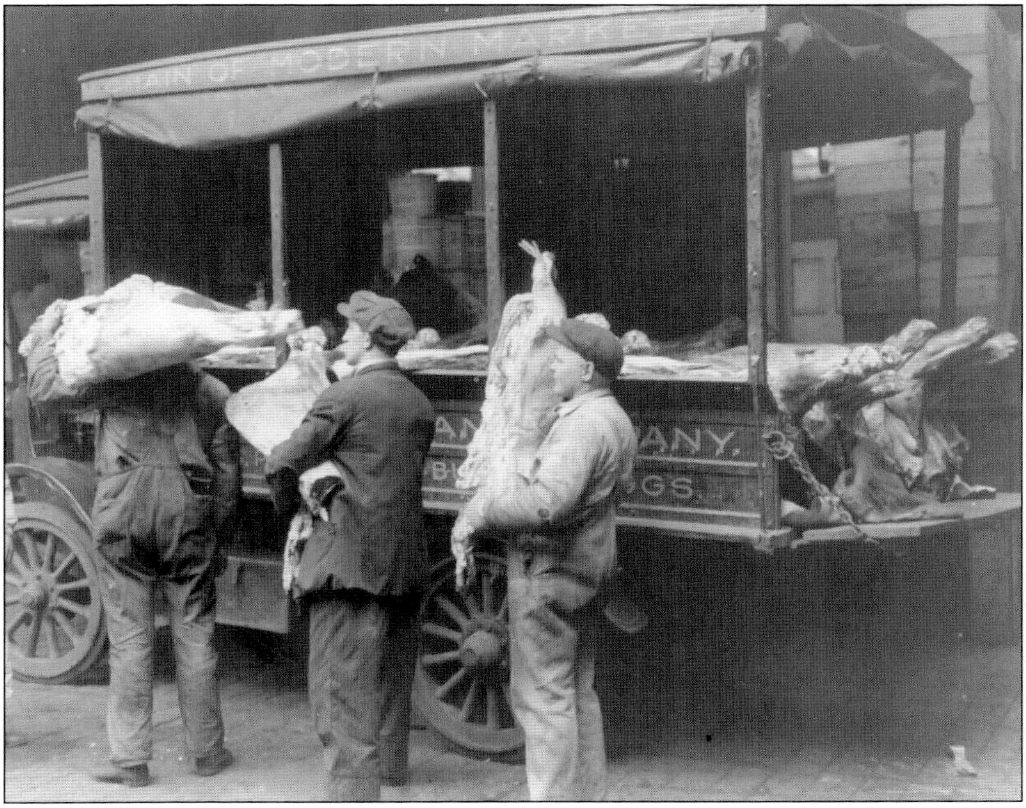

Unidentified butchers are featured in this undated photograph. Buffalo was considered to have the second-largest stockyards and meatpacking industry in the country (after Chicago). After roughly 80 years of holding that title, the stockyards and meat transportation business so central to Buffalo began shifting to the Midwest in the late 1950s. The growth of refrigeration technology decreased the need for animal transportation, since animals could be slaughtered closer to the farms, then the prepared meat could be frozen for shipment.

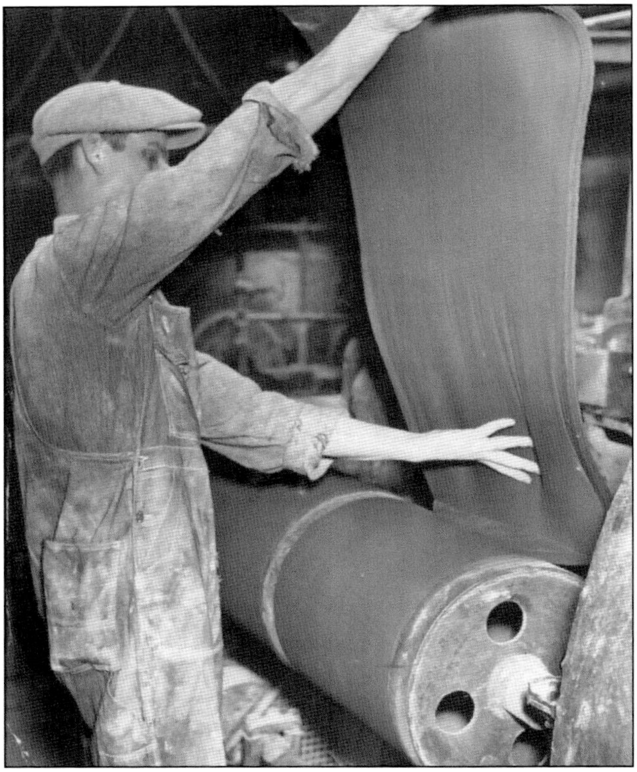

Here, Henry Babula is removing rubber from a cylinder in 1940 while working at the US Rubber Reclaiming Plant at 724 (New) Babcock Street (off Clinton Street). The company opened in 1929 and closed in 1957. It recycled 46 million pounds of tires each year, using the repurposed rubber to make other rubber products.

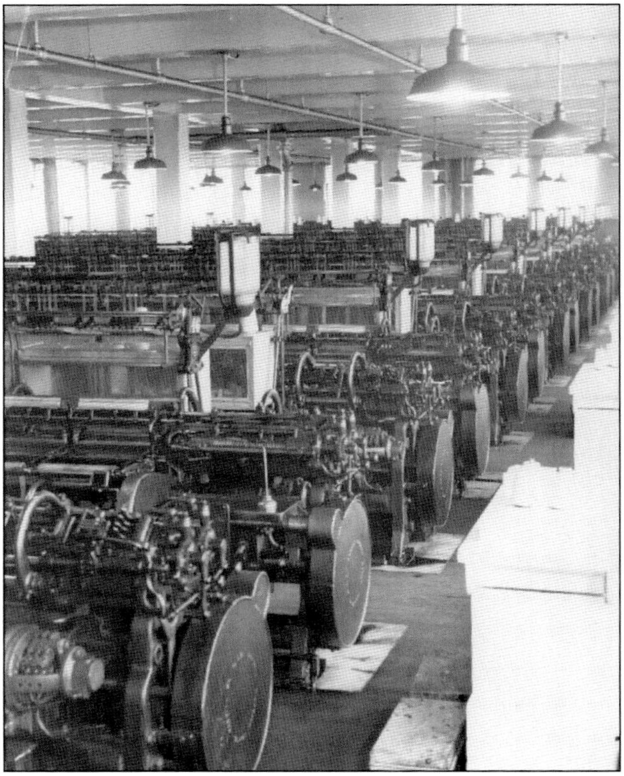

The Millfay Manufacturing Company, located at 22 Fay Street off West Shore Drive, started as a hosiery company in 1928. It produced various hosiery for woman and aided in the wartime effort by preparing nylon for use in military cords and parachutes. The name changed to Hemmerrich Knitting Company in 1949, and the company closed in 1951. Machinery in the legging department is shown in this 1941 photograph.

Started by two barbers, the Wildroot Co., Inc., produced hair tonic for men. It began operations in 1911 and quickly opened a plant at 1490 Jefferson Avenue. In 1945, it moved into a facility at 1740 Bailey Avenue, and in 1951, it took over the Millfay Manufacturing Company building directly across Fay Street while also expanding the Bailey Street location by 45,000 square feet. At right is an example of the ornate Wildroot letterhead from 1920, and below is the plant at 1490 Jefferson Avenue.

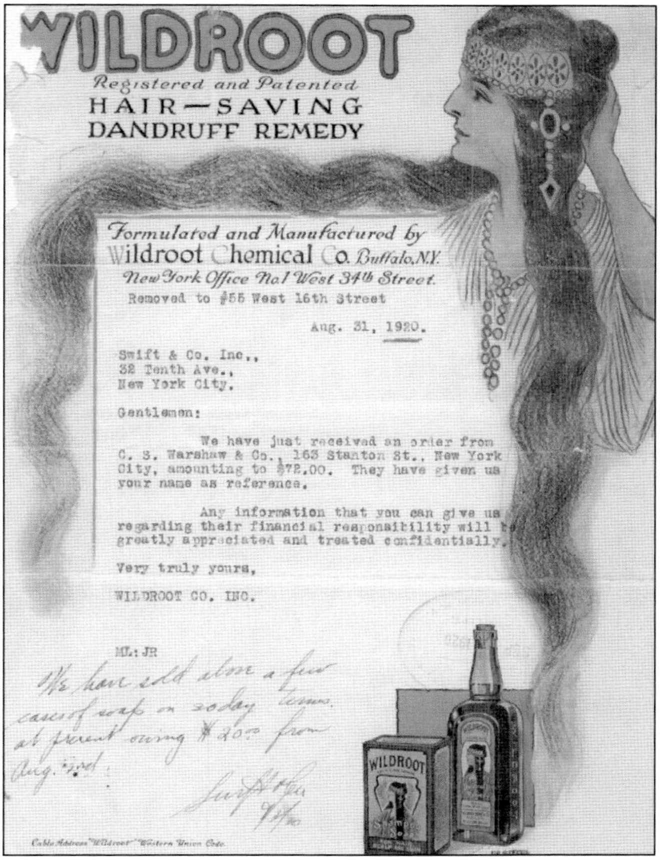

WILDROOT
Registered and Patented
HAIR—SAVING
DANDRUFF REMEDY

Formulated and Manufactured by
Wildroot Chemical Co. Buffalo, N.Y.
New York Office No. 1 West 34th Street.
Removed to #55 West 16th Street

Aug. 31, 1920.

Swift & Co. Inc.,
32 Tenth Ave.,
New York City.

Gentlemen:

We have just received an order from C. S. Warshaw & Co., 163 Stanton St., New York City, amounting to $72.00. They have given us your name as reference.

Any information that you can give us regarding their financial responsibility will be greatly appreciated and treated confidentially.

Very truly yours,

WILDROOT CO. INC.

ML:JR

We have sold above a few cases of soap on 30 day terms at present owing $20.00 from Aug. 23rd

Cable Address "Wildroot" Western Union Code.

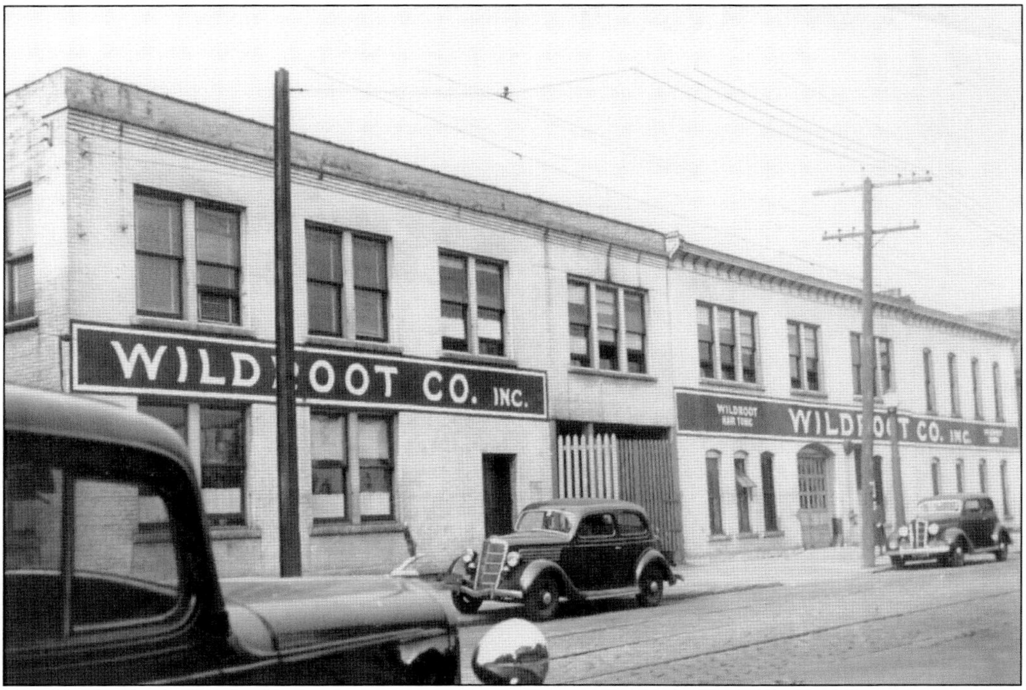

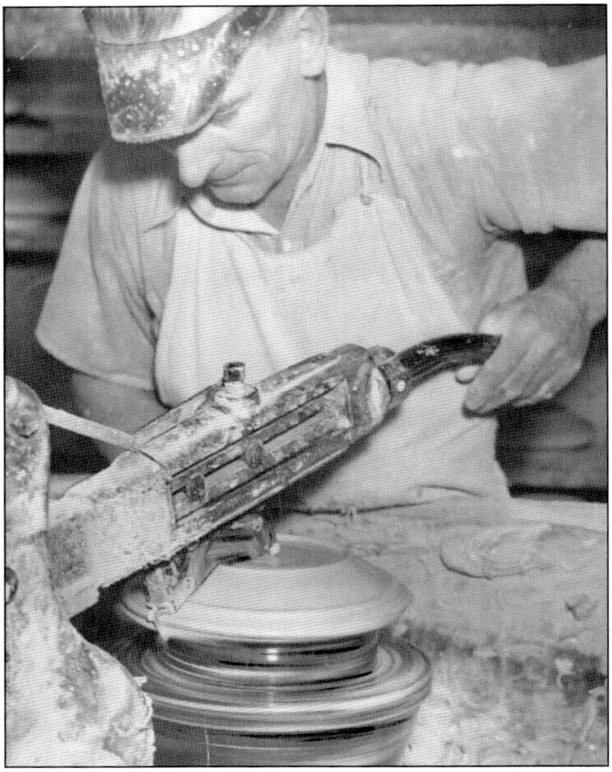

Established in 1901, Buffalo Pottery was a subsidiary of the Larkin Soap Company. The pottery could be "purchased" with a certain number of Larkin certificates that were sent to customers when they bought soaps or other products. The photograph at left shows Sylvester Burt jiggering a plate. The 1915 photograph below shows the plant near the corner of Seneca Street and Hayes Place. Buffalo Pottery became Buffalo China, which operated until 2004, when it was purchased by Niagara Ceramics, which closed in 2013. Buffalo Pottery employed many skilled workers, such as pottery molders, cutters, trimmers, painters, and designers. Over its 112 years in operation, it employed roughly 350 men and women each year.

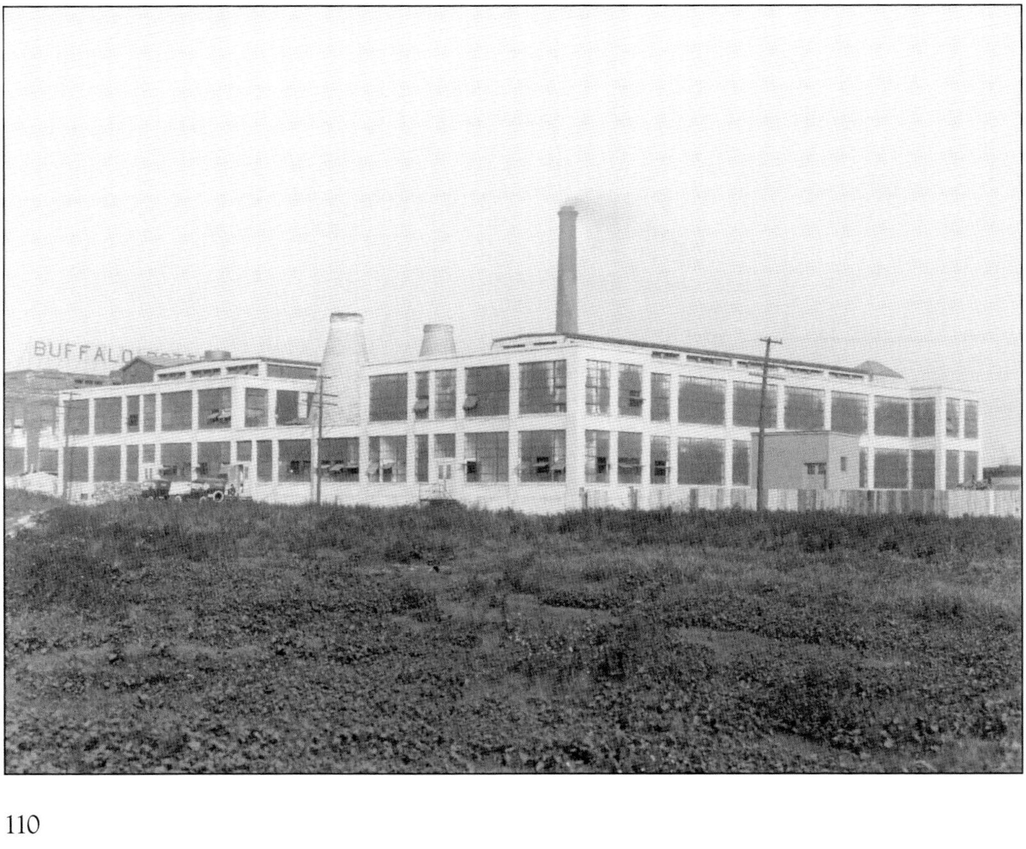

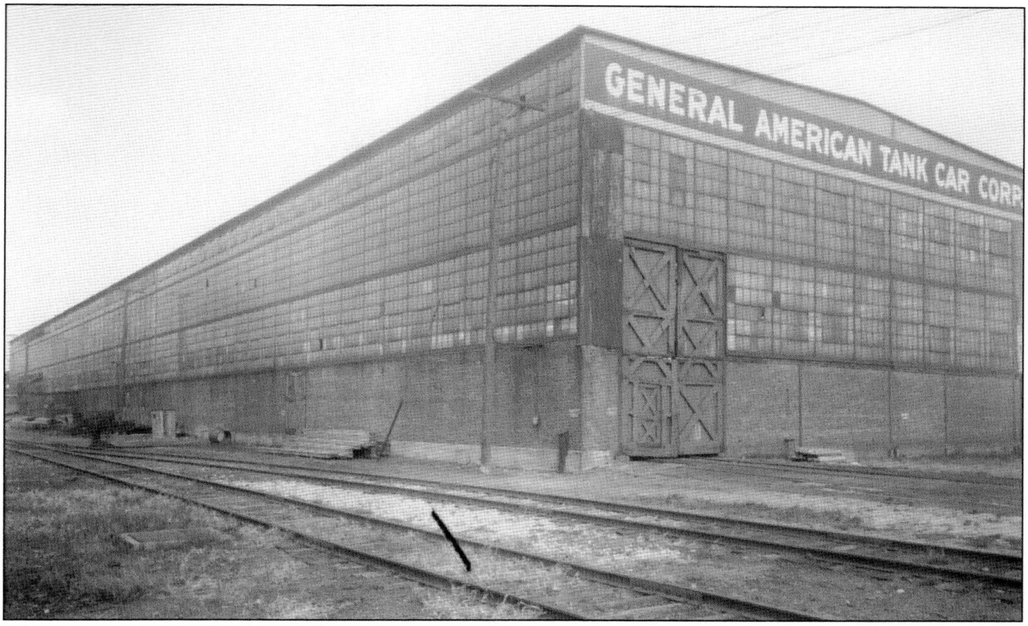

This image shows the massive footprint of the Buffalo Steel Car–General American Tank Car Corporation on Walden Avenue (near the city line). Founded in 1900 as the Buffalo Street Car Company (and later known as Buffalo Steel Car), it was acquired by the General American Tank Car Corporation in 1926. It remained at the Walden Avenue location from 1933 until it closed in 1935. For 35 years, the company produced and repaired freight rail cars.

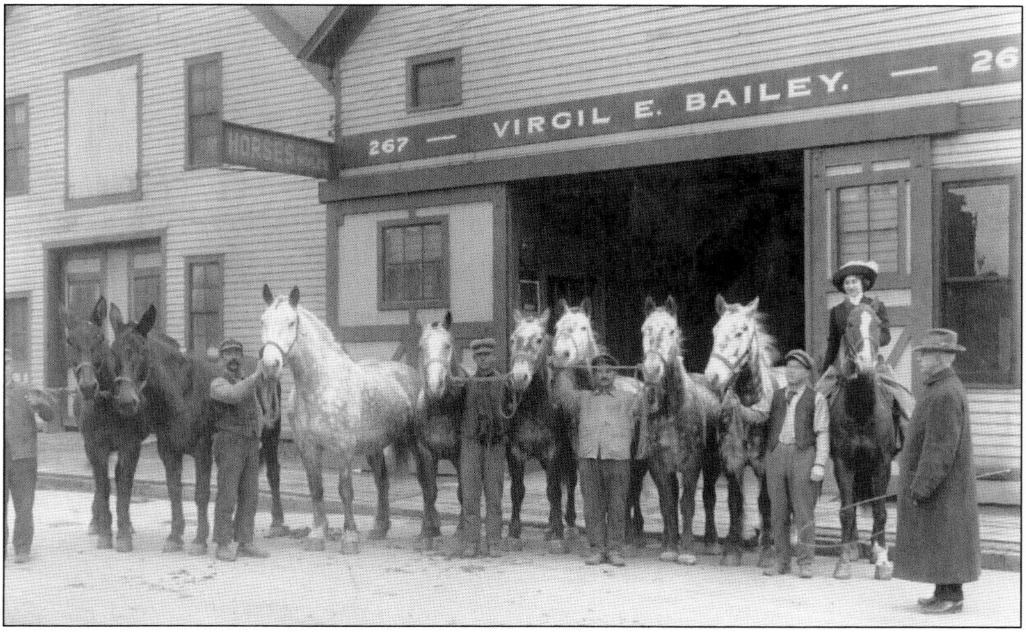

The Virgil E. Bailey Stables were located at 267 Lewis Street near the Buffalo stockyards and slaughterhouses. The company first appears in the city directory in 1906 as a horse dealer at 24 Lewis Street. By 1910, the company was listed as a dealer in both horses and mules, and in 1912, it was listed as offering stabling services at an expanded location at 267 Lewis Street. The stables were short-lived, though, as the company is not mentioned after 1914.

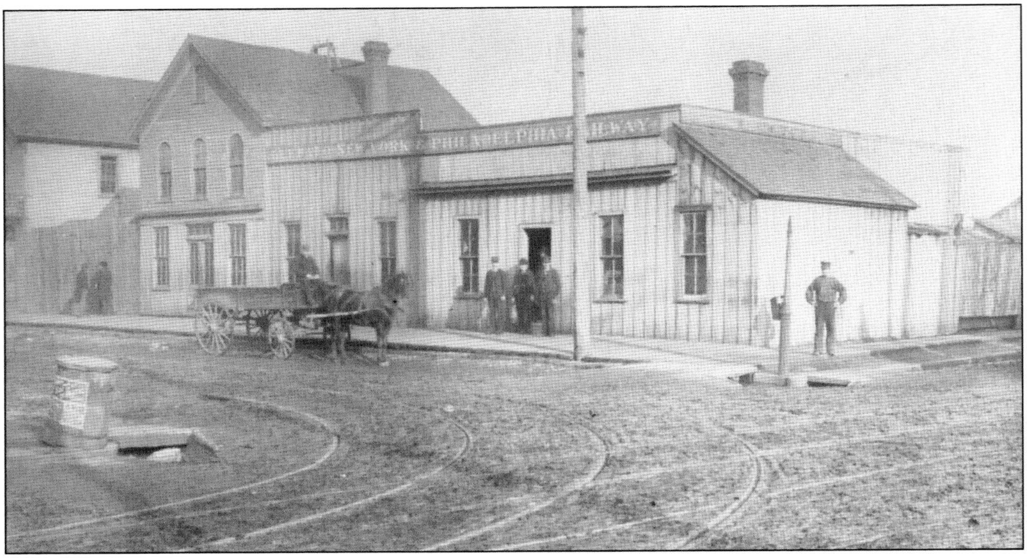

Pictured is one of the many rail lines that entered Buffalo. After the Civil War, rail line construction increased across the country. The Buffalo, New York & Philadelphia Railroad expanded up through Olean, New York (at the border of New York and Pennsylvania), and was primarily a passenger line. This station, pictured in 1880, was located at the corner of Louisiana and Exchange Streets.

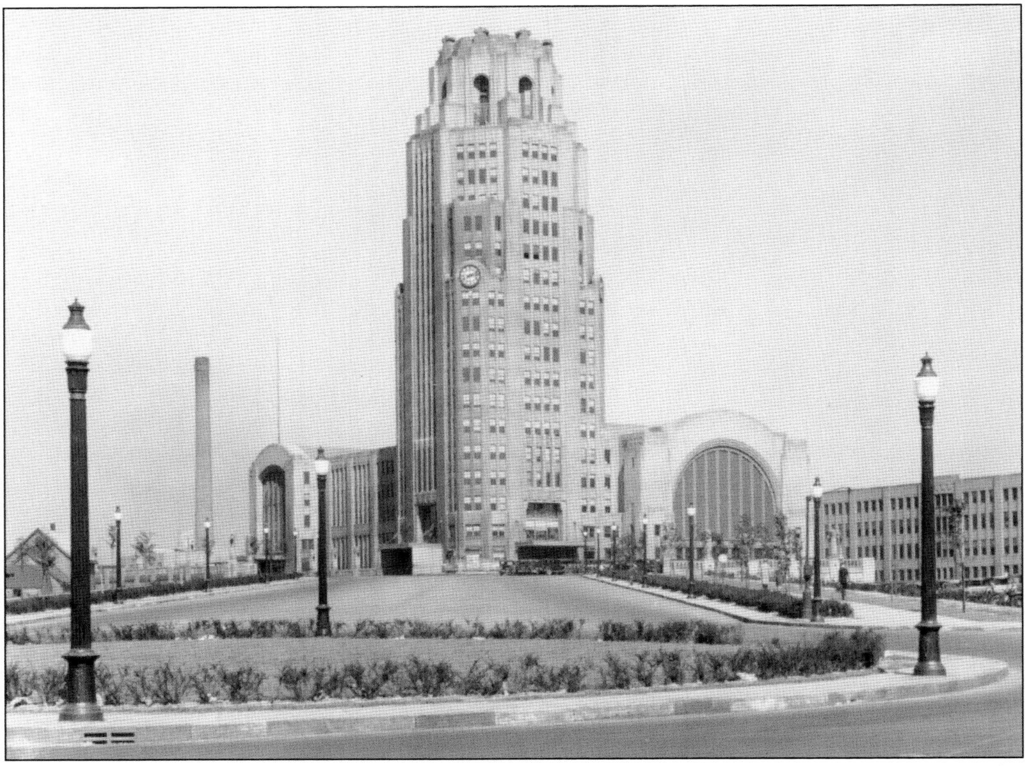

Buffalo contains two major Art Deco masterpieces. One is the ornate Buffalo City Hall, and the other is this structure—the Buffalo Central Terminal, built in 1929. This view shows the approach from Paderewski Drive, with the Memorial Drive Circle in the foreground. The expansive footprint of the building is visible in this photograph, which was taken in 1929.

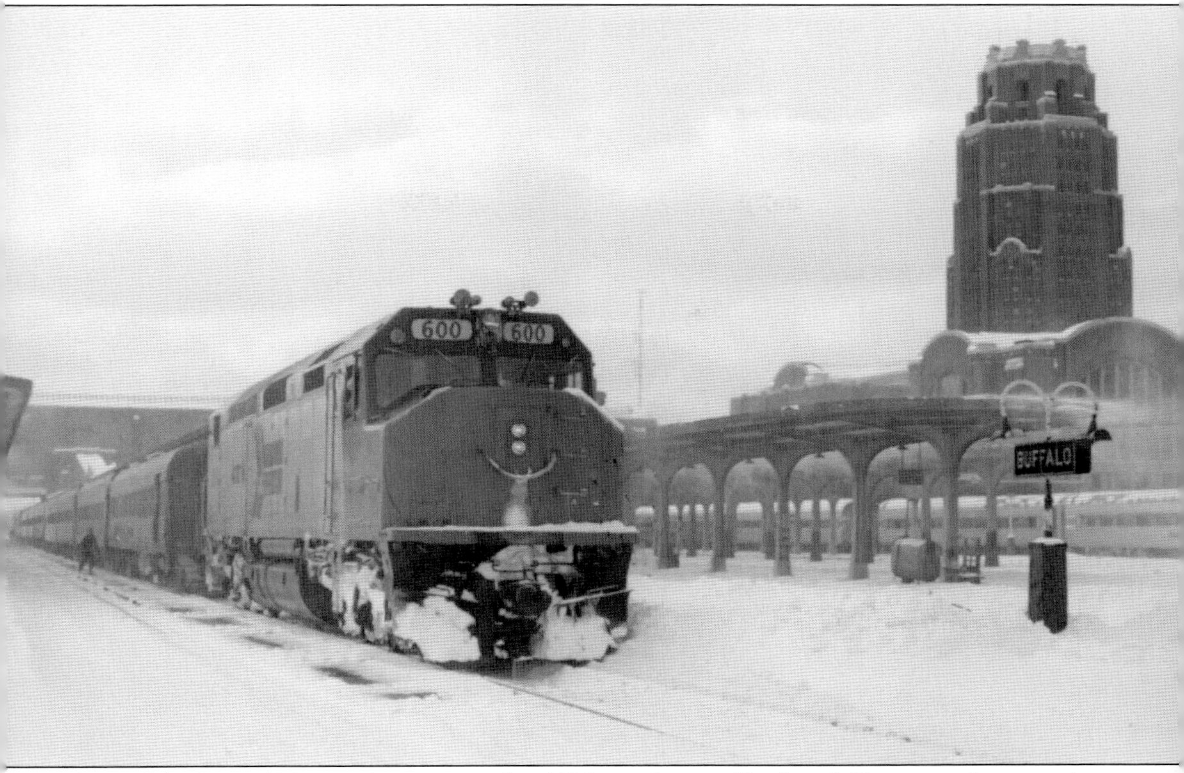

The Buffalo Central Terminal, constructed in 1929, was designed by famed Chicago architectural firm Fellheimer & Wagner. The firm designed railroad terminals around the country, including the Cincinnati Union Terminal in Ohio; Union Station in Erie, Pennsylvania; and Grand Central Station in Manhattan. In 1924, the New York Central Railroad decided to construct a new terminal farther away from the city because of downtown congestion. The railroad had managed Buffalo's Exchange Street station, located on the site of a station originally built for the Attica & Buffalo Railroad, since 1870. By the early 1920s, management realized that the station needed more space. Here, the "Niagara Rainbow" is pulling out of the station around the time of the blizzard of 1977.

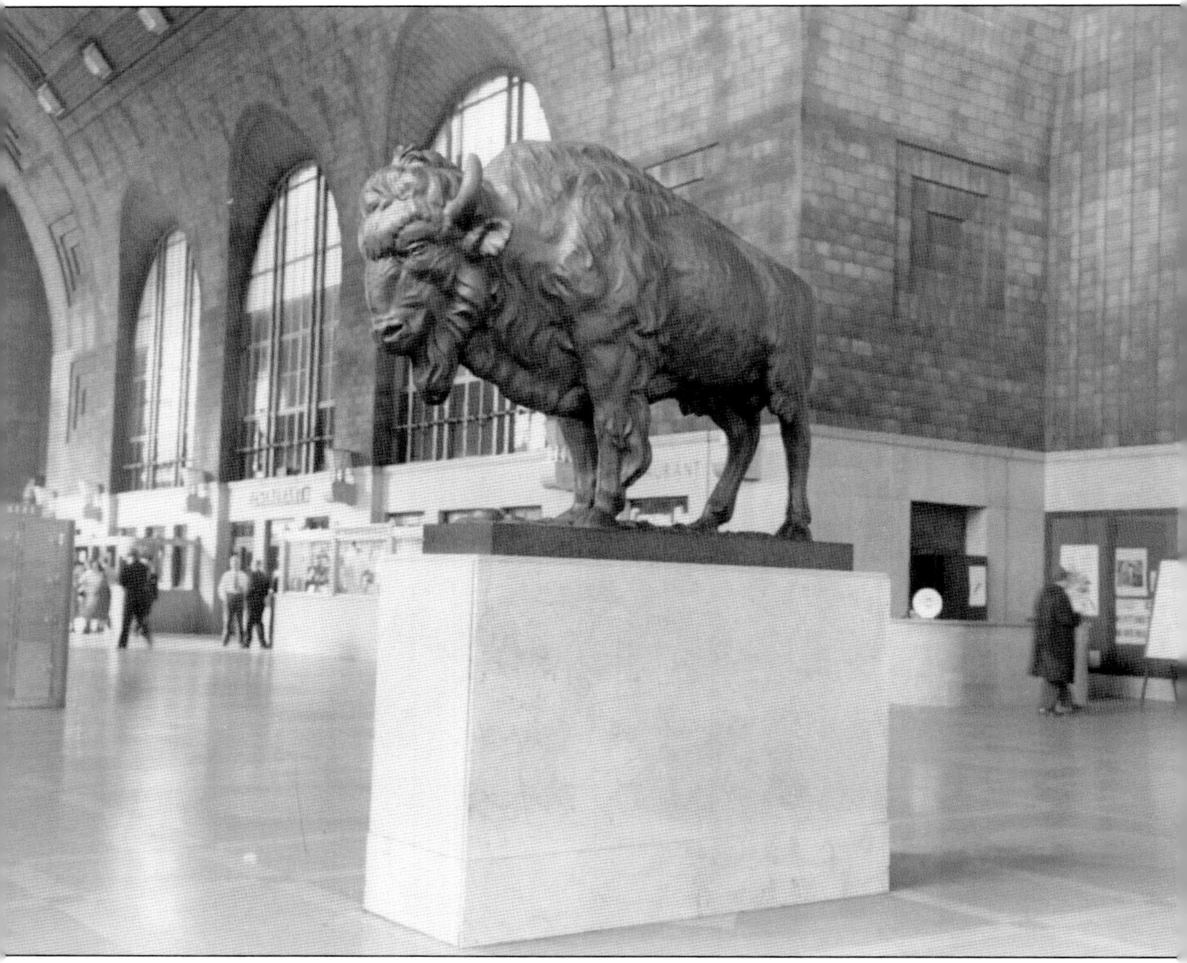

The famed bronze buffalo statue located in the Buffalo Central Terminal concourse is shown here around 1955. Because the terminal was constructed outside of downtown, coupled with its opening at the start of the Great Depression, it never realized its full potential—except during World War II years, when troops would leave and arrive at this station. The last passenger train left the station in October 1979, and the Amtrak offices that took over the station closed in 1980. In 1997, the Buffalo Central Terminal property was transferred to the Central Terminal Restoration Corporation, which has worked tirelessly to raise money, restore parts of the terminal, and host events—all to shed light on this Art Deco masterpiece. This buffalo statue was destroyed when a trucked backed into it, knocking it over; thankfully, the statue has been reconstructed and again adorns the concourse.

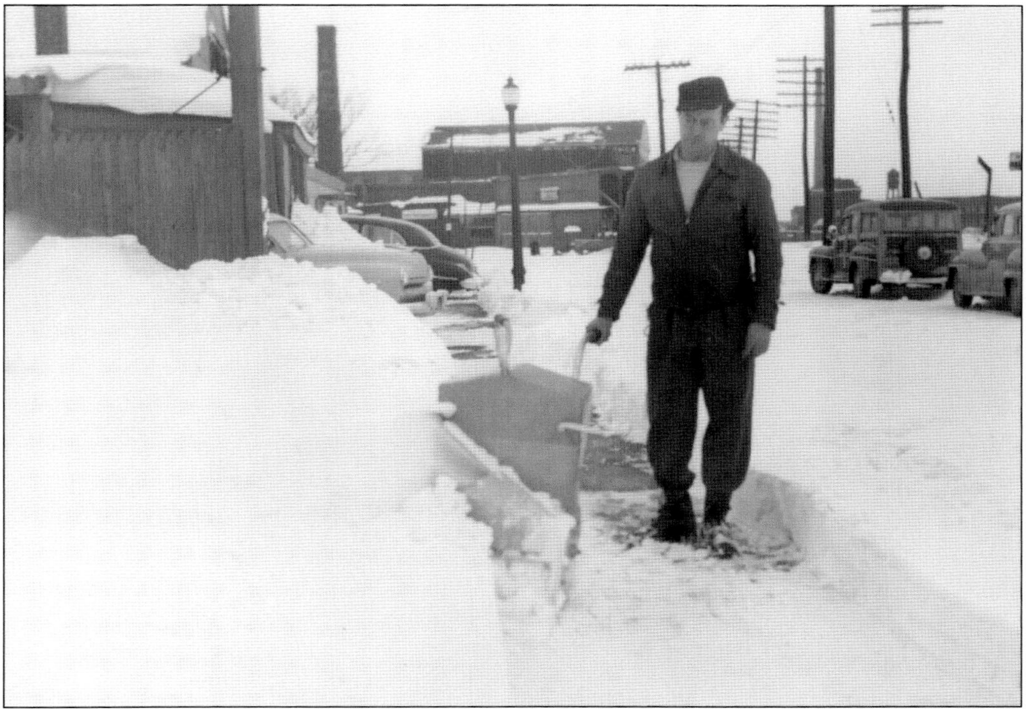

GN Metal Products opened in 1947 at 26 Gillette Avenue between Kensington and East Delavan Avenues. The company produced tools, dyes, and metal stamping, also designing special machines, like this Sno-Star snowblower (pictured around 1949). The company remained at this location until 1965, when it moved to 4490 Broadway in Depew, New York. In 1971, GN Metal moved again, to 3901 Union Road, where it soon closed.

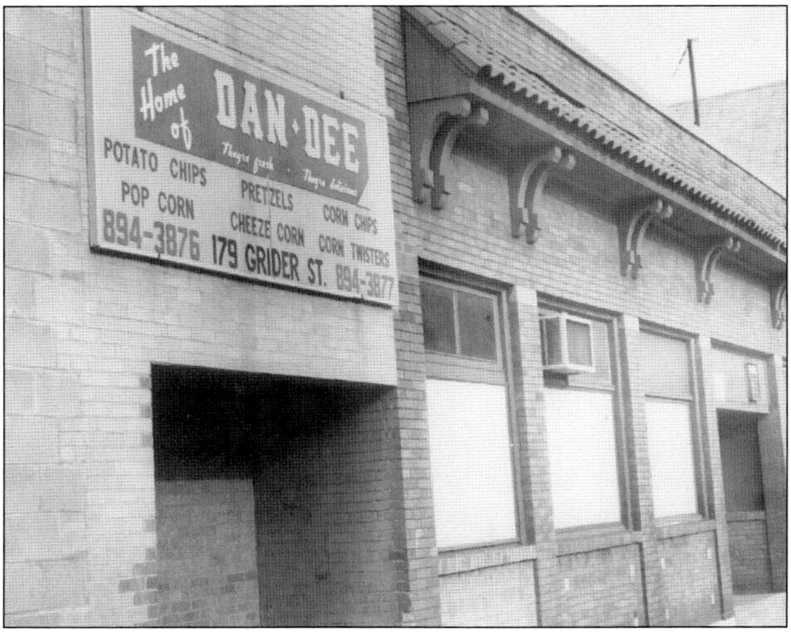

The Empire Potato Chip Company opened in 1950 at 179 Grider Street between Northland and East Delavan Avenues. The company added pretzels and other corn-chip snacks to its production lines in 1951. In 1980, the company's name changed from the Empire Pretzel & Potato Chip Co. to Dan-Dee, and in 1985, it closed its doors.

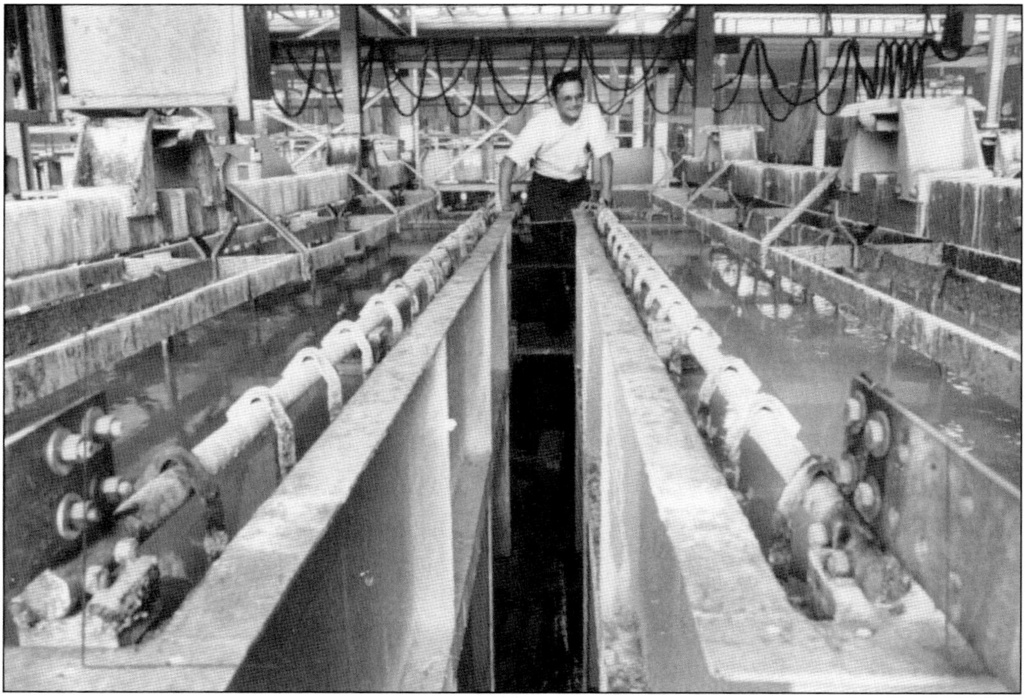

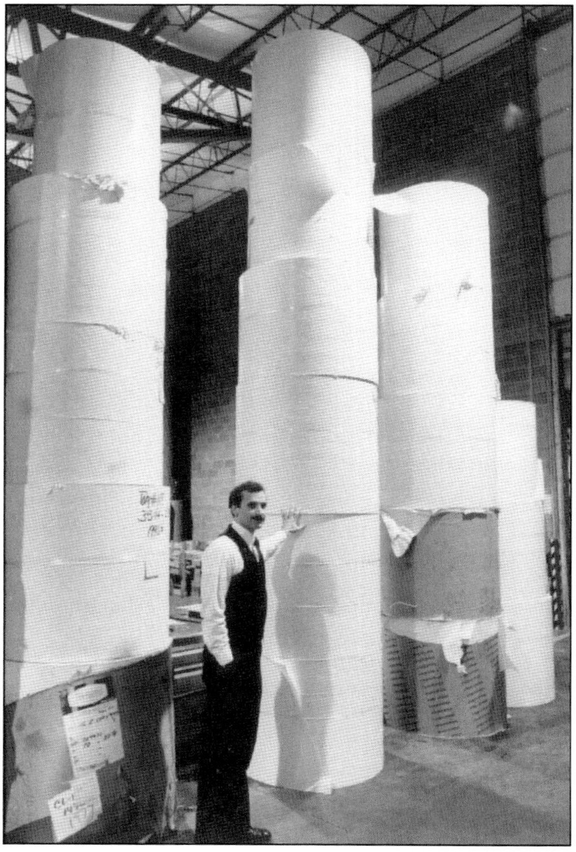

The Marlette Plating Company started in 1908 as a nickel and chrome plating company, with most of its production going to the Pierce Arrow Motor Car and Thomas Motor Car Companies. Originally located at 200 Cornwall Avenue, it moved to 25 Rano Street in the 1980s. In this photograph, Daniel Ruszczyk is checking chemical baths for metal plates. After 100 years in business, the company closed in 2008.

A worker stands in front of industrial paper rolls at the Niagara Frontier Paper Company. Niagara Frontier opened its doors in 1975 at 36 Depot Street but eventually moved to Bud Mil Drive, a suburban-style industrial complex off William Street. The company closed in 1987, but its building was home to other paper companies, such as Millcraft Paper Company, and currently houses the International Paper Buffalo Sheet Plant.

Eight

Old Meets New
The East Side of Yesterday and Today

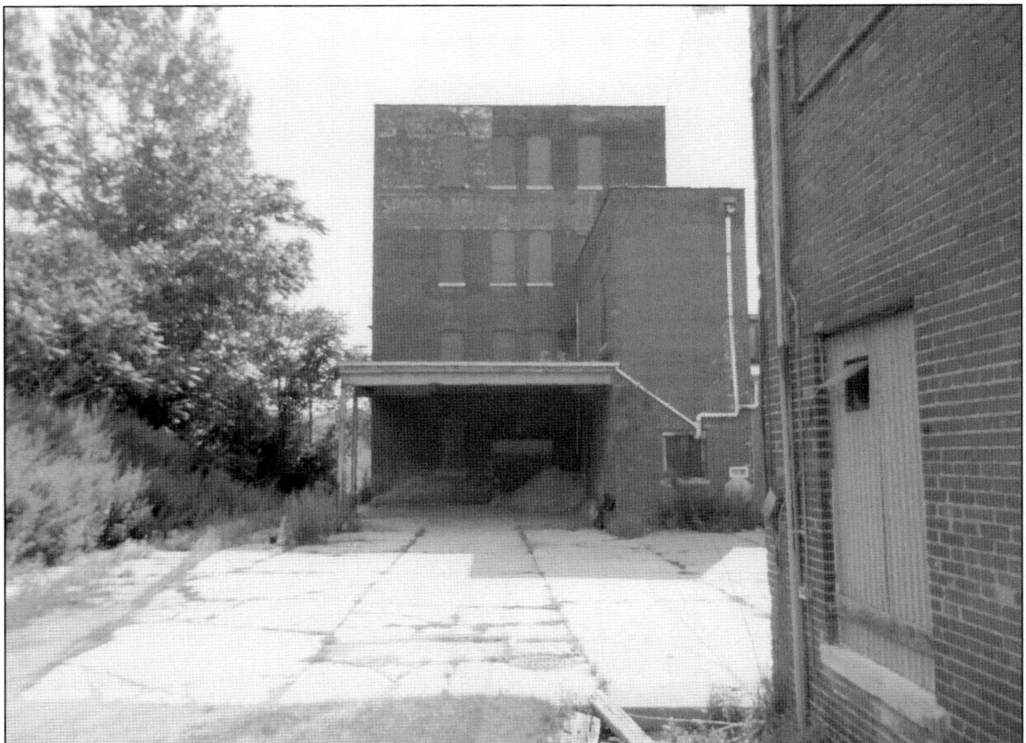

The Spencer Kellogg & Sons Company left a huge mark on Buffalo manufacturing. This building, located at 697 Elk Street, opened in 1903, where it remained open until 1931. The company was founded in 1878 and was the largest producer of linseed oil in the country; it opened plants in China and Argentina in the 1920s and operated 187 presses at its height. Its research facility was located on the northwest corner of Niagara Square. In 1961, the company merged with Textron Agro-Chemical Group. In 1985, NL Industries bought the companies and closed all remaining Buffalo facilities. (Courtesy of the author.)

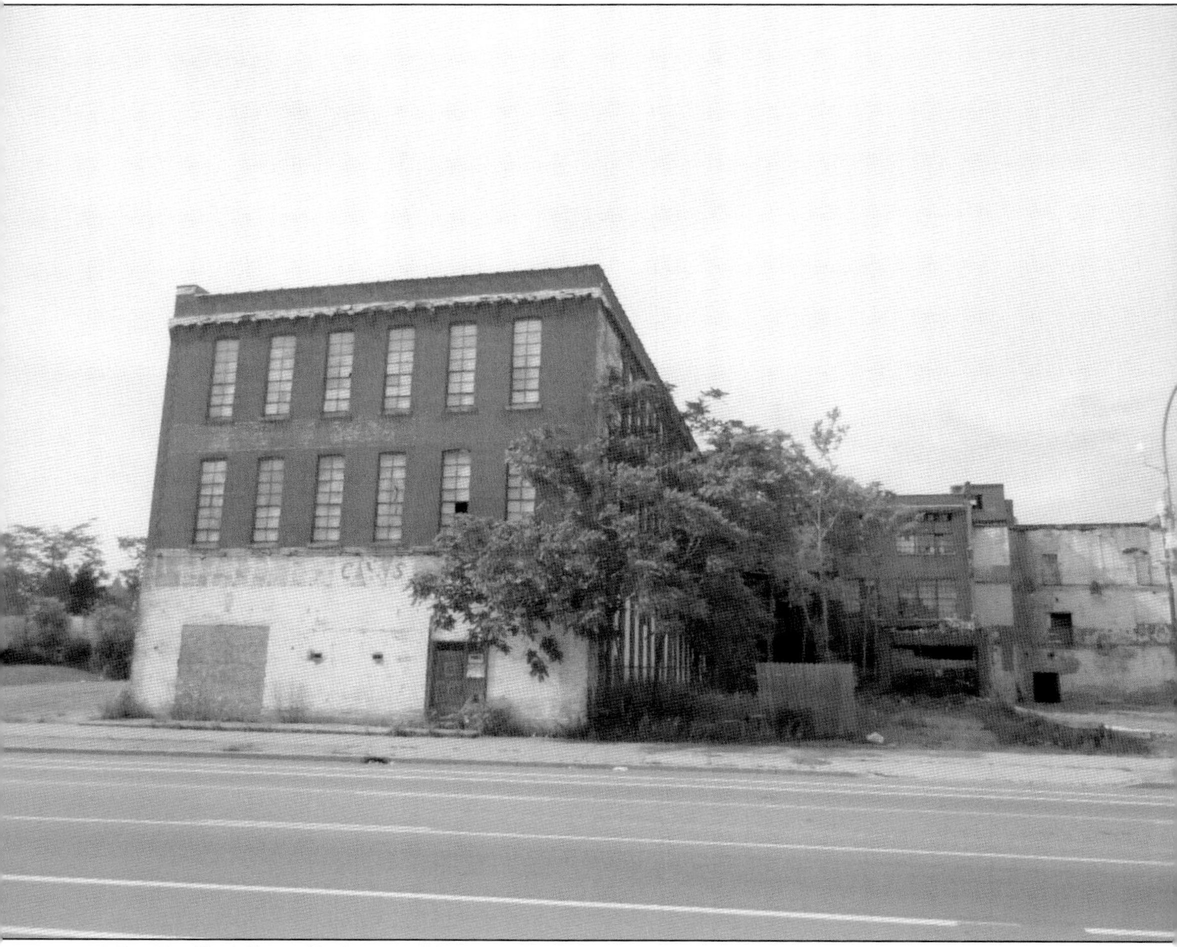

The Duffy Silk Mill, designed by noted Buffalo architects Esenwien & Johnson, is shown as it has appeared since a 2014 windstorm caused the collapse of part of the building. Charles Duffy opened his business in 1903 at 1226 Broadway, and expanded three years later to the pictured location at 1270 Broadway. By 1930, work at the plant had increased enough for the company to expand, and Duffy purchased the Guilford Manufacturing Company, which was located at 207–225 Guilford Street. City directories reveal that it took one year for the company's name to change, and by 1932, the Duffy Silk Mill was listed at both 1270 Broadway and 207-225 Guilford Street. During World War II, with major silk suppliers cut off in the Far East, the company reverted to making and processing nylon. A third factory, located at 980 Northampton Street, opened in 1945 and was likely added to increase wartime production. By 1959, the company had closed its three plants. The building at 1270 Broadway was repurposed for new tenant Buffalo Leather Sporting Goods. (Courtesy of the author.)

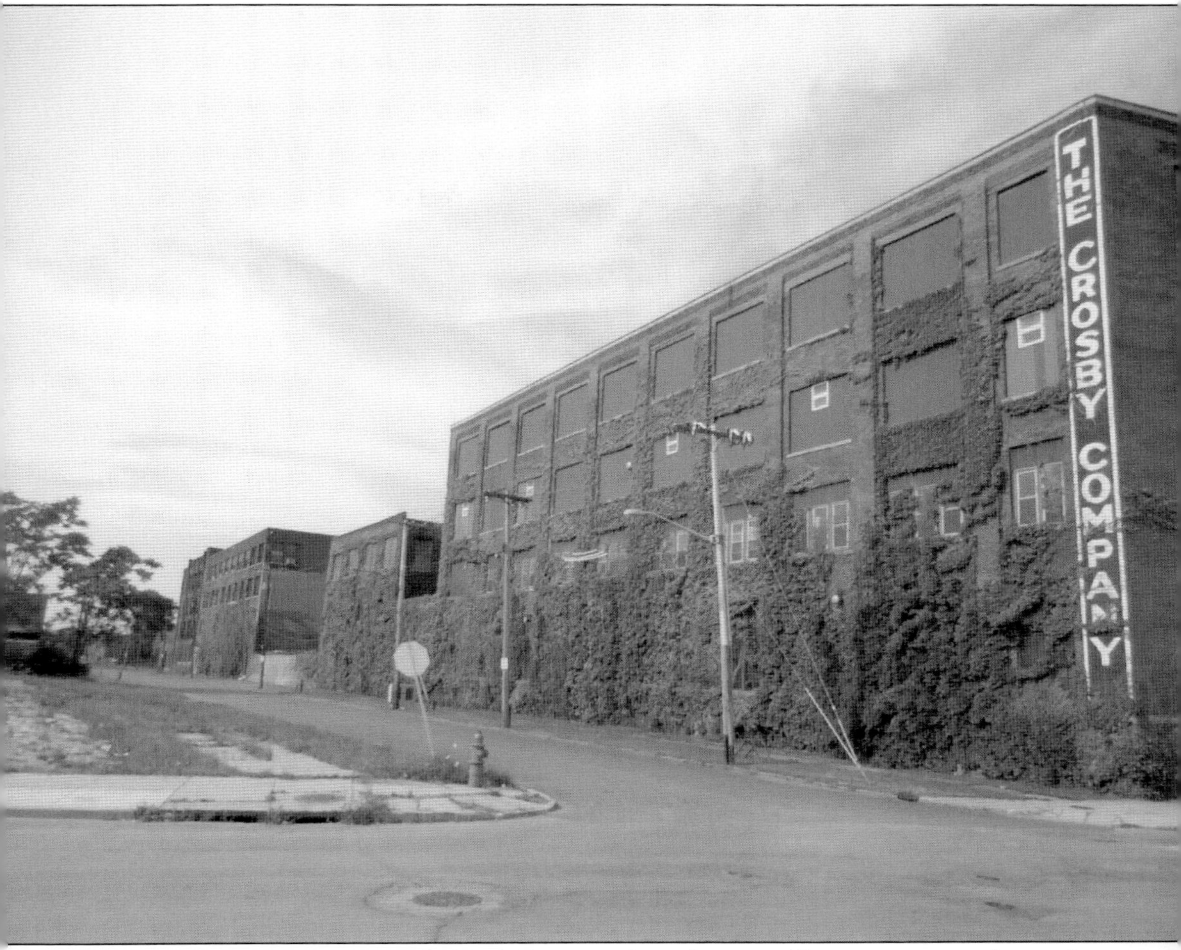

The Crosby Company's mammoth 300,000-square-foot plant is still in operation today and currently employs 50 people. The plant, located at 183 Pratt Street and bound by William and Spring Streets, is as a testament to the industrial might of the city and the East Side. The 1925 edition of the Sanborn Maps for the City of Buffalo shows the Crosby Company complex with at least 17 buildings, including Fire House Hook and Ladder No. 3, which is built into the structure. The company, founded in 1896 by William H. Crosby, began producing stamped metal for bicycles to make them lighter, stronger, and more cost-effective. Now run by fourth-generation CEO Peter Crosby, the company currently produces stamped and 3D laser-cut metals, fabrication, and assembly. Crosby Company manufactured products are used in the medical, surgical, agricultural, food, aerospace, and military sectors. The company currently works with aluminum, brass, bronze, carbon, and stainless steel and continues to have a strong East Side presence, with $10 to $20 million in annual sales. (Courtesy of the author.)

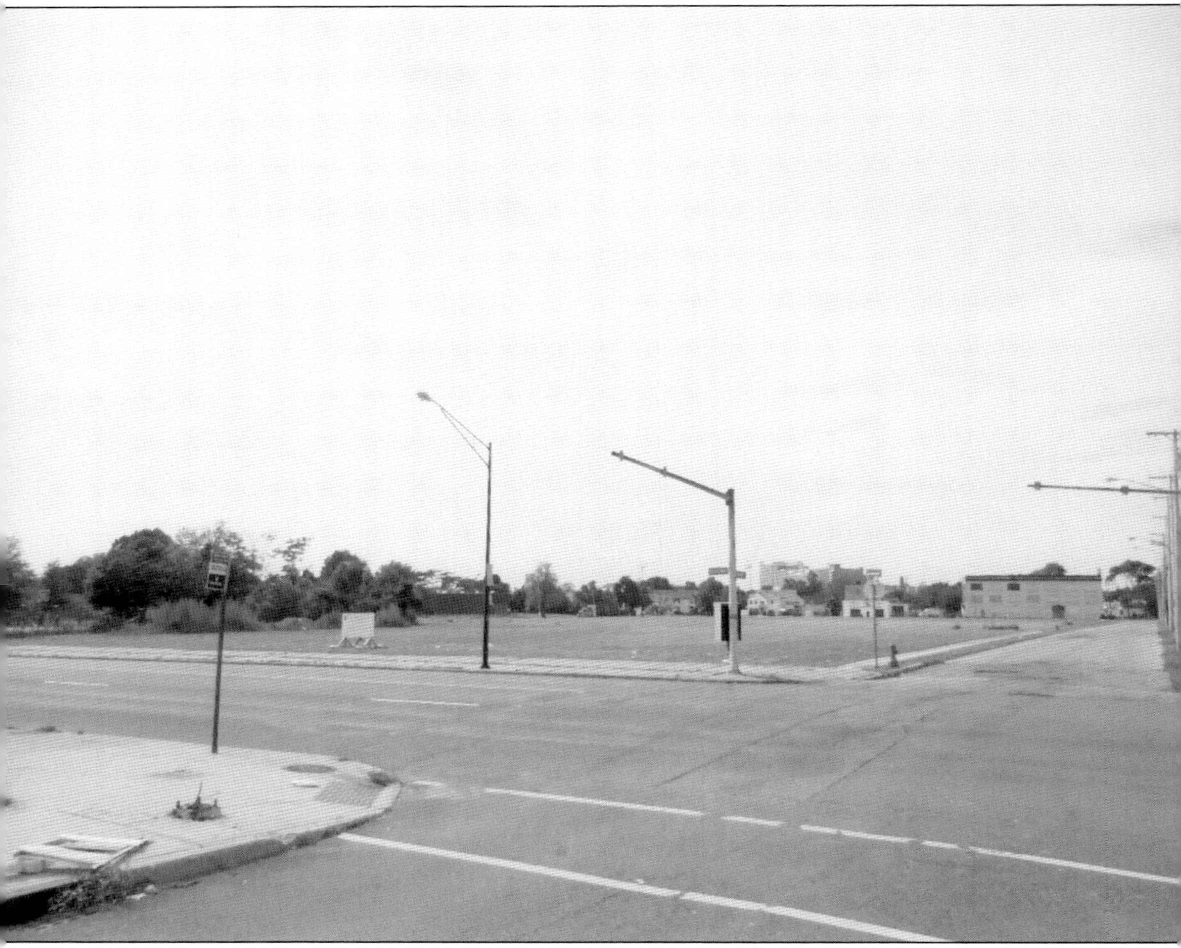

Buffalo Forge Company was located at 490 Broadway (the pictured block); contrast this modern photograph with the image on page 32 and 33. The storage facility and "dust lab" in the background are also visible in the image at the top of page 17. Over time, Buffalo Forge purchased and absorbed the Buffalo Steam Pump Company and the George L. Squire Manufacturing Company. The land has looked like this since 2006, when Howden Buffalo, which purchased Buffalo Forge in 1993, razed the structure after not being able to find a buyer. Buffalo Forge also opened a plant in Canada, the Canadian Blower & Forge Company, in Montreal, Quebec, in 1903, then opened another in Kitchener, Ontario, in 1914. At the height of its production, the Buffalo Forge Company was a $125-million business. Although the production facility is gone, Buffalo Forge continues to have a positive impact on the lives of Buffalonians through the Margaret L. Wendt Foundation. Margaret, daughter of William Wendt (one of the brothers who founded Buffalo Forge), created the foundation to support youth, community, arts, energy, and educational organizations throughout the city and region. (Courtesy of the author.)

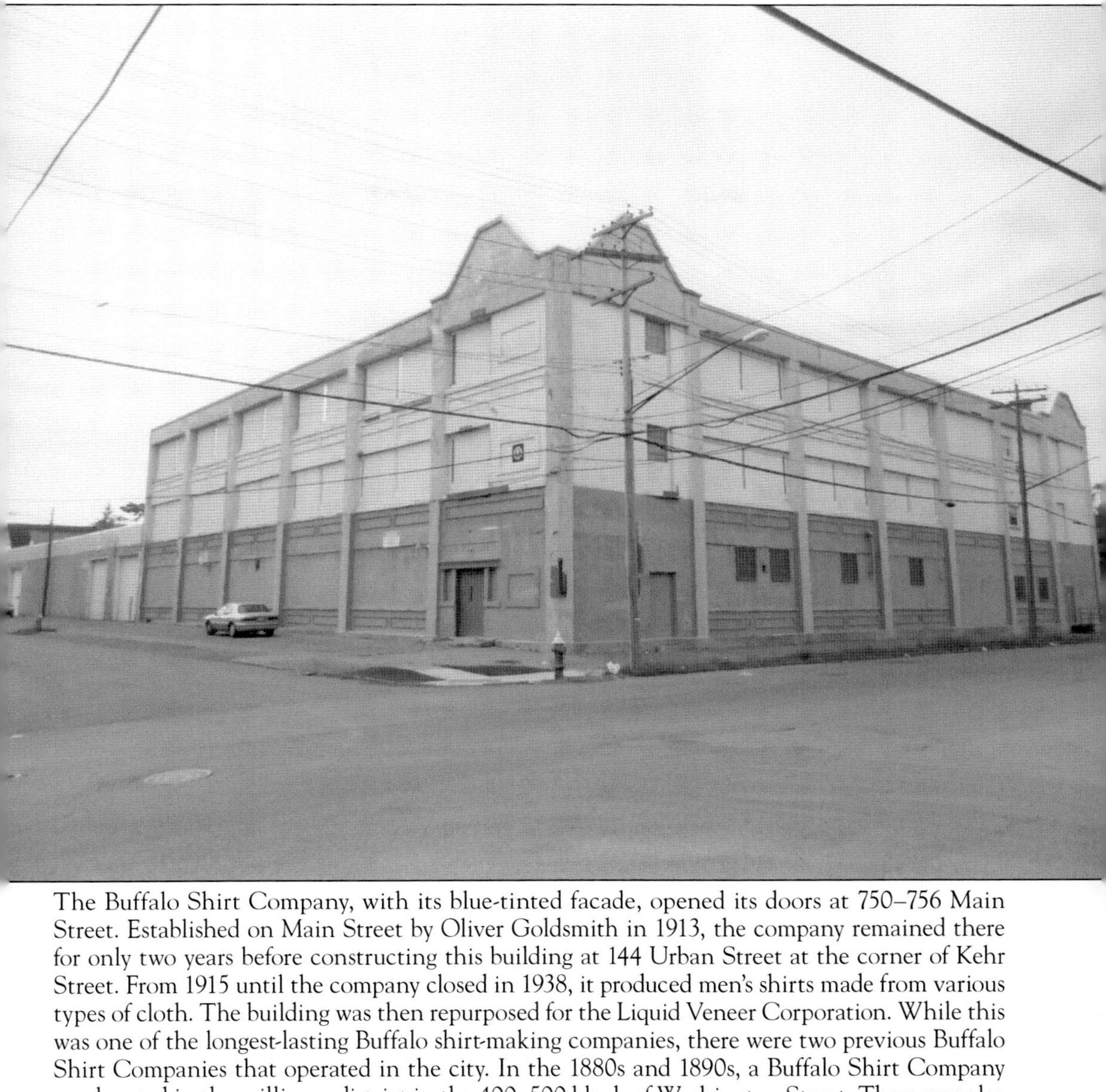

The Buffalo Shirt Company, with its blue-tinted facade, opened its doors at 750–756 Main Street. Established on Main Street by Oliver Goldsmith in 1913, the company remained there for only two years before constructing this building at 144 Urban Street at the corner of Kehr Street. From 1915 until the company closed in 1938, it produced men's shirts made from various types of cloth. The building was then repurposed for the Liquid Veneer Corporation. While this was one of the longest-lasting Buffalo shirt-making companies, there were two previous Buffalo Shirt Companies that operated in the city. In the 1880s and 1890s, a Buffalo Shirt Company was located in the millinery district in the 400–500 block of Washington Street. There was also a Buffalo Shirt Company that operated for four years at 106 Hampshire Street on the West Side. (Courtesy of the author.)

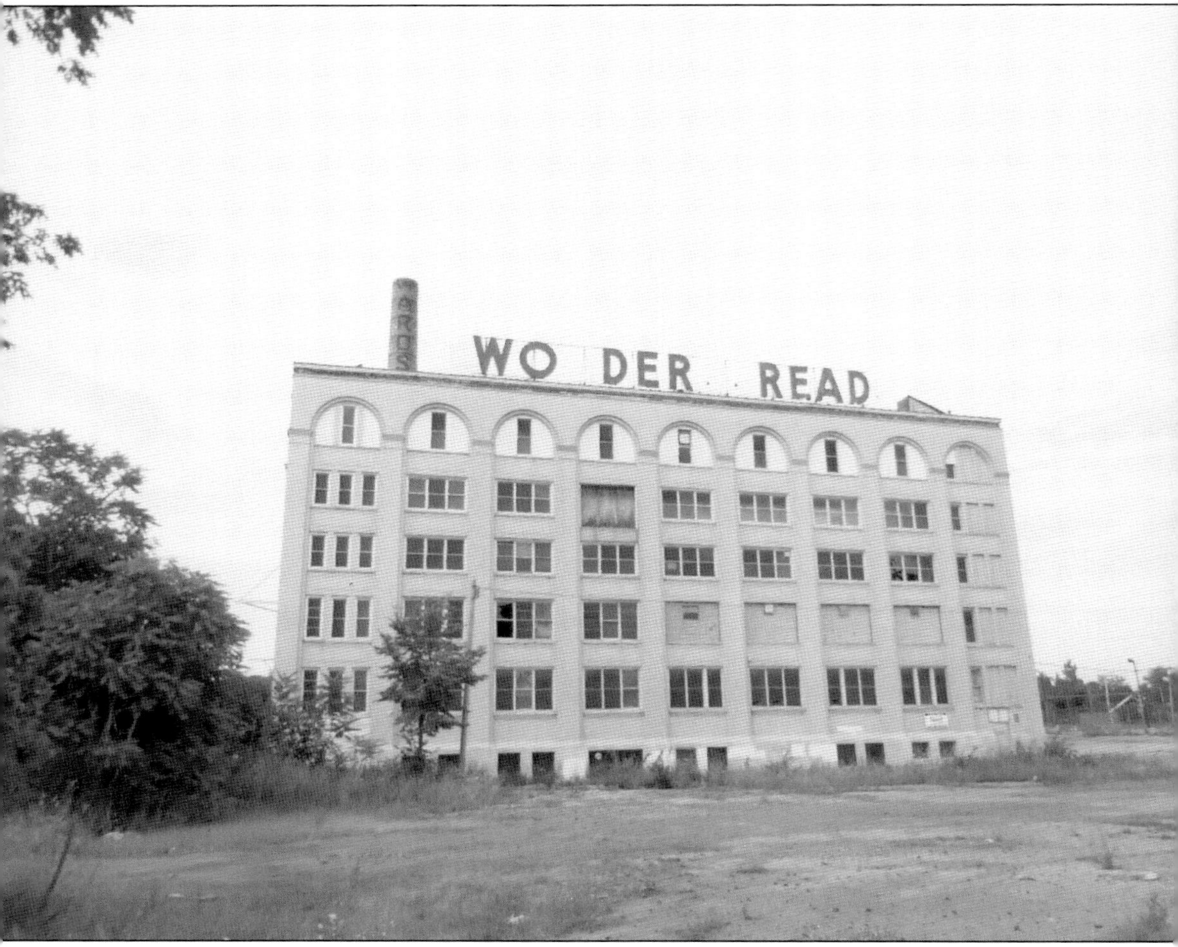

One of the iconic buildings on the East Side is the Ward's Baking/Wonder Bread factory at 313 Fougeron Street. This image shows the battered Wonder Bread sign that must have been a sight to see when it was lit. There are some discrepancies regarding the companies once located in this factory. Buffalo city directories show that Ward & Ward Bakers opened at "Genesee and the Belt Line" in 1916. By 1930, the company—through consolidations, mergers, and antitrust settlements—became Continental Wonder at 313 Fougeron Street, the location of this plant. In 1965, the name changed to Wonder Bread. In 1972, it underwent a change in ownership, becoming ITT Continental Baking Company. This factory also served a site where Hostess Cake products were made. The plant was shuttered in 2004. (Courtesy of the author.)

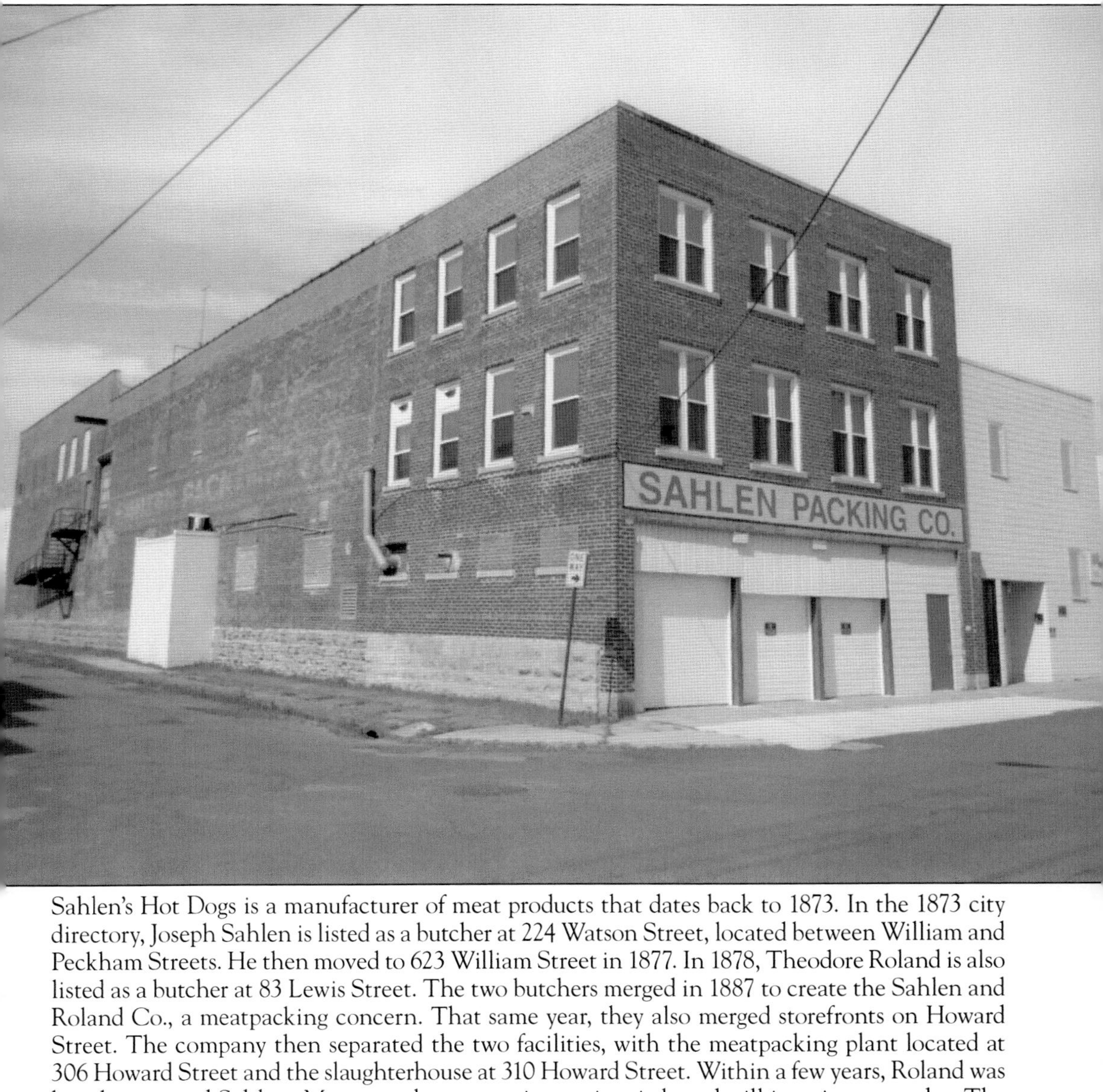

Sahlen's Hot Dogs is a manufacturer of meat products that dates back to 1873. In the 1873 city directory, Joseph Sahlen is listed as a butcher at 224 Watson Street, located between William and Peckham Streets. He then moved to 623 William Street in 1877. In 1878, Theodore Roland is also listed as a butcher at 83 Lewis Street. The two butchers merged in 1887 to create the Sahlen and Roland Co., a meatpacking concern. That same year, they also merged storefronts on Howard Street. The company then separated the two facilities, with the meatpacking plant located at 306 Howard Street and the slaughterhouse at 310 Howard Street. Within a few years, Roland was bought out, and Sahlens Meats was born, creating an iconic brand still in existence today. The company produces roughly seven million pounds of ham and five million pounds of hot dogs a year, which are distributed throughout 20 states. Pictured is the facade of the structure at 310 Howard Street, which is still in use today after 129 years in business. (Courtesy of the author.)

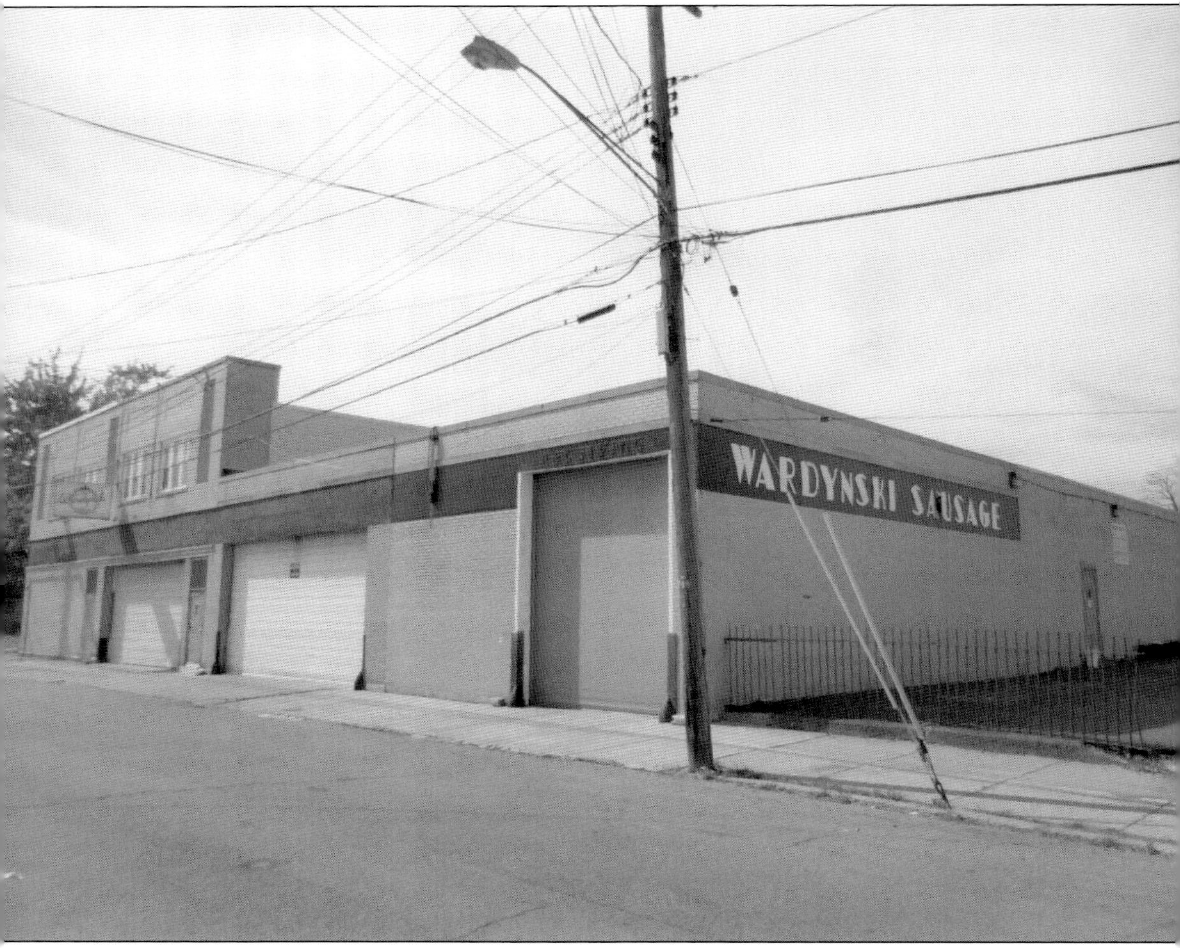

Within the yellow brick of the Wardynski Sausage Company facade is a red brick from Kazimierz, a district of Krakow from which the Wardynski family hails. The connection to the old world that is important to this third generation family-operated business. Frank Wardynski is first mentioned in the city directories in 1919, with a butcher shop at 336 Peckham Street, where it still continues. In 1954, after many successful years, Wardynski decided to turn to wholesale production of sausages, along with bologna and hotdogs. When his son Raymond came into the business, the company became F. Wardynski and Son's Co. Since 1954, father and son have continued the tradition of making meat products using old-fashioned recipes brought from Poland. For the past 25 years, Raymond's son Raymond "Skip" Wardynski has run the business, continuing the tradition his grandfather started. In 2005, Wardynski's purchased the rights to the Szelagowski "Shelley" brand hotdogs and began making hotdogs the same way Anthony Szelagowski did over 100 years ago.

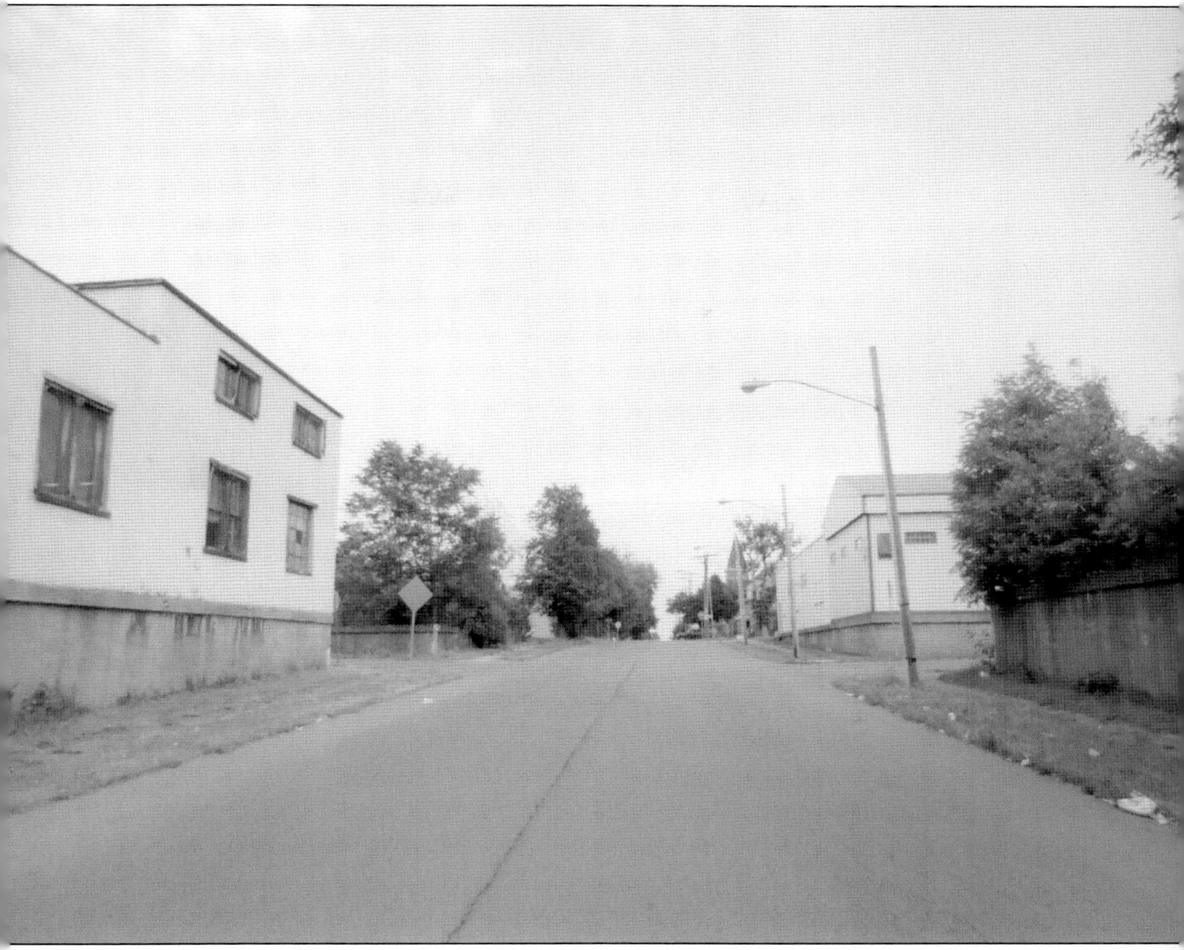

In this 2015 photograph, the intersection of Doat Street and Rapin Place is shown. This photograph shows the location on page 13, but the contrast is evident, as all of the houses on the left have been removed and only the concrete wall and iron fence remain. When Reiber Roofing and Sheet Metal Works, which had occupied the structure since 1957, closed, Eskay Metal Fabricating moved in soon after. Still located on this site after the owner purchased the building in 1987, the company manufactures fabricated stainless steel, brass, cooper, aluminum, and embossed metals, currently employing six people. After the Mohawk Machinery Company at left closed, the site became occupied by American Welding and Fabrication. Since 1990, American Welding and Fabrication has been producing metal products for building construction. (Courtesy of the author.)

INDEX

Bibliography

Buffalo Architectural Guidebook Corporation. *Buffalo Architecture: A Guide*. Cambridge, Massachusetts: MIT Press, 1981.

Jablonski, Fred Francis. *The Dynamics of an East Buffalo Ethnic Neighborhood*. Buffalo, New York: self-published, 1976.

Rizzo, Michael F. *Nine Nine Eight: The Glory Days of Buffalo Shopping*. Morrisville, North Carolina: Lulu, 2007.

www.clintonbaileymarket.com

www.crosbycompany.com

www.eberliron.com

www.preservationready.org

Other resources utilized include Buffalo History Museum photographic collections (General Collection, Goldome-Nagel, George Hare, Houser Bob), Buffalo History Museum ready reference and vertical file resources, the Buffalo Collection at the Buffalo & Erie County Public Library, and Buffalo City Directories.